Setting the Captives Free

Setting the Captives Free
A Christian Theology for
Domestic Violence

Ron Clark

Cascade Books
A division of Wipf & Stock Publishers
199 West 8th Avenue, Suite 3 • Eugene OR 97401

SETTING THE CAPTIVES FREE
A Christian Theology for Domestic Violence

ISBN: 1-59752-424-7

Cataloging-in-Publication Data

Clark, Ron
Setting the captives free : a Christian theology for domestic violence / Ron Clark.

    p. cm.

    ISBN 1-59752-424-7 (alk. paper)

    1. Church work with abused women. 2. Abused women—pastoral counseling of. 3. Church work with abusive men. 4. Abusive men—pastoral counseling of. I. Title.

BV4445.5 .C550 2005

Contents

List of Figures

Acknowledgments

This book is the result of years of study, work, research, teaching, and mistakes. I have been blessed enough to see the heart of God in all of this, and Jesus has not only given me a chance to change my life but a chance to make a difference in the lives of others. My wife, Lori, has been with me every step of the way. The night she came home from a domestic violence training class angry about what she heard from a victim's testimony was the day we started this journey together. She has been my partner, lover, best friend, and advisor throughout. I look forward to many more years with her and in this ministry. My sons Nathan, Hunter, and Caleb have been a joy to come home to. They make it easy to unwind. I appreciate their patience while I have been preoccupied with this book. I couldn't ask for better sons.

I would like to thank my various friends who have provided editorial comments on this work. Dr. Chris Huffine, Dr. David Livingston, Don Voeks, and Song-Cha Bowman have provided important advice from the batterer intervention perspective. Michelle Weldon, Bettie Williams-Watson, Katy Pendegraft, and Dr. Chiquita Rollins have all been valuable as victims' advocates in editing this work. Dr. Ken Durham, Dr. Chris Altrock, Dr. Paul Watson, and Candy Wood have also provided invaluable advice from their ministry perspectives. Thanks to Mary Anne Owen and the New Way Shelter in Bonne Terre, Missouri, for our first introduction into the world of domestic violence.

I also have appreciated the hard work and support from Communities Against Domestic Violence (CADV) in Gresham, Oregon, as well as the Multnomah County Domestic Violence Council in Portland. Your support for me as president has been uplifting and I have learned so much from all of your trainings, work, and comments in our workshops. The Metro Church of Christ has provided a good forum to develop these ideas in a safe and supportive environment. Metro's Abuse Ministry has also been a great team of Christians who have worked with Lori and I to dream and have a vision for a new and powerful ministry to others. Preaching has been a great joy, and I hope that the church continues to see the fruits of this ministry.

Thank you to Dr. Shawn Jones, Academic Dean at Cascade College. Your friendship has been a blessing and your pushing me to teach has challenged me to grow and rethink issues in my ministry. I appreciate what you and your family have meant to my family. My students at Cascade have always been a joy to teach and their willingness to allow me the opportunity to integrate faith, ministry, and scholarship in the class and their assignments. I look forward to what they will accomplish in the future.

A special thank you goes to Sue Tester, who did the final proofreading and editing on this manuscript. Thanks for seeing past the poor grammar and errors and encouraging me to push on for publication.

Finally, I want to acknowledge all of the victims and families who have endured the emotional and physical pain and humiliation of abuse. I am in awe of their courage and will continue to devote energy to this ministry. I also appreciate the support of the victims and former victims. They have been our biggest cheerleaders and we pray that our words represent their courage as much as their words have given me courage.

Ron Clark
Metro Church of Christ
Gresham, Oregon

Preface

It was the third time that I had seen Forrest Gump. I don't remember where I was (or why I was watching it for the third time); I just remember the thought that flashed through my mind as I watched one of the scenes. Jenny had come back to see Forrest at his home in Alabama. They went by her old home, which was now abandoned, and she began to get angry. She yelled and threw rocks at the house. That's when I got it. She had been abused as a child! It all came together. Her erratic behavior in the movie, her distant love of Forrest (the only man who truly loved her), and her choices in life were all understandable now. How could I have missed it?

You are probably thinking "Everyone saw it but you—why did you have to watch it three times to get it?" My answer, I don't know. I wonder the same thing. But this helps me to understand why faith communities don't "get it." That's right, sometimes faith communities don't get it. We watch it over and over again until someone grabs us and says, "Mary is being abused and you have done nothing." Then it makes sense; yet we still might not know what to do about it.

My wife, Lori, and I have been working with abuse victims and shelters for over ten years. We have given countless sermons, classes, and trainings on abuse and have helped victims and abusers find resources. Sometimes even we have to see the movie a third time to get the message. Other times we see it coming but feel we can do nothing about it. Lori and I have been working with those who have been abused since 1992.

In the beginning we served the women, children, and staff at a small safe house in southern Missouri. We felt compelled to help, and we rallied the church to provide pizza parties, build fences (literally) and playground equipment, help with odd jobs for the house, provide clothing and gifts for the children, and offer a safe place for the families to worship. The director of the shelter encouraged us to attend domestic violence trainings that were provided by local service providers and counselors. She later offered us the opportunity to provide counseling and trainings for others in the community as well as the shelter guests. Wherever we are, the memories of the staff and guests in that small safe house, who courageously pushed us to get involved, drive us forward.

Yet God was not finished with us. When we came to Portland in August 1998, we were introduced to a new view of domestic violence. The abusers I had so hated and ignored became flesh and dwelt among us. I began to attend workshops presented by batterer intervention specialists and anger management counselors. We learned that accountability, change, mercy, and, lastly, forgiveness needed to become part of our abuse awareness language. Abusers had always been among us; we had just ignored them and focused on the victims. We learned that when we say "Mary was/is abused" rather than "Steve abused Mary," our very language suggests that women are at fault.

I believe that my family lives in one of the best states in the country. Oregon is not only full of natural beauty, but it has excellent domestic violence intervention programs. I have learned much from the domestic violence advocates and counselors. The number of opportunities to gather and present research in the area of theology and domestic violence has grown immensely in the Northwest. The advocates have also been willing to listen to and seek advice from this preacher, and I will always remember the times we have prayed together for their work. At our church's annual domestic violence conference, I introduced a local batterer intervention trainer to my son as "the man who is teaching me to be a better dad." God has truly used these servants to teach my family how to be more like Jesus. I look forward to what God will continue to do through them in the future.

This book has been part of a journey as well as an emotional roller coaster ride. Not everyone has shared our enthusiasm. At times I have felt various degrees of anger originating from critical comments such as "you preach about abuse too much" or "there they go with abuse stuff again," to statements suggesting that abuse is not a real problem. All of these comments have stirred us to respond. We have been frustrated over the apathy of many colleagues who suggest that there must be "balance" in their ministries (meaning that they don't think this is as important an issue as victims do) and disappointed over the continual stories of church leaders who have refused to help victims. In the community, we have been angered over the loss of quality domestic violence advocates whose positions were eliminated due to budget cuts. Above all, there is the grief over the suffering of victims, the witnessing of abuse by innocent children, and the manipulative excuses from abusers and their families. We, like God, are angry with abusive people as well as with the overwhelming prevalence of domestic violence.

At times we have felt despair. Despair over the size of this problem and the costs involved in trying to educate the world. Despair over the abuser who clouds the conversation with "no one is perfect, can't you just give me a break?" Despair over the men who continue to use power and control to manipulate their partners, children, and others around them. Despair over the victims who have come for help only to return to their abuser. Despair over the children who can't get away. Despair over the churches who tell me "Thanks, but we have it under control," or "It doesn't exist in our church."

Sometimes the victims' stories have caused me to have nightmares and feel a sense of helplessness as a healer. The prevalence of abuse and the enormous emotional investment needed to help adds to this sense of helplessness. The struggle to help, to care, and to become emotionally involved is heightened as we try to keep a certain distance so that we can empower, rather than control, those seeking help. The struggle between being a healer/helper and a savior is a constant battle within. As a male, I feel a sense of duty to deliver, save, and protect every woman and child who is being abused. I am constantly faced with this question, "Do I empower or rescue them?"

There are also times of excitement. The smiles of the women who have said, "I am safe now," "I am free," "Thank you for caring," "I have a job," "I am ready to be baptized," or "I now know that God loves me," are memories that keep us going. Seeing the children relax, play, and laugh helps to replace the despair and anger with a sense of joy. Seeing the men accept responsibility and grow reminds us that our work is worthwhile. Seeing families who support those in abuse and parents who help their daughters leave their abusers shows us that things are changing. The support from service providers and advocates is also encouraging and reminds us why we entered ministry in the first place.

This excitement can take an emotional toll on us personally. Sometimes it seems that working with domestic violence can become a mosh pit of emotion. All of the swirling emotions can make it is easy to burn out. I admire those who daily work with victims, families, and abusers and continue to stick with them. I admire those who ride on the emotional roller coaster and refuse to abandon it. I can retreat into theological studies, hospital visits, Bible studies, and teaching. I can take a break from the roller coaster and ride other rides at the park. If my stomach is queasy, I can get off the ride for a while. Our local providers cannot. I continue to thank God and pray for them, because their courage has brought Lori and me to this point. Their persistence has prepared us to inform others. They reflect the heart of the prophets more than anyone else I know. At times they, rather than the faith community as well as myself, have been the loyal representatives of God. Their eyes have been open while ours have been closed. Sometimes it seems that we have watched the movie and missed the message.

Hopefully, this book will help you to "get it" the first time you see it. If you are a church leader, my hope is that you will become an advocate for families that suffer from abuse. If you are a former victim, my hope is that this book will validate your struggle and journey to freedom. If you are a family member or friend of someone who feels the pain of abuse, I hope that you will learn how to be a good listener, helper, and friend. If you are abusing your partner/wife, my challenge is that you stop, repent of this sin, and enroll into a batter intervention or anger management group. I also challenge you to confess this sin to your family, friends, and those you are abusing. This book is designed to help you learn about domestic violence and what it is like to experience abuse. Many victims who have experienced pain have told us their stories. Contrary to what Forest Gump said, life is not always "like a box of chocolates."

Special Message For Those Being Hurt By Their Partner or Family Member

If you are now being abused or afraid of being hurt by your partner, my hope and prayer is that you will learn how to get help and be safe. My hope is that you will not have to live the life that Jenny lived and that you will see that all people, including yourself, are in the image of God. All people should be loved and respected. You should be loved, respected, and honored as one who is created to be like God.

Introduction

Is Domestic Violence a Problem?

Some people try to tell me that domestic violence isn't a big problem in their congregation or community. The facts don't bear that out.

- In America two to four million women have indicated that their spouses or live-in partners physically abused them during the year.[1]
- Twenty to twenty-five percent of all women reported that their partners abused them at least once.[2] One out of four American

[1]The statistics vary but each year the range of reported statistics falls between two and four million. Angela Browne, Violence Against Women: A Majority Staff Report, Committee on the Judiciary, U.S. Senate (Oct. 1992) 3; P. Tjaden, and N. Thoennes, Full Report of the Prevalence, Incidence, and Consequences of Intimate Partner Violence Against Women: Findings from the National Violence Against Women Survey (NCJ 183781) Washington, D.C.: U.S. Department of Justice, National Institute of Justice, 2000; Lundy Bancroft, Why Does He Do That? Inside the Minds of Angry and Controlling Men (New York: Berkely Books, 2002) 7.

[2]Evan Stark and Anne Flitcraft, "Spouse Abuse," Surgeon General's Workshop on Violence and Public Health Source Book, 1985; Sarah Glazer, "Violence Against Women," Colorado Researcher 3:8 (Feb. 1993) 171. For a more statistical analysis of domestic violence in America and other countries, see "Physical Assault on Women by an Intimate Male Partner, Selected Population-Based Studies, 1982–99, Table 1," Population Report Series L: Number 11, <www.infoforhealth.org/pr/l11/l11tables.shtml>.

women report having been raped and/or physically assaulted by a current or former spouse, live-in partner, or date at some time in their life.[3]

- Twenty-five to forty percent of dating couples experience physical violence.[4]

- Hospital emergency rooms indicate that twenty to thirty percent of women seeking treatment are victims of battering.[5]

- Every day in America at least three women are murdered by their husband or intimate partner.[6]

- Throughout the world, one in three women have confessed to having been beaten, coerced into sex, or experienced other forms of abuse.[7]

- Domestic violence is estimated to be much higher within the United States military than within civilian families.[8]

---

[3]Ending Violence Against Women: Population Reports, Series L., Number 11, 27:4 (1999). See also the Population Report Series L; National Center for Injury Prevention and Control, Intimate Partner Violence (Oct. 2003)<www.cdc.gov/ncipc/factsheets/ipvfacts.htm>; Samantha Levine, "The Perils of Young Romance," US News and World Report (Aug. 13, 2001) 46. National Women's Health Information Center, Violence Against Women (Sept. 2001) <www.4woman.gov/violence/index.htm>.

[4]Sherry L. Hamby, "Acts of Psychological Aggression Against a Partner and Their Relation to Physical Assault and Gender," Journal of Marriage and the Family 61 (1999) 968.

[5]International Journal of Health Services 20 (1990) 21; and Mary Susan Miller, No Visible Wounds: Identifying Nonphysical Abuse of Women by Their Men (New York: Random House, 1995) 7.

[6]Bureau of Justice Statistics Crime Data Brief, Intimate Partner Violence from 1993–2001 (Feb. 2003). In 2000, 1247 women were killed, while 440 men were killed, by intimate partners. Estrella suggests that every fifteen seconds a spouse kills his wife. Rosa Emily Nina Estrella, "Effects of Violence on Interpersonal Relations and Strategies that Promote Family Unity," LaFamilia Unida: La Fuerza Del Futuro 4th Annual Power in Partnership Bilingual Conference, June 20, 2003, Portland, Oregon.

[7]Population Report Series L. Estrella reports that 50% of the women of the world are abused by a spouse and that four million women are involved in sexual trafficking. The statistics vary from country to country. Estrella indicates that 20.8% of women in the Dominican Republic report having been physically abused while Palacios reports that in El Salvador four out of five women live with violence in their families. Maria Aracely Linares Palacios, "Strategies for Working with Latinos Who Have Experienced Family Violence," LaFamilia Unida.

[8]Christine Hansen, "A Considerate Service: An Advocate's Introduction to Domestic Violence and the Military," Domestic Violence Report 6:4 (Apr/May 2001). The study

Domestic violence is an ongoing problem in the United States and throughout the world. This problem not only affects the spouse who is targeted by the abuser, but it also affects the children in the home.

- One-third of abused women indicate that they were abused the first time during pregnancy.[9] Research suggests that this may contribute to low birth weight of infants and other negative effects for infants.[10]
- In a study done by Boston Medical Center over one-third of children reported seeing violence by fathers against mothers when a parent reported that no violence occurred.[11]
- Children brought up in abusive homes have a higher risk of being abused.[12]
- It is estimated that 5 million children per year witness an assault on their mothers.[13]
- "Around forty percent of abusive men extend their behavior pattern

---

suggests that in 1985, one in three military spouses were victims of abuse. In 1987, research indicated that military victims were four times more likely to be choked into unconsciousness. A study done at the Pentagon from 1992–96 also indicated that domestic violence in the military occurred at a rate five times higher than that among civilians. While serious incidents decreased from 1997–99, the amount of moderate to severe domestic violence incidents increased. The results suggest that domestic violence in the military is much higher than in civilian families. Also see: Marianne Szegedy-Maszak, "Death at Fort Bragg," US News and World Report (Aug. 12, 2002) 44.[9]Jacquelyn Cambell, "Correlates of Battering During Pregnancy," Research Nursing Health 15 (1992) 219–26; Cambell et al, "Why Battering During Pregnancy?" Clinical Issues in Perinatal and Health Nursing 4 (1993) 343–49. As many as 324,000 women each year experience intimate partner violence during pregnancy. J. A. Gazmararian, R. Petersen, A. M. Spitz, M. M. Goodwin, L. E. Saltzman, and J. S. Marks, "Violence and Reproductive Health: Current Knowledge and Future Research Directions," Maternal and Child Health Journal 4:2 (2000) 79–84.

[10]Carol J. Adams, Woman-Battering, Creative Pastoral Care and Counseling Series (Minneapolis: Fortress, 1994) 12.

[11]Boston Medical Center Pediatrics, "Child Witness to Violence Project," see <www. childwitnesstoviolence.org/care_givers/for_caregivers_facts.html>.

[12]A national survey of more than 2000 American families reported that 50% of the men who abused their wives also abused their children. Jennifer Talbot, "Children Witnessing Domestic Violence," presented at the Working with Abusive Men workshop, Portland State University, Portland, Oregon, May 2002.

[13]Bancroft, 8.

to other family members."[14]

- In Portland, Oregon, the statistics are similar. While I believe we have excellent domestic violence resources, the problem is still prevalent. In a survey of over 739 women, ages 18 to 64, fourteen percent confessed to having been physically or sexually abused in the previous year by a partner, and twenty percent had been abused at least once during their lifetime.[15] Most of these women were college educated and had a yearly income of over $25,000. The abusive men commonly had problems with alcohol and drugs, were college educated, and had an income of over $25,000. Fifty-percent of the children exposed to domestic violence were less than five years old, and two-thirds of the children saw or heard an act of domestic violence at least once per month.

These statistics don't even include emotional, verbal, and other forms of abuse. Men commit 85 to 90 percent of the reported abuse.[16] The remaining 10 to 15 percent of cases involves women abusing their male intimate partners, and intimate partner violence between gay and lesbian couples. Thus, it is clear that men are overwhelmingly the major cause of pain and suffering on others.

It is sad that women are safer on the streets than in their own homes while men are safer in their own homes than on the streets.[17] We know that most women who are assaulted know their attacker.[18] Most often it is a woman's intimate partner who abuses her, not a stranger. Men, however, are more commonly attacked by strangers.

[14]Bancroft, When Dad Hurts Mom: Helping Your Children Heal the Wounds of Witnessing Abuse (New York: Putnam, 2004) 53.

[15]The following statistics are taken from the publication by Multnomah County Health Department, Domestic Violence in Multnomah County, February, 2000. More recent research was done in 2004 with a survey of over 2900 women, ages 20–55, in which 10% indicated that they had been physically and/or sexually abused by an intimate partner in the five years preceding the survey. 3% of these women experienced intimate partner violence in the twelve months preceding the survey. Oregon Department of Human Services, Intimate Partner Violence in Oregon: Findings from the Oregon Women's Health and Safety Survey (Feb. 2004).

[16]Callie Marie Rennison and Sarah Welchans, Intimate Partner Violence, Bureau of Justice Statistics Special Report (May 2000) 1.

[17]Adams, 12.

[18]Browne, Violence Against Women.

The statistics are alarming. The following should help put this in perspective. If our nation were a church of 400 people, one could estimate that 160 would be adult women, twenty would be teenaged girls, 160 would be adult men, and twenty would be teenage boys. According to national statistics, forty of the women would experience some form of physical abuse in their life. Twenty of the women would be currently experiencing physical abuse. Four or five of the teenaged girls would experience some type of dating violence. If abuse is expanded to include verbal and emotional abuse, then at least eighty of the women would be experiencing the humiliation and degradation of verbal criticism from a spouse or boyfriend. Approximately sixty of the men and boys would have assaulted their girlfriend or wife at some time. It could also be expected that half of the congregation (200 people) would have witnessed abuse in their family or their spouse's family and 150 of them would know of a woman who has been abused in the past year. Even more than this, some of the men and boys in the congregation would be actively abusing some of the women.

Do you think this is being an alarmist? Remember, these statistics are only the reported cases. Most abuse goes unreported. Most victims keep quiet. Most abuse is hidden from the outsider. Ministers should be talking about abuse so that victims can feel safe to come forward. Churches should be talking about abuse because statistically some of our men are abusing women. I would suggest that any minister who preaches about abuse will probably have the greatest outreach program any church has known. How many sermons are preached for the five percent who really want to hear about a topic, and how many sermons really connect with the majority of the congregation? Abuse is a topic that will impact at least one-half of the congregation.

Faith communities need to integrate domestic violence resources into premarital counseling, marital counseling, men's and women's studies, sermons, ministries, teen classes, and missions programs. We must open our eyes the first time we see the movie and tell the world we are willing to deal with this epidemic.

I have been frustrated with colleagues who feel that this is not worth their time. I have found that many will avoid our clergy trainings until they personally have to deal with a domestic violence situation. Yet when these ministers do come, it is an opportunity to teach them how to help victims. One of my neighbors, an elder of a church, came to an abuse training we conducted and invited his minister to attend the next training. The minister told him, "It's not a problem here." When my neighbor shared this with me, I suggested to him that within a month someone would come forward about abuse. Three days later he told me of a church member's neighbor who was being abused. They went to the minister, and he asked not to be involved. My neighbor was frustrated to realize that while his eyes were open his pastor's were not. It is a shame that someone close to us has to be beaten before we decide that it is a problem.

Domestic violence is not only a crime against humanity, it is a sin against God. The community of faith is called to protect victims and prevent the abuse of power.

> Open your mouth for those who cannot speak
> to bring justice to the weak.
> Open your mouth and judge righteously,
> and bring justice to the oppressed and poor. (Prov 31:8-9)[19]

The faith community is called to represent God and call men and women to love, compassion, gentleness, and respect for themselves and each other. The community of faith must deal with domestic violence because it has penetrated our families, our neighborhoods, our community, our churches, and our world. Domestic violence crosses all racial, ethnic, cultural, social, and gender boundaries and is destroying families, children, businesses, friends, and the structure of our society. Yet a greater crime exists. It is the crime of apathy and silence. To ignore this violence and humiliation is to ignore the voice of God. To pat the victims on the head and minimize their pain is to slap God in the face. To go to our homes and sleep at night, without being compelled to act, while others live in terror and fear is ignoring our duty to God and our neighbor.

As this book was being written, the United States was at war with Iraq. It is striking to realize that our government will spend millions of dollars to stop terrorism, yet it largely ignores the "domestic terrorism" that occurs every day in someone's home. It also amazes me that American citizens will support our president in his attempt to remove bullies and

---

[19]All Biblical quotations are my translations.

terrorist leaders in order to protect the innocent, yet those who call for the arrest and conviction of men who terrorize and abuse their families are seen by some as fanatics! Abuse is a problem that needs to be understood, addressed, and challenged. The abused are humans in the image of God who need to be protected, loved, and empowered to stand with us and walk through life with respect and dignity. When God brings a victim to us, we have a responsibility to love them as we want to be loved and be faithful to that responsibility. We must make sure that they and their children are safe, protected, and given the chance to live in peace and love. Abusers are also humans who are in the image of God, and they need to be taught how to live and respect all others. They must be confronted and challenged to change or face prosecution by our legal system and our spiritual communities.

I believe that the faith community is in a great position to address this problem. We have a God who grieves over the violence that occurs in families. Yet we have a God who grieves even more over the fact that spiritual leaders have failed to act as servants of Yahweh in this respect.

Figure 1:
Email from an Advocate

Hi Ron,

My name is Mary and I'm the director/advocate for Advocate Services which is a crisis center working with victims of domestic violence, sexual assault, elder abuse and child abuse. One of the Portland advocates gave me your address and said that you might have some ideas that will help me with working with the pastors in our area.

#1. The pastors will not return any of my phone calls; rather I call for information or need assistance.

#2. In the past I had three clients return to their abusive homes because the batterer suddenly became religious, and they ended up getting marriage counseling. Of course restraining orders were dropped, etc. Then this past week I moved a domestic violence victim into another small neighboring town so that she could have some peace of mind, and one Pastor called another Pastor and they tracked her down and confronted her on her front lawn at 8:30 pm. Her interpretation of the contact was that she was a bad wife for leaving her husband, she should receive marriage counseling to work it out, and that her husband has been going to church so he's sorry for what he did. Needless to say I had a very long crisis call to this client's residence after they left.

I relish the fact that some of my clients consider the church to be like family and they have these resources to help them through the hard times ahead. But this client states that she will not go back to the church and now she's not only dealing with the loss of a husband who was never there, but also a loss of faith which to me is worse. How do I bridge a gap that I'm not allowed to cross? I know that our Pastors mean well but they do not understand the dynamics behind DV. The women are the ones that suffer in our area. We have had clients kicked out of the congregation until they went back to their husbands.

I'm truly at a loss. We look for any resources that a victim has to help us through the process, and the faith community is slowly becoming more of a hindrance than a resource.

Any ideas of help would be greatly appreciated.

The rest of this book is an appeal to you to gain an understanding of what it really means to face domestic violence and how to help bring peace and wholeness to victims and their children caught in the web of abuse. It is an appeal to you to confront those who abuse others rather than shut your eyes to the message of the movie.

Part 1
Understanding Domestic Violence

I will forgive but I won't forget
I hope you know that you've lost my respect
Does it run in your blood to betray the ones you love?
—Papa Roach[1]

---

[1] Jacoby Shaddix, "Blood," on *Getting Away With Murder* (Geffen Records Inc. Universal, 2004).

1
Definitions of Domestic Violence

There are many different definitions for words such as *abuse, violence,* or even *beating.* Whenever I speak to groups on the subject of abuse, it is important to begin by defining the terms. I once was talking to a group of Russian-speaking students and asked them what came to their mind when I mentioned the word abuse. They all said that they thought of drugs and alcohol. When I asked about domestic violence, they weren't clear on what I meant. When I asked about spousal abuse they said, "When a man beats his wife." When I mentioned that sometimes mom hits dad, the group roared with laughter. People have different stereotypes and definitions of abuse that need to be clarified.

People approach this discussion from various backgrounds, contexts, and experiences. Some of those attending my seminars and workshops have a very strong knowledge of the material including the issues of power and control in the area of domestic violence. Their nods, smiles, and "amens" when we are defining terms of abuse show that these listeners are crossing into familiar territory. Others who are listening from a mindset of abuse that has been influenced by popular myths, media, or assumptions may need a clearer understanding of the definitions and dynamics of abuse. Many times these listeners are taking notes and asking questions, and they sometimes are fascinated by the material presented. There are also people who have been directly or indirectly affected by abuse and are interpreting domestic violence through their own cognitive filters. These filters are the result of complex coping mechanisms that have given them the strength to survive. These participants are usually hit hard by much of the evidence and communicate this through looks of amazement, tears, lowered heads, and sometimes a hug after the presentation. Often there are those present who are currently abusing power over others. They may express hostility, be argumentative, or attempt to flatter me with praise. Yet each one has come, I believe, out of concern about this issue.

As you read this book, you may find that you are one of these people. I cannot see your face, but I can hope and pray that you read this entire book carefully. Our experiences many times affect our interpretation of events. If your coping skills involve minimization, silence, or ignoring the pain, then these may be the skills you pass on to others. If you believe that you have heard it all before, then you may miss something if you read too quickly. If you read this book in order to gain knowledge and help others, then you may find it to be another valuable tool in your box of resources. Set your experiences on the table next to this book. Your experiences are who you are and hopefully this book will help you see those experiences as valuable or invaluable to your growth and development as a person in the image of God.

The terms used for individuals that are caught in the cycle of violence and abuse will be as follows:

- Those who perpetrate the violence and abuse will be referred to as *abusers*.
- Since the majority of abuse is done by males on females, the abuser will be referred to in the masculine gender.
- Those who are the recipients of the intimate partner violence will be referred to as *victims* and in the feminine gender. This is not an attempt to suggest that women are always victims or that men cannot be victims, but it is a term with which most readers are familiar.
- While children may also be victims, the focus will be on intimate partner violence. The children will be separated from victim terminology and referred to as *children*.

- Child abuse is a sin and a dangerous issue in our society, but the focus of this book is on intimate partner violence.
- *Family* will be referred to as those who are not part of the nuclear family but are related to victims or abusers.

Definition of Abuse

The Oregon Domestic Violence Council has given a good definition of abuse that will be used as a model for this discussion. The Oregon Domestic Violence Council defines abuse as:

> A pattern of coercive behavior used by one person to control and subordinate another in an intimate relationship. These behaviors include physical, sexual, psychological, and economic abuse. Tactics of coercion, terrorism, degradation, exploitation, and violence are used to engender fear in the victim in order to enforce compliance.[2]

Three key points in this definition will be discussed more fully. First, the definition uses the term *coercive behavior*. This suggests manipulation of another person to get what one desires. The definition mentions that the goal of the abuser is to enforce compliance. *Coercion* suggests control and an expression of "power over" another person. This coercion and control can occur through the use of threats, violence, humiliation, exploitation, or even self-pity. Abuse is not about anger; it is about control and forced compliance.

In order to understand how power and control interact in an abusive relationship, let us look at the Power and Control Wheel in Figure 2. This diagram was created by the Domestic Abuse Intervention Project in Duluth, Minnesota, and has become a standard diagram used in domestic violence trainings.

---

[2]Domestic Violence in Multnomah County, 2.

Figure2: Abuse Power and Control Wheel

The wheel, in Figure 2, indicates that at the center is *power and control*. The main focus of abusers is controlling and displaying power over others. Abusers do not always use physical violence. They use whatever they must in order to enforce compliance. They may intimidate and threaten their victims. If these do not work then they will use something else. Usually they become more controlling in an attempt to gain control.

The aim of all abuse, unlike that of sadism, is not the pleasure of inflicting pain, but the need to control: domination is the end in itself. While a man may explain his actions by saying: 'I lost control,' in fact what he did was *gain* control.[3]

---

[3]Miller, 17.

The spokes of the wheel (Figure 2) are the different forms or types of control that abusers may use. Abusers use various tactics to force compliance in another person.[4] Patricia Evans illustrates two realities of the abusive relationship and the imbalance that exist (Figure 3). The realities of the abuser suggest that the world of the abuser is one of selfishness and control rather than love and compassion.

Figure 3: The Reality of the World of the Abuser[5]

What is present in the relationship is:	*What is lacking in the relationship is:*
Inequality	Equality
Competition	Partnership
Hostility	Mutuality
Control	Goodwill
Negation	Intimacy
	Validation

We tend to view abusers as angry people who are out of control.[6] The goal of abusers is control.[7] Abusers react to anxiety in a dysfunctional

---

[4]In some presentations, domestic violence advocates or service providers have expressed disagreement with the power and control wheel. Citing research in immigrant communities and drug and alcohol studies, they suggest that abuse is not only about power and control but about socio-economic factors, stress, or intoxication. While this sounds tempting these other factors may influence or aggravate an abuser's condition. We need to be careful that these do not become excuses for their behavior. Abusers are responsible for their actions, and they make a conscious choice to abuse their intimate partners.

[5]Patricia Evans, *The Verbally Abusive Relationship: How to Recognize it and How to Respond*, 2d ed. (Holbrook, Mass.: Adams Media, 1996) 42.

[6]"The emotionally abusive person has an agenda, and that agenda is to be in control. In his attempt to be in control he will dominate, suppress, tyrannize, persecute, and attempt to conquer anyone he relates to on a consistent basis. Among his repertoire of control tactics are insults, denigrating comments, derogatory words, threats, and constant criticism, along with an extensive array of other intimidating behavior designed to make others feel inadequate and helpless." Beverly Engel, *The Emotionally Abused Woman: Overcoming Destructive Patterns and Reclaiming Yourself* (New York: Fawcett, 1990) 47.

[7]Bancroft, *Why Does He Do That? Inside the Minds of Angry and Controlling Men* (N.Y.: Berkeley, 2002) 112.

manner. They may use anger or other emotions to gain control of a situation or another person. Abusers can also use apologies, self-pity, and sympathy to control a situation. As a high school wrestling referee, I have been the brunt of coaches' and parents' anger during matches. At times I have seen intense displays of hostility toward me during the meet. Later, after apologizing, some tell me that this behavior is uncommon for them. Since I was making *bad* (and other adjectives) calls, I am expected to understand that they "just lost it, but only this once." They tend to be somewhat hostile when I persist in stating that their actions are unacceptable under any circumstances. Sometimes they leave and other times they push the issue passive-aggressively. Some believe that they were pushed to lose their cool, and I should accept their actions.

This is an example of *coercion.* The coaches who try to justify their anger or blame me are trying to coerce me into accepting their actions. When abusers want to have their own way, they will use anger, apology, instruction, and anything else available to *win their case* or *enforce compliance.* This control is grounded in an unwillingness to admit wrong and take the necessary steps to change *their* behavior. It is also grounded in a narcissistic attitude, which will be discussed further in a later chapter. Narcissism is a preoccupation or infatuation with one's self. For abusers the issue is not about changing themselves but about coercing others to change or accept their behavior. Abusers do not feel that they are wrong; they believe that they are misunderstood and need to help others understand their actions! They seek to control others' perceptions about their behavior.

"I didn't mean to hurt her," he said.

"But you did," I replied.

"It's just, it's just that I want her to understand me," he slowly muttered.

"What do you mean, 'understand you'?"

"When I get mad and cuss at her, she just leaves and won't let me explain. That's why I grab her and try to talk to her, but she won't listen."

"Why don't you just let her walk away? Isn't it better to let her go and cool off and then talk to her later?" I asked.

"She might not come back and I don't want her to think that that is how I am," he said.

"So it is OK for you to use violence to make her understand?" I asked.

"No, but I try to tell her that those actions are not me," he responded.

"What do you mean, not you? Is someone else doing this?"

"Well, it's not me; I mean it is but it is a part of me I need to shove down—it's a bad part that I am trying to control," he said. "When she doesn't listen, the bad comes out and I just can't stop it. I tell her that, but sometimes she makes it worse."

"Steve, Jesus says that you will know them by their fruits. I believe that we do what we choose to do. This is who you are and it is not about Karen understanding you, it is about you changing your behavior. Grabbing another person so hard that they bruise is wrong, especially when they want to walk away and cool off."

"But she bruises easy," he said.

"I don't buy that," I responded.

"Then how do I make her understand me?"

"You don't," I said, "you start by trying to understand yourself."

The second key point in the council's definition is . . . *to control and subordinate another . . . to engender fear*. This suggests an unequal relationship between two human beings. "The term *abuse* is about *power*, it means that a person is taking advantage of a power imbalance to exploit or control someone else."[8] People are meant to live together in harmony and equality, not fear. The marriage/dating relationship does not change this basic human right. No one has the privilege, from God or anyone else, to *control* or *subordinate* another person. No one has the right to cause fear in a relationship. We do not accept this in our friendships, and we should not accept it in our intimate relationships. Abusive relationships do not involve shared power. They are foreign to God's method of relationships. God gives us free will and is not willing to force or control others ("Choose this day whom you will serve," Josh 24:15).[9] Those in a

---

[8] Ibid., 123.
[9] This will be discussed further in chapters 5–6.

relationship with God are empowered to reflect the divine nature of the creator. They are not forced to obey or serve God.

Finally, the council's definition states that the victim is in an *intimate relationship* with the abuser. This intimacy creates a strong bond between the abuser and the victim and is difficult to break. This produces a dangerous interplay of emotion and passion expressed by the abuser who is trying to control both his environment and his partner. This interplay then causes the abuse to become cyclical. The cycle of abuse involves violence, forgiveness, guilt, shame, and further manipulation (see Figure 4). David Livingston suggests that this interplay continues to intensify rather than end the relationship.

> It seems absurd that a relationship that is supposed to be based on love can become violent and demeaning. The incredulity is stretched even further when the relationship does not dissolve but instead continues in a cycle of apparent forgiveness and sentimental love followed by increased violence.[10]

Our family is a fan of the reality show *The Amazing Race*. We often comment on how intense the conflict seems to be among couples who are in an intimate relationship. Those who are friends or have parent-child relationships generally seem to handle the stress and frustration with little verbal abuse and criticism. Yet some of the married, dating, or formerly intimate couples use harsh criticism and abusive language toward each other. This seems especially prominent with the men toward the women. It makes one wonder what would happen without the presence of a film crew! While the couples, and sometimes siblings, who verbally abuse each other during times of stress are not representatives of all Americans, it does seem interesting that in this show couples in intimate relationships seem to be more abusive in their treatment of each other. It is also interesting that the period of "forgiveness" seems short but "sweet." Yet the stress of the race continually flushes out the abusive tendencies in these couples.

---

[10]David J. Livingston, *Healing Violent Men: A Model for Christian Communities* (Minneapolis: Fortress, 2002) 7.

Abuse continues not only because the abuser is controlling the victim, but also because the victim feels loved by the abuser and a sense of duty to stay in the relationship to keep the family together. Sometimes the good memories of their intimacy can override the painful memories.

> While those who emotionally abuse others don't always intend to destroy those around them, they do set out to control them. And what better way to control someone than to make her doubt her perceptions? What better way than to cause her to have such low self-esteem that she becomes dependent on her abuser? Emotional-abuse victims become so convinced they are worthless that they believe no one else could possibly want them. Therefore, they stay in abusive situations because they believe they have nowhere else to go. Their ultimate fear is that of being all alone.[11]

I understand that sometimes relationships should focus on the good, but destruction and harmful behavior is unacceptable in a relationship. If the couple has children sometimes the fear of being a single parent causes the victim to continue in the relationship.[12]

> Children are far better off—as a number of studies demonstrate—living in peace with their mother than being exposed to a man who abuses her. In fact, the studies indicate that children are better off living with a

---

[11]Engel, 11.

[12]In the past, single parenthood has been blamed for the increase in delinquent teen behavior. The rise in divorce and backlash of the church has caused us to view single parents as being handicapped in raising their own children. The fear and financial strain of being a single parent can prevent women from leaving an abusive relationship. Any statistics suggesting that children of single parents are more likely to be dysfunctional ignores the fact that dysfunctional behavior can be modeled. Children do not become abusive, violent, or substance abusers only because they experience divorce. While divorce does traumatize children, it is less traumatic than experiencing violence, neglect, and dysfunction. The level of trauma induced by divorce may also be related to the degree of dysfunction in the husband-wife relationship. P.R. Amato and A. Booth, "Consequences of Parental Divorce and Marital Unhappiness for Adult Well-Being," *Social Forces* 69 (1991) 895–914; and L. Gabardi and L.A. Rosen, "Intimate Relationships: College Students from Divorces and Intact Families," *Journal of Divorce and Remarriage* 18 (1992) 25–26. Children are actually much more susceptible to dysfunctional behaviors if they live in dysfunctional and violent homes.

single parent than being around parents who fight frequently even *without* abuse.

The research that purports to show how damaging single mothering is to children has failed to control for income and for prior exposure to abuse, so that the difficulties observed are actually the effects of poverty and of the fact that many children witnessed abuse while their parents were together—and that is why the mother is now single.

It is worth noting that we never seem to hear reports claiming that children are damaged when they are raised by single *fathers*. The reality is that single parenting is difficult, exhausting, sometimes isolating work, but both women and men can do it well, and the world is full of well-adjusted, successful people who grew up with one primary parent, male or female. What matters above all is to live in a home where there is safety, love, and kindness—and adequate economic resources.[13]

Society has long instilled the idea that unless children are raised by two parents . . . they will grow up somehow warped; as a result mothers often suffer prolonged abuse for what they explain as "the good of my children."[14]

The truth is that it is far better to have no father than to have a destructive one, because as psychiatrists have found, one nurturing parent is sufficient to foster a child's healthy development. A child who grows up hearing his father's constant put-downs of his mother, who absorbs his father's manipulative skills like osmosis through his pores, who models his father's macho domination and watches his mother submit in fear—this child cannot grow up whole. He will instead grow up twisted by the dread he felt, guilty over his inability to protect his mother, and angry that, too small and helpless, he couldn't cry out.[15]

Many women choose to stay in the relationship out of fear. One thing must be understood: the victim is not choosing the abuse, they are choosing to strengthen or stay in the relationship. Most humans desire intimacy and fear rejection. This is a driving force in continuing the relationship.

---

[13]Bancroft, *When Dad Hurts Mom*, 321.
[14]Miller, 137.
[15]Ibid., 137–38.

Abuse is Cyclical

The first characteristic of the methodology of abuse is that it is *cyclical*. Abuse usually is not a one-time event. Figure 4 illustrates how abuse can be cyclical. The relationship seems to progress in three phases.[16] There is tension, followed by a violent storm, followed by the cam after the storm. This cycle occurs because the abuser is not able to effectively address his anxiety.

Calm After the Storm

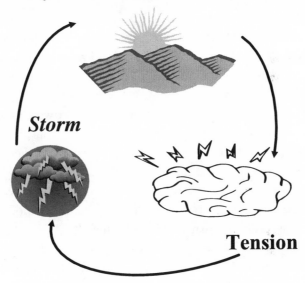

Storm

Tension

Figure 4: Cycle of Abuse

---

[16]Some of the domestic violence trainings have left the three-phase model behind and adopted a more complex cycle. They suggest that this cycle is too simple and makes the victim feel responsible for the activity. A police detective indicated to me that he had redrawn the cycle and inserted this cycle for serial criminal behavior. This produced a cycle that involved stalking, manipulation, and other forms of predatory behavior. While research is continuing on serial criminal activity and abusive behavior, I think that many batterer intervention specialists would suggest that all abusers are not as calculated and predatory as serial criminals. The three-stage cycle is still the best overview of the abuse cycle, and it does not assume more about the abuser's or victim's behavior than is available to the observer. I have decided to use this model because I find that it is easy to understand and see in action when working with victims, abusers, advocates, and family and friends.

An abuser may explode, be bitter, or become aggressive, but the test is how he expresses his anger.

> The harder we try to pin down one explanation, the more certain we are to fail. The reason, I will argue, is that anger is not a disease, with a single cause; it is a process, a transaction, a way of communicating. With the possible exception of anger caused by organic abnormalities, most angry episodes are social events: They assume meaning only in terms of the social contract between participants.[17]

Is their anger used to control, intimidate, coerce, or manipulate others? Can they switch from anger to sympathy and still attempt to "win?" An abuser may not use anger, especially if they know it will not work in a situation, but may use different emotions to control and coerce others.

> One of the earliest lessons I learned from abused women is that to understand abuse you can't look just at the explosions, you have to examine with equal care the spaces *between* the explosions. The dynamics of these periods tell us as much about the abuse as the rages or the thrown objects, as the disgusting name-calling or the jealous accusations. The abuser's thinking and behavior during the calmer periods are what cause his big eruptions that wound or frighten.[18]

Abusers many times feel they are in control of their emotions and surroundings. While abusers may suggest that they are in control of the situation, the opposite actually happens. They are losing control over others, since people and human behavior are not always predictable, and this brings about fear and a desire to achieve more control.

Phase one of the cycle is the *tension phase*. In this phase the tension mounts. The abuser may display higher amounts of anxiety and emotion. Pressures from work, sleep deprivation, or other events may increase their level of anxiety. The abuser becomes edgy and critical around those with whom they have an intimate relationship. The victim and/or children become scapegoats of the abuser's problems and are made to feel responsible

---

[17] Carol Tavris, *Anger: The Misunderstood Emotion*, rev. ed. (N.Y.: Touchstone, 1989) 19.
[18] Bancroft, *Why Does He Do That?* 137–38.

for the abuser's behavior. The victim can usually sense this phase and predict its intensity. Some call it the "walking on eggshells phase." Tension builds and the abuser acts out as a result of his anxiety. This generally is the time when a victim will reach out to others, knowing that the storm is about to erupt. The victim tries to avoid making the abuser angry, hoping that the storm will pass. The family revolves around the anxiety level of the abuser. One woman told me, "When he came home smiling, we all breathed a sigh of relief. When he came home angry, we were on edge."

Phase two of the cycle is the *storm phase*. At this point the abuser uses whatever is at his disposal to control others. This may be the point when the husband first cusses out his wife or when the wife degrades her husband. The abuse escalates. It may develop into physical violence, depending on the behavior of the abuser or intensity of the cycle. For some, it takes years before physical abuse happens; for others, it happens immediately. Rarely is it disclosed the first time this happens. After counseling women and men in abuse, it has become clear that this is a pattern or cycle that occurs but the level of intensity many times differs in intensity. It doesn't matter what the victim has done to try to avoid the storm; it comes and there is little they can do to stop it. A family may bring temporary relief and silence the storm for a time, but the tension will return and the storm will happen. In this phase the abuser acts out by abusing those around him.

Phase three is the *calm after the storm*. During this phase the abuser is sorry. He verbally repents, makes promises, gives gifts, and/or weeps with the victim. He does not seem to be an angry person, but he still attempts to control the victim. He fears that the victim will leave and not return so he promises to change his behavior. He worries about how this looks to others. He can be kind, sweet, charming, and even romantic. He uses coercion and control to "keep the family together," not realizing that he is acting out of fear and selfishness. He will offer to go to counseling, but it is usually only a concession.[19] He may deny the event happened or minimize the abuse. The victim who asked for help during the tension phase now feels that everything is better and they were exaggerating the situation. Children many times are conceived during this period.

---

[19]The Portland batterer intervention trainings I have attended indicate that only 50% of the men who attend batterer intervention groups return for a second session.

Commitments are made in the religious community, counseling sessions are started, and sometimes new things are bought for the family. As with any storm, the scars and damage are still visible. The calm is temporary. Sadly though, the victim sees the cycle begin again. Yet this time there are more responsibilities and attachments as a result of the honeymoon period. The abuser has not changed, but he has coerced his partner to invest more into the relationship, which makes it that much harder to leave. The victim is reminded by the abuser that she could have avoided the storm. Each time the cycle repeats, the storm is more violent and the honeymoon period becomes shorter.

Abuse Escalates

The second characteristic of the methodology of abuse is that it is *likely to continue or escalate unless there is intervention*. When the calm passes, the abuser's attempt to control intensifies. The abuser is narcissistic, which means that he is focused on his own needs and emotions. This attitude causes the victim to be in danger if she leaves, and if she returns he will remind her that he is in power.[20] The abuser feels that he almost lost his partner but has now increased the investment in the relationship through gifts, commitments, and promises. The abuser continues to control but may introduce new methods of coercion into the relationship. He may say that the victim made him angry and give subtle reminders concerning the "night of the storm." This again is an attempt to intimidate and warn the victim not "to cross me again." A raised hand, fist, or threat will remind the victim that the storm can come at any time. Depending on the intensity of the relationship and abuse, the transition from the honeymoon phase to the tension phase can range from a few days to years. It does come

---

[20]The narcissistic attitude of the abuser is illustrated by the research that suggests that the two most dangerous times in an abused woman's life are when she leaves and when she becomes pregnant. The abuser feels that his needs must be met. Rebecca L. Burch, Rebecca L. and Gordon G. Gallup Jr. "Pregnancy as a Stimulus for Domestic Violence." *Journal of Family Violence* 19:4 (2004): 246; and Sandra L. Martin, April Harris-Britt, Yun Li, Kathryn E. Moracco, Lawrence L. Kupper, and Jacquelyn C. Campbell. Changes in Intimate Partner Violence During Pregnancy. *Journal of Family Violence* 19:4 (2004) 201–10.

around again and the cycle repeats, only with more intensity. The cycle abuse can escalate like a violent storm or tornado and subside quickly (Figure 5).

> Abuse *never*—and I use the word never fully aware of its pitfalls—goes away of its own accord; it escalates. Name-calling grows into public humiliation, isolation, and eventually threats, at which level a union may continue until death do them part; on the other hand, threats may become the reality of beatings and murder.[21]

The abuser acts as if he controls the weather and the victim determines the type of weather. The abuser becomes similar to the Canaanite god Baal who rides the clouds, throws the thunderbolt, and brings pain or relief. The victim's only responsibility is to be good and please their Baal.[22]

Figure 5: Escalation of Abuse

The best way to break this cycle is through intervention. Someone has to break the cycle and stop the escalating danger. Sometimes the police arrest the abuser and the cycle ends for a brief period of time. Other times

---

[21]Miller, 10.

[22]There is a play on the Hebrew word for Baal and husband/master found in Hos. 2:16-17, which sound similar.

the victim leaves; however, the abuser is more likely to kill his victim if she leaves home for a time.

> The abusive man becomes more dangerous when he loses all contact
> with his partner. There is a sense of urgency for a man when he feels out
> of control or abandoned. He may even experience this abandonment as
> a threat to his very existence, so that he feels that regaining control or
> reestablishing the relationship is a matter of life or death.[23]

The abuser feels abandoned by his spouse or partner and may violently pursue them, not because of a sense of remorse but because of a need for control.

Sometimes the family or a community intervenes, protects the victim, and holds the abuser accountable. If the abuser attempts to revive the relationship and is successful, the cycle may continue. The cycle will continue until the abuser practices shared power and mutual respect with the partner or until the victim leaves for good. If the relationship continues, the abuser must change his behavior in order for the cycle to end. The abuser is responsible for the cycle, not the victim.

> As long as we see abusers as victims or as out-of-control monsters, they
> will continue getting away with ruining lives. If we want abusers to
> change, we will have to require them to give up the luxury of
> exploitation.[24]

In interviews with victims I have found that some try to display a sense of control in order to survive in the abusive relationship. Victims have taken beatings for their children or parents. Some have found the tension phase so stressful that they have challenged the abuser in order to get past the storm. One woman shared that her mother was coming to

---

[23]Livingston, 22. The victim's greatest physical threat is when they leave their abuser for their first few weeks. Victimization rates in married women separated from their abuser are three times higher than those divorced from an abuser. Caroline M. Clements, and Caryn M. Sabourin, and Lorinda Spiby. "Dysphoria and Hopelessness Following Battering: The Role of Perceived Control, Coping, and Self-Esteem," *Journal of Family Violence* 19:1 (2004) 25.

[24]Bancroft, *Why Does He Do That?*, 157.

visit in two weeks, so she felt that it was better to get a black eye now so that it would heal before her mother arrived. Some found that they could avoid the storm phase occasionally but they also knew that other times there was little they could do about to stop it. This attempt at control is dangerous and happens when the victim sees no way out. Intervention must occur so that the victim does not have to live with this imbalance of power.

While this seems odd to many, it is a typical method of survival. One of our local probation officers has stated, "When you're in survival mode you don't have time to grieve. You don't have time to process."[25] Victims do what they have to do to survive. Victims should never be judged for why they have suffered abuse; they should be supported for their desire to survive. They should be encouraged to be strong rather than be humiliated for trying to adapt. The cycle of abuse is dangerous and violent, and victims many times feel that they are alone. They have been isolated, intimidated, manipulated, humiliated, and violated. They feel powerless. They have been told that the abuse is their fault. They need to be validated. They need to be strengthened to stand, with the rest of the community, and call the abuser to accountability. They need to know that they can remove themselves from the cycle of abuse.

Domestic violence involves coercion, control, subordination, and an intimate relationship. The goal of the abuser is to enforce compliance and engender fear. The cycle of abuse continues because the abuser enjoys the benefits of this cycle. "Over time the man grows attached to his ballooning collection of comforts and privileges."[26] These characteristics are not requirements for an abusive relationship, but they help to define this type of relationship. One person is attempting to exert power over another individual. This is destructive to the spiritual development of others. Healthy relationships are grounded in love, respect, and encouragement. God empowers people to make their own choices and gives free will. Church leaders are not to enforce rules but are to empower members to

---

[25]Naomi Morena, "Cultural Specific Interventions for the Hispanic Domestic Violence Offender," Batterer Intervention Workshop, May 30, 2003. Portland State University, Portland, Oregon.
[26]Bancroft, *Why Does He Do That?* 152.

minister and mature spiritually (Heb. 13:17; Eph. 4:11-16).[27] People are to encourage others to be the best they can be.

Types of Abuse

Abuse can take many forms; therefore, definitions of abuse may differ. This list is not exhaustive, but it introduces the main types of abuse. We are most commonly aware of *physical abuse*. This is usually the type displayed by the media. Physical abuse involves any form of physical action used to control another person. The most obvious forms are hitting, punching, slapping, kicking, shoving, choking, pulling hair or other body parts, and throwing objects at another person.[28] These forms of physical abuse involve abusers directly attacking the victims in an attempt to punish or control their actions. The abusers are invading the other individuals' personal space in an unwelcome manner. This form may often leave bruises, marks, or other signs of trauma that others may or may not be able to see.

> Your partner may have hit you hard enough to leave bruises, but he was careful to hit you only on parts of your body where others would not see them. He may have grabbed you and twisted your arm sufficiently to cause real pain, but he didn't leave a noticeable mark. If he threw you against a wall or pushed you to the floor, no one else would have known.[29]

---

[27]The common translation of Hebrews 13:17 is "Obey your leaders and submit to their authority." Usually the word *peitho* is translated "obey" but it means, "to be persuaded." "Submit" is also the Greek word to "listen intently" (*hypoakouo*). Hebrews 13:17 does not suggest that leaders have power over the members. The passage suggests that Christians respect and listen to their leaders so that the leaders may serve with joy. This, of course, assumes that the leaders are moral and authentic representatives of God. Timothy Willis, "'Obey Your Leaders': Hebrews 13 and Leadership in the Church," *Restoration Quarterly* 36:4 (1994) 316–26.

[28]Meg Kennedy Dugan and Roger R. Hock, *It's My Life Now: Starting Over After an Abusive Relationship or Domestic Violence* (New York: Routledge, 2000) 6; Al Miles, *Domestic Violence: What Every Pastor Needs to Know* (Minneapolis: Fortress, 2000), 111–13; and Susan Weitzman, *"Not to People Like Us": Hidden Abuse in Upscale Marriages* (New York: Basic, 2000) 88.

[29]Dugan and Hock, 5–6.

The forms of physical abuse that may not be as obvious are grabbing/restraining another person by the hair or body parts, and forcing another to stop their movement. These are not as obvious to outsiders because they usually do not leave bruises or marks and can be interpreted by the abuser or victim as "rough housing" or simply a warning. The abuser may also suggest that if they wanted to hurt the other person, they would have used a direct attack on the individual. They may tell the other person that they didn't mean to act so roughly. These forms of physical abuse also force the victims to change their behavior or use a physical response themselves. An example of this occurs when the abuser blocks the door so that the victim cannot leave. The victim is forced to stay where they are or physically attempt to move the abuser. This is still physical abuse because it is an attempt by the abuser to intimidate, control, or coerce the other person. It is also a violation of and unwelcome entry into a person's physical space.

Another type of abuse is *verbal and/or emotional abuse.*[30] While physical abuse is the most obvious, verbal and emotional abuse is the most common. Very few people feel confident reporting this type of abuse because they assume that the abuser is only "losing their temper" or "not thinking before they talk." While at times this may be true, it becomes abuse when it is used to control another person. Verbal and emotional abuse is usually a direct attack on the individual. The abuser uses words and emotions to humiliate or shame the other person. They may resort to name calling, threatening the other person's emotions or personal items, yelling, insulting, blaming, disregarding the other person's feelings, criticizing the other person's language skills, culture, or physical appearance, or harming their pet.[31] This direct abuse causes the other person to feel guilty, ashamed, afraid, and humiliated, and it encourages them to be silent. "As with physical violence, verbal abuse can take many different forms, but the result is to change your view of yourself."[32]

---

[30]While Dugan and Hock separate verbal and emotional abuse, I believe that these work together and therefore can constitute one type of abuse.

[31]There is an increasing awareness concerning the correlation between animal abuse and domestic violence. Veterinary conferences have included sessions concerning domestic violence in families and the effects on animals. Abusers may injure or kill a family pet in order to cause fear in or control the rest of the family. Miles, 112.

[32]Ibid., 6.

Emotional battering, then, runs the gamut from a steady grinding down of a woman to emotional trauma. While her bones are never broken, her flesh never bruised, her blood never spilled, she is wounded nonetheless. With self-confidence and self-respect gone, she lives, empty, with no self left to assert. She cedes control of her life to her abuser. She is helpless.[33]

Dr. Grace Ketterman wrote that verbal abuse is more damaging to the soul of victims than physical abuse. She believes that *verbal abuse precedes other forms of abuse and neglect and also affects a person's self esteem.*[34] Patricia Evans also suggests that verbal abuse affects an individual's personal view of life:

> Verbal abuse is damaging to the spirit. It takes the joy and vitality out of life. It distorts reality because the abuser's response does not correlate with the partner's communication. The partner usually believes the abuser is being honest and straightforward with her and has some reason for what he says—if only she could figure out what it is. When the abuser's response does not correlate with her communications to him, the partner usually tries again to express herself more adequately so he will understand her.[35]

Ketterman also writes that verbal abuse has seven different ingredients.[36]

1. Verbal abuse causes *emotional damage* because of the victim's sense of *rejection* of their value as a person.
2. Verbal abuse may *isolate* a person from friendships by *destroying* the self-esteem needed for these relationships.
3. Verbal abuse *creates terror* in the victim.
4. Verbal abuse *ignores* the victim's basic needs.

---

[33]Miller, 32.

[34]Grace Ketterman, *Verbal Abuse: Healing the Hidden Wound* (Ann Arbor: Servant, 1992), 13.

[35]Evans, 50–51.

[36]Ketterman, 12–13. See also Evans, 50. Evans also has a list of consequences and affects of verbal abuse on the victim that is quite exhaustive.

5. Verbal abuse *corrupts* the values and behaviors of the victim.
6. Verbal abuse *degrades* the victim by robbing them of self-esteem.
7. Verbal abuse *exploits* the victim to the benefit of the abuser.

Physical bruises may heal in a few days, but emotional bruises can last a lifetime. Verbal abuse is designed to humiliate, control, and cause self-doubt in the partner. One victim told me that the bruises healed but the words burned in her mind. Whoever said, "Sticks and stones may break my bones but words will never hurt me," was wrong![37]

Indirectly one may use verbal and emotional abuse to evoke a response or change in the other person. They may threaten to injure or kill themselves, friends, or relatives. They may badger, beg, plead, or harass their partner into consenting to their wishes. They may tell the victim, "You're not really hurt, suck it up." They may withhold information or affection from the victim. The abuser can turn the abuse inward to cause the victim to feel sorry and apologize for their actions. "You made me do this," or "Can't you see what you have done to me?" are examples of verbal and emotional abuse that attempt to take the focus off of the victim's feelings and onto the abuser's. This keeps the abuse cyclical and moves the relationship from the honeymoon phase to the tension phase.

> After each incident of abuse, your partner probably tried to make it seem as though you caused it. It may have gone something like, "I'm so sorry but if only you hadn't . . . " [H]e created a way to seem repentant while telling you it was really all your fault.[38]

This *indirect* form of verbal and emotional abuse causes the other person to be confused and lowers their self-esteem and trust in their own feelings, language, and emotions.

---

[37] "The resilient body mends with ointments and splits—physically battered women know that in their pain. But so deep is the wounding of emotional battering, so down-reaching the anguish, so hopeless the mending that, as the Spanish maxim says, 'He that loseth his spirit loseth all.' The emotionally battered woman loses herself." Miller, 32.
[38] Dugan and Hock, 8.

23

The emotionally abused woman is a particular type of woman, a woman who has established a pattern of continually being emotionally abused by those she is involved with, whether it be her lover or husband, her boss, her friends, her parents, her children, or her siblings. No matter how successful, how intelligent, or how attractive she is, she still feels 'less than' other people.[39]

Sexual abuse is another form of abuse that causes pain to victims. Coercion of sexual activity with another person with or without their consent is rape. When the abuser expects, forces, or initiates unwanted sexual contact upon the other person, it is abuse. A relationship between two people does not give one a right to force or manipulate another into having sex.[40] While sex is meant to be an enjoyable experience, an abuser may try to control the experience of pleasure in the other person. In this manner sex will either be enjoyable only for the abuser or a form of punishment or control over the victim. The victim usually feels humiliation, shame, and guilt when this type of abuse happens.

I believe that sexual abuse can also happen *indirectly*. Whenever a person, organization, or community manipulates others into consenting to have sex with another, it is abuse. The abuse may involve badgering, coercing, or verbally assaulting another person into consenting to have sex, engaging in prostitution, or spouse swapping.[41] While the person

---

[39]Engel, 7.

[40]In 1 Cor 7:1-5 Paul wrote, "Do not deprive one another." This has been used as a text to remind the spouse that they must fulfill their marital duties to the husband. In the Roman Empire having extramarital affairs was a method of sexual fulfillment for most upper class families. Women usually stayed home, managed their families, and accepted whatever their husband chose to do. Sexual fulfillment many times was enjoyed by the husband rather than the wife. Yet the text is encouraging *both* spouses to meet the sexual and emotional needs of the other. The husband and wife are to serve each other sexually so that the relationship may be enjoyable and the other is not tempted sexually. It goes without saying that a husband must be compassionate with his wife.

[41]I have worked with a few women who carried tremendous guilt over extramarital sex due to the fact that their husbands wanted them to be in a "spouse swapping" group. Their unwilling "affairs" with other men who were friends or clients of their husbands usually were coerced. God has opened my eyes to the "coercion" that these women experience when their husbands encourage or force these sexual encounters, and I have been convicted that we often blame the women for "making a choice to have sex" rather than accepting the fact that they may have been manipulated into this behavior.

may have "willingly consented" to sexual contact, this is still a form of coercion and manipulation.[42] The abuser may also manipulate others to coerce the victim through religious teachings, cultural values, humiliation, money, bartering, or marital roles to consent to sexual contact. Spouses coerced into spouse swapping are also victims. The victim feels confusion, shame, and guilt in this situation because they are convinced that they chose this action.

Two shelters contacted me to mediate an issue between Robert and Cecilia. Cecilia was at the women's homeless shelter and Robert was at the men's shelter. She had filed abuse charges against him and had filed for divorce after Robert was convicted. The two shelters were in disagreement over how to handle the situation. The women felt a need to empower Cecilia, and the men felt the same for Robert. Yet the men felt that Cecilia was not acting within God's will when she filed for divorce

After meeting with the counselors of each shelter I had found that the men knew of Robert's abuse conviction and were holding him accountable. Cecilia had told the women counselors that Robert was still harassing her and threatening her over the telephone. Since they were staying in different shelters, he was not able to see her but he still found ways to talk to her. Robert's counselors, unaware of his telephone calls, felt he was coming along and were trying to arrange conjugal visits between Robert and Cecilia. Cecilia and her counselors were uncomfortable with this. The men counselors had a difficult time understanding why this was uncomfortable for Cecilia. This frustrated the women counselors, hence the need for mediation. Cecilia was being

---

[42]I have also spoken during young mothers' programs at our public high schools about dating violence. The school system provides an opportunity for teen mothers to attend school while placing their children in the school day care. I always enjoy talking with these young ladies about their dating relationships and why they have come back to school. Teenage females who are in a dating relationship with older boys do experience pressure to have sexual intercourse. Many have been coerced by the constant nagging of these boys. It is unfortunate that they bear the guilt and shame of what has happened, but it is a clear reminder that "yes" does not always mean "yes." We need to empower our young women to be strong and confident and feel comfortable "loosing" their boyfriend if he does not respect who they are.

placed in a vulnerable position that was being controlled by Robert. He was controlling the counselors who, in turn, were using the Bible (unknowingly) to coerce Cecilia into further victimization. The use of scripture and "theology" to coerce her into sex was an example of direct and indirect sexual abuse by all of the men involved.

God created us male and female to share a sexual relationship out of love, respect, and compassion. Agur tells us that the way of a man with a maiden is wonderful (Prov 30:18-19).[43] This is how a sexual relationship is meant to be—with shared power and respect!

Another form of abuse that is common is *neglect*. Current research suggests that neglect and poor parenting (antisocial behavior) is a powerful indicator of children repeating abuse in their adulthood.[44] Neglect is defined as behavior that withholds emotional or physical needs from another individual. An abuser may withhold food, liquids, clothing, protection, emotional support, verbal communication, finances, or anything else needed by the other person for survival or daily needs.[45] They may fail to properly guide, develop, and nurture their children due to their own selfishness. They may also isolate people physically, emotionally, and geographically in order to prevent them from developing relationships with others. The victim will feel abandoned and unloved as a result of this neglect.

Indirectly abusers may also manipulate victims into sacrificing their needs for the abuser or others. Through coercion and control, abusers

---

[43]The use of *pala'* in the niphal suggests that it is wonderful, great, or amazing.

[44]"Although witnessing family violence uniquely contributed to prediction of psychological spouse abuse, it was childhood neglect that accounted for the largest amount of unique variance in physical spouse abuse scores." Emma Bevan and Daryl J. Higgins, "Is Domestic Violence Learned? The Contribution of Five Forms of Child Maltreatment to Men's Violence and Adjustment," *Journal of Family Violence*, 17:3 (Sept. 2002) 239. Simons, Lin, and Gordon wrote that ineffective parenting increases the chance of dating violence in their children rather than modeling or exposure to harsh corporal punishment. "Children are at risk for developing antisocial patterns of behavior when they are exposed to ineffective parenting practices such as low supervision, rejection, and inconsistent discipline." Ronald L. Simons, Kuei-Hsiu Lin, and Leslie C. Gordon. "Socialization in the Family of Origin and Male Dating Violence: A Prospective Study," *Journal of Marriage and the Family* 60:2 (1998) 468–69.

[45]While some list financial abuse as a separate category, I feel that the withholding of finances seems to fit better under the definition of neglect.

evoke sacrifice and giving from the victim for their own benefit. They may try to manipulate clergy into suggesting that their wives "serve" more. While this form of abuse is hard to see, it is common among spiritual communities and families that may appear deeply religious. While the victim may feel a sense of worth by giving, it is second to the sense of satisfaction and control that is experienced by the abuser.

> The impact of severe neglect on persons is as damaging as acts that are more intentionally and actively perpetrated. In addition, the worst forms of human-induced trauma are those in which some violent act against a person is followed by a period of neglect and lack of support.[46]

When a man becomes violent, those in the intimate relationship become confused. The Dr. Jekyll and Mr. Hyde behavior causes the victim to question the character of the abuser. The refusal to acknowledge wrong and change behavior leaves the victim asking the question, "Is this really his/her nature?" As discussed with Steve earlier (pages 6–7), the abuser must acknowledge his actions and take responsibility for his behavior. Neglect can involve an unwillingness to be accountable for one's actions to those who have been wronged.

Finally, I would like to suggest another form of abuse not commonly discussed, *second hand abuse*. Just as research has proven the harmful effects of second hand smoke, research indicates that children who witness acts of domestic violence are harmed in their emotional, mental, and physical development.[47] Children who witness physical abuse between both parents are subjected to horrible acts of violence. Children who also witness intense

---

[46]J. Jeffrey Means, *Trauma and Evil: Healing the Wounded Soul* (Minneapolis: Fortress, 2000), 16.

[47]Ibid., 223–45; Stephen A. Anderson and Darci B. Cramer-Benjamin, "The Impact of Couple Violence on Parenting and Children: An Overview and Clinical Implications," *American Journal of Family Therapy* 27:1 (1999) 1–19; Bancroft, *The Batterer as Parent*, 37–41, and *When Dad Hurts Mom*, 76, 145–46; Ernest N. Jouriles, Renee McDonald, William D. Norwood, Holly Shinn Ware, Laura Collazos Spiller, and Paul R. Swank, "Knives, Guns, and Interparent Violence: Relations With Child Behavior Problems," *Journal of Family Psychology* 12:2 (1998) 178–94; Jack C. Straton, "What is Fair for Children of Abusive Men?" *Journal of the Task Group on Child Custody Issues of the National Organization for Men Against Sexism*, 4th ed., 5:1 (2001) 1–10.

verbal abuse between both parents are also affected mentally.[48] Children may be the victims of physical, emotional, verbal, or sexual abuse that actually was intended for the other adult. Sometimes pregnant victims have lost their unborn babies due to a physical blow by the abuser. In Oregon, abusers who use physical violence on their partner in front of a child are given stricter punishment in the legal system due to the realization of the effects of second hand abuse. Children who witness domestic violence suffer from sleep difficulties, somatic complaints, aggressive behavior, Attention Deficit Disorder (ADD), Post Traumatic Stress Disorder (PTSD), and depression.[49] The saying is true, "Little pictures have big ears (and eyes)."

Abuse may take many forms, including physical, verbal, emotional, sexual, neglect, and second hand. While these forms are not exhaustive, they give us a good framework with which to begin. Usually domestic violence involves more than one form. All of the forms of abuse may contribute to the dysfunction in an abusive home as well as to the behaviors and coping skills used by the family to survive. Unfortunately, not all of the forms are illegal. While they are all gross violations of human rights, a victim being able to obtain a restraining order for neglect is unlikely. Even though our legal system will prosecute someone committing many of these forms of abuse, there are forms of abuse that occur in the home everyday without prosecution or conviction. A man can verbally and emotionally abuse his wife in front of a police officer and not be charged with abuse.

Fortunately, in faith communities, we can communicate that these forms of abuse are sinful and unacceptable for the people of God to practice or allow to be practiced. In the Hebrew Bible, *Yahweh* revealed divine glory and honor to the nation of Israel and expected them to reflect this glory to the world.

> If a person sins, because they do not speak up when they hear a public
> charge to testify regarding something they have seen or learned about,
> [that person] will be held responsible. (Lev 5:1)

---

[48]Straton, 5.
[49]Boston Medical Center.

An Israelite or alien, living in Israel, who sacrifices any of his children to Molech must definitely be put to death (punished). The people are to stone him. . . . If the people of the community close their eyes when that man sacrifices one of his children to Molech and they fail to put him to death (punish), I will turn my face away from that man and his family and will cut him, and those who follow him, off from their people. (Lev 20:4-5)

If there is a girl who is a virgin engaged to a man, and another man finds her in the city and lies with her, then you shall bring them both out to the gate of that city and you shall stone them to death; the girl, because she did not cry out in the city, and the man, because he has violated his neighbor's wife. Thus you shall purge the evil from among you. But if in the field the man finds the girl who is engaged, and the man forces her and lies with her, then only the man who lies with her shall die. But you shall do nothing to the girl; there is no sin in the girl worthy of death, for just as a man rises against his neighbor and murders him, so is this case. When he found her in the field, the engaged girl cried out, but there was no one to save her. (Deut 22:23-27)

In the Deuteronomy verse, God assumed that if a woman who was raped cried out, someone would rescue her. God opposes the oppressors and protects victims. God also expected the community of faith to speak out against abuse and sexual violence against women and children. God expects the community to respond to the cries of victims.

The Apostle Paul wrote that the fruits of the Spirit are love, joy, peace, endurance, compassion, goodness, gentleness, faithfulness, and self-control (Gal 5:22-23). These are opposite the works of the flesh that include violence, selfishness, and hatred (Gal 5:19-21). In Islam *Allah*, the Creator, is not violent but compassionate and merciful. In the *Quran* every *surah* (chapter) but one states, "*Allah* is beneficent and merciful." All communities of faith should clearly teach the practice of love and peace in community as well as in personal relationships. The types of abuse listed above are contrary to the spirit of the creator and the God who loves and frees the people. In an attempt to reflect the nature of God, faith communities can adopt a zero-tolerance policy for any of these forms of abuse and encourage shared power in relationships rather than coercion, control, and power over one another.

Since abuse is about control and power over another person, we must look at how abuse is used to control others. Once we understand how abuse is used, it will help to dispel the myths of abuse that so saturate our understanding of domestic violence. Again, look at the cycle of abuse (page 11). This cycle repeats until it is broken.[50] The cycle often escalates in intensity and violence as it is repeated.

> The research of clinicians and the studies of criminology, psychology, and sociology allow us to present the three basic dynamics of intimate violence . . . First, intimate violence has a repetitive or cyclical pattern. Second, the repetitive nature of intimate violence creates a psychosocial dynamic within the relationship, in which the perpetrator and survivor become intensely bonded because of, not in spite of, the violence. Third, stalking and homicide can become serious dangers when the survivor of the violence terminates a violent relationship.[51]

Domestic violence is not about anger or losing control. It is about power and control. Abusers use various types of abuse to control and coerce those with whom they are intimate. Unless this cycle is broken, those who try to exert power and control over others are breaking basic human rights as well as spiritual values. Since we are created, male and female, in the image of God, then it should not be in our nature to control others. *Yahweh* is one who empowers people to grow and develop physically, emotionally, and spiritually. Since we are in God's image we must also empower others through shared power, respect, and love.

In this chapter I have suggested that abuse is an attempt to coerce another person in an intimate relationship by using power over them and forcing them to comply. This abuse can be verbal, physical, emotional, sexual, and/or second hand. The abuser is someone who uses these methods to control and subordinate another to comply with their will. Abuse

---

[50]If no one intervenes to break the cycle, the problem will not continue forever. As men grow older their violence decreases. After years of living with an abuser, a wife may find that the cycle will end or that she has learned to adapt to the abuser and avoid conflict. This is still not healthy, but it explains why abuse escalates until older men finally stop abusing their wives. Yet the long-term exposure to abuse has still affected the woman and the children.

[51]Livingston, 11.

involves power and control issues, but it can be intensified by stress, chemical use, or anxiety. Confronting abuse involves addressing these power and control behaviors and educating others about empowering people in relationships.

My belief is that the spiritual community must address domestic violence from the perspective of abusive power and control issues. First, the source of spirituality, God, is not abusive or controlling. Second, the community must reflect our Creator by confronting abusive behavior and empowering victims to be strong and safe. Third, victims are to be protected by the faith community. Instead of further oppressing them or humiliating them, we must empower them to be safe and loved. Too often the faith community calls the victims to forgive rather than the abusers/oppressors to repentance. This will be discussed in a later section.

2
Issues in Domestic Violence

In the first chapter we defined some of the terms that are used in domestic violence. It was suggested that abuse involves power and control rather than anger and loss of control. Anxiety and stress may intensify power and control issues in an individual, but they are not the source of abuse. An abuser may use physical, sexual, verbal, or emotional abuse or neglect to coerce a person into submission. It was also suggested that these tactics may be direct or indirect. Intimate partner violence is cyclical and can escalate when continuing over a long period of time.

Because of the issues of power and control, escalating violence, and various types of abuse, the effects of domestic violence on the family are very traumatic. The affected families are caught in an intricate web of deceit, violence, submission, and manipulation. When trying to work with victims, children, or abusers, one should understand the family system and how it affects the members. This chapter discusses the issues that victims, abusers, children, and other family members will face while living in an abusive home.

Victims

Most of the victims that we work with are women. It has been suggested by many of those working in domestic violence that eighty-five to ninety percent of abuse happens to women by male intimate partners.[1] This involves married, cohabiting, and dating relationships. The victims in these relationships face tremendous obstacles both in surviving and finding safety. Too often outsiders try to rescue victims. Popular songs and movies on the subject of abuse have the woman killing the abuser, running to a protective lover, or having a friend plot to kill the abuser. This hero and rescuer mentality is based on the assumption that the victim wants to be *saved*. The victim wants to be *safe* and respected, but trying to "save" them is further manipulation. This does not empower the victim to confront the abuser and abuse. The victim is being taken away from their home and placed in another environment, sometimes against their will. This is not what the victim needs.

She told Lori and me that she had been abused in the past. Tammy and Mike had come to me for counseling and both admitted that he had hit her. After further discussion, Tammy told me of an incident where she called the police after Mike had beaten her. The police officer had told Tammy that she was crazy to go back to Mike after what he had done. This caused me to think that Tammy and Mike were minimizing the abuse. After a month Tammy called me from her trailer. Lori and I rushed out to help protect her. She had four children, and they lived in a trailer park about ten miles outside of town. Mike had disconnected the telephone and was planning to move further out in the country. Lori and I spent a half hour at the next-door neighbor's home calling the shelter to see if they had room. They were full but willing to make room. The time was right. Mike was drunk and at a friend's trailer down the road. He had his gun and had been drinking all afternoon.

We spent an hour persuading Tammy to leave with the children. We talked and talked and persuaded with everything we had. The adrenaline was flowing and we were on a roll, not even thinking about

---

[1] Note that any statistics are reported statistics. There are men who do not report being abused by women often because of a sense of shame. There are also women who are not able to report abuse. There are also studies among the gay and lesbian communities that indicate a prevalence of abuse. This book focuses only on intimate partner violence in heterosexual relationships. While the number of reported male abuse victims is increasing, it is still a safe assumption to suggest that the majority of abuse comes at the hands of men.

what could happen if Mike came home. Would he attack Tammy and/or the kids for informing me about his abuse? Would he actually "shoot the preacher?" Would he consider us the enemy? She finally consented, and then it took her another hour to get ready. Tammy loaded the kids with a few belongings into the old van. They followed us to the shelter and spent the night there. Lori and I went home exhausted but feeling good. We had saved another one.

The next day Tammy called Mike and went back home. From what the shelter worker told me, he told Tammy he had a good stash of marijuana for her and promised not to hit her any more.

What a roller coaster ride! What a disappointment! What a shame! What manipulation! I am not talking about the husband—I am talking about Lori and me, who obviously *coerced* a woman to leave when that was not what she wanted to do. Would we do it again? If we felt we had to. Was it the right thing? Maybe. Could we have done it differently? Yes! All these questions can be answered better once one is removed from the situation. We did what we felt we had to do at the time, but helping victims is not about whisking them away on our magic carpets. Helping victims is about empowering them to be strong. When working with victims, it is important to understand what they want from others. Studies illustrate that almost ninety-two percent of abused women surveyed indicate that what they want most from another person is a listening ear.[2] This suggests overwhelmingly that victims want to be heard. The first issue that is important to victims is *validation*.

The people of Israel were comforted when God validated their suffering: "When they heard that *Yahweh* was concerned about them and had seen their misery, they bowed and worshipped" (Exod 4:31). Victims cannot worship or be free until they feel validated. Many times victims are afraid that their confession or experiences will be met with "I can't believe it!" or "Are you sure?" Sharing the painful experience of abuse with others is very humiliating, and victims take a great risk when they open up to another person. An abuser has minimized their pain, and they

---

[2]Nancy Nason-Clark, *The Battered Wife: How Christians Confront Family Violence* (Louisville: Westminster John Knox, 1997) 41. See also Adams, 38. Adams indicates that victims want someone to listen to them and acknowledge their suffering.

have been manipulated and confused for so long that they question their own experiences.[3] They have also been taught by both the abuser and many times unbelieving family members and friends to ignore the inner voice. They need to know that they do not deserve to be mistreated. Above all else, when others hear a victim's story they should say, "I believe you," "I want to listen," or "I am sorry that this is happening to you."

> The traditional view of psychotherapy holds that once you sort out your inner conflicts, your behavior will change. Insight precedes action. But when it comes to the abused upscale wife, I have found that outsight—the validation that others bring from the outside by concretizing the experience with words and recognition—precedes insight, which in turn precedes action. Validation must occur before the woman will recognize what is happening and take action on her own behalf.[4]

A second issue for victims is *silence and confidentiality*. Victims have had to cover bruises, scars, tears, cuts, or public outbursts. In order to survive and keep the family together, they have had to give the appearance of a "happy," "normal," and "loving" family. This is an expectation and burden that the abuser has placed upon the victim. The victim feels that it is their responsibility to keep the violence quiet and hidden from the public. Many times they have paid the price for others hearing or seeing the abuser attack them. They also carry a sense of shame for living in this relationship. When a victim shares their suffering, they are risking their own safety as well as their own emotional security. Victims may share their deepest pain with someone and never return for help. The fear of public humiliation and shame keeps them from seeking help. The abuser has convinced them that public exposure is bad for the victim, when in reality it is the reverse.

---

[3]"Chronic mistreatment gets people to doubt themselves. Children of abusive parents know that something is wrong, but they suspect the badness is inside of them. Employees of an abusive boss spend much of their time feeling that they are doing a lousy job, that they should be smarter and work harder. Boys who get bullied feel that they should be stronger or less afraid to fight," Bancroft, 49.

[4]Susan Weitzman, *"Not to People Like Us": Hidden Abuse in Upscale Marriages* (New York: Basic Books, 2000) 35.

Third, victims want *peace and safety*. "I just want him to stop hitting me," is a phrase I hear women say to judges as they submit a restraining order. Children, when taken out of the home, just want the abuse to end. No victim asks to be mistreated. They resist outsiders threatening or punishing the abuser. They want to protect the abuser, but they also want to be protected in their own right. Countless women never tell their fathers or brothers when their husbands or boyfriends abuse them. "If my father would have known I was being abused, he would have killed him!" As a father myself I could understand the passion of their fathers. Why not tell dads about the abuse? Because they love their partners, and they do not want to be alone. They also expect condemnation from friends and family who suggest, "How could you have married such an abuser?" While this may be strange for advocates to understand, it can be damaging for the advocate to react with anger or communicate a hatred for the abuser. The victim hopes that the abuse will stop and that peace will be restored to the family. They love this person and are committed to them. They may see themselves as the problem and just want peace.[5]

Finally, victims *want to be loved*. They truly hope for the best and believe that he can change. While it may be hard to understand why and how the victims can stay in abuse, we do know that victims want to be loved and treated with respect. Many victims have had a history of intimate relationships with men who have been abusive, but this does not mean that they seek abuse. One member in the church where I preached said, "I don't know why they just don't get out. They must enjoy being treated this way." This was an insensitive comment and made out of ignorance. Abusers are manipulators, and they have a powerful way of making someone feel that they are being loved. Victims are like all of us—they want to be loved and respected. They, like anyone else, deserve this. Their hesitance to leave may come from a fear of being rejected and unloved.

Fear, finances, and fantasy of change are three major reasons why women do not leave their abusers.[6] While women may fear their husbands, they also believe that their husbands will change or that they can change

---

[5]Self-blame is a common coping mechanism for victims in abuse. Clements, 33.
[6]Catherine Clark Kroeger and Nancy Nason-Clark, *No Place for Abuse: Biblical and Practical Resources to Counteract Domestic Violence* (Downer's Grove, Ill.: InterVarsity, 2001) 34–35.

their husbands. What happens when they leave their abuser? They have to raise their child, find a job, and live in transition. They are at greater risk of being attacked or killed by their partner. They feel at times as if they made a mistake. Then they come to church and see families that seem happy. They hear sermons on how people divorce too easily or that adultery is the only scriptural grounds for divorce. They hear how wives must submit to their husbands and through patience and submission can turn them around. These women feel alone and out of place. They feel guilty and responsible for the direction of the marriage. Instead of feeling like they made a wise choice, they feel ashamed and feel they are failures. They hear the abuser's voice from the pulpit saying, "You can't leave me because no one will accept you." Even though the abusive relationship is dangerous, they feel a sense of love, support, and acceptance in that relationship. They do not feel validated in the community.

Imagine what it is like to be a child who is being bullied at grade school. Maybe someone at school bullied you when you were younger. How did you react? While others said it's not that bad, was it real in your mind? Did you worry every time you saw the bully? When he/she stared at you, did you feel overwhelmed with fear? When he made a punching motion with his hand or she acted like she was going to slap you, did you react defensively? How many teachers did you tell? Do you remember the warning "If you tell anyone I will get you after school." If the teacher asked if you were OK, in front of the bully, what did you say? Above all, how did it feel when the bully came to you and acted as if everything was good? How did it feel when she put her arm around you and acted like she was your friend? Remember that sigh of relief mixed with uneasiness? "Good," you thought, "today is a day I won't get pummeled!"

> Most of us start a relationship thinking we have certain limits in terms of what we will or won't tolerate from other people. But as the relationship progresses, we tend to move our boundaries back, giving in more and more until we end up tolerating more and more and even doing things we were determined not to do. Not only do we begin tolerating unacceptable and abusive behavior, we begin to convince ourselves that these behaviors are normal or acceptable.[7]

---

[7]Engel, 159.

Abuse victims live on that playground every day, and they usually won't tell a soul because they know what will happen when there are no teachers around. Yet, whenever a teacher intervenes and protects them, while they may resist, deep down the victims appreciate the help.

One of my favorite Dr. Seuss stories is *Horton Hears a Who*. In the story Horton, an elephant with big ears, hears a cry from a Who person who is in a tiny city that exists on a small flower. Throughout the story Horton listens and speaks to these unknown tiny people. When the community where Horton lives tries to destroy the flower, not knowing the Who people, Horton tries to convince them that these people exist. The community does not believe Horton and continues the plan to destroy the flower. Finally, Horton convinces the Who people to make so much noise that the friends of Horton hear them. The city is saved because someone with *big ears* hears the cries of the little people and convinces others that they exist.

God has big ears and hears the cries of the oppressed and abused (Ps 95:1-9; Jonah 4:9-11). While the faith community has, at times, been oblivious to the voice of the little people, God continues to challenge Christians to hear their cries. When the faith community supports women who are being abused, it needs to *validate* the victims by listening to their story and showing empathy. The community also needs to appreciate the great risk that these victims have taken when they share their story. It is the victim's right to expect *confidentiality* until they decide to share their story with others. The faith community should also be concerned about providing *peace and safety* to the women who seek help. Finally, the spiritual community has a great opportunity to show *love* and *acceptance* to those who have been abused. It is the responsibility of the faith community to listen, protect, love, and provide safety to victims. We must empower them to be strong rather than humiliate them back into submission, self-blame, and fear.

A woman cannot escape an abusive marriage unless she first realizes that she is being battered and puts a name to her situation. Often this insight comes through others. . . . Most women report that it was input from external sources—friends, relatives, therapists, lawyers, even strangers—that ultimately helped them recognize they were in an abusive marriage and gave them the courage and permission to get out.

When others witness or comment on abusive behaviors, the little voice that the upscale abused wife once heard inside her and ignored or muffled becomes amplified. Slowly she starts to recognize that she must stop enduring the abuse.[8]

Abusers

Since we have defined domestic violence as power and control rather than anger, it is important to discuss the major issues that abusers face. This is important to discuss before anyone attempts to help or confront someone who has been abusive. The power and control issues are such that even an outsider can get caught in the web of manipulation, coercion, and control. Abusers are not monsters. They are human beings whose views of life are dysfunctional and need reform.[9]

First, abusive partners usually feel that *they are the victims*. One batterer intervention specialist has told me that when he talks with couples that experience domestic violence he asks, "Who is the victim?" The abuser tends to be the first one to speak up and say, "I am." The world of the abuser is one that revolves around him. Abusers tend to be narcissistic and have the feeling that they are being victimized in the domestic violence justice system.[10] They sometimes view disagreements as win/lose situations rather than as win/win. As perceived victims, they feel that their actions are always in response to others. They feel that they are reacting to tension and strife. If other people would behave, they often reason, they would not lose their temper or become violent. Abusers spend much of their lives reacting to the actions of others rather than practicing self-control. They feel that it is the responsibility of others to understand their actions.

Second, abusers *attempt to control* others because they are concerned about self-image. This may stem from low self-esteem or deep insecurities.[11]

---

[8]Weitzman, 112–15.

[9]Bancroft, 36.

[10]This is illustrated by the fact that the highest risk a partner has of being abused is when they leave or return to the abuser and when they become pregnant. The first means abandonment to the abuser; the second means competition.

[11]Bancroft, *Why Does He Do That?*, 42, suggests that this is a myth (abusers have low self-esteem) but my trainings at the Men's Resource Center in Portland and my own personal

They may practice control in different ways, but they do attempt to control others. While the abusive man may seem like the perfect gentleman in public, he is controlling how others view him. No one would know that he goes home and beats his wife or verbally humiliates her. Her family may see him as a nice guy. If he ever explodes in public, he will quickly try to smooth over his actions to others, while later taking it out on his partner behind closed doors. *Men who are violent outside of the home usually are violent within the home, yet men who are violent within the home usually are not violent outside the family.* When pressure is on the family (the wife leaves, the children tell someone about the abuse, or the husband feels others know about the problem), the abuser will become very concerned about convincing others that it is not his fault. He may suggest that he was overstressed or sleep deprived or that it was just this once. He may also tell others that it was her fault by saying "She attacked me and I was defending myself." Excuses and perceptions are important to the abuser because he is concerned about self-image.

"I was told by my sister-in-law to call you," the voice said on the telephone.

I had never met him but had seen his picture. It was the family picture I glanced at as we convinced his wife to get the two children and leave for her parents' home. Her sister was a member of our congregation and we had worked up this escape plan for a few weeks. We helped her out that day and he was calling me that night.

"What do you want to talk about?" I said.

---

experience suggests that the men who I have dealt with do have low self-esteem. I think that it is important to make a distinction between overconfidence and self-esteem. Overconfidence is a front or an appearance that an individual will display because they feel inferior and do not want their true identity to be seen. Jackson Katz calls this the "Tough Guise" that men use to mask their true feelings. An excellent video on this issue is: Jackson Katz, *Tough Guise*, (Northampton, Mass.: Media Education Foundation, 1999). I also feel that this is a result of low self-esteem. Many of the men I have observed who have been abusive also have problems developing relationships with others, especially men. An individual with low self-esteem is acting out of fear rather than self-respect. I think that most abusers are overconfident and this gives batterer intervention specialists the impression that they do not suffer from self-esteem issues. This also explains their fear of being abandoned or second in an intimate relationship.

"Well, I'm really hurtin' here. My wife left and won't talk to me. She took the kids away from me. She says I have been verbally abusive to her and had some anger problems. She says I neglect them because I won't work and when I'm home I won't help her out around the house."

"Anything else?" I asked.

"Yes, I guess I have hit her sometimes but I was drunk," he finally said.

"Why are you calling me?" I asked.

"My sister-in-law told me maybe you can help. Says you work with this stuff."

"Yes, I do," I said. "To be honest with you, I was there to get your wife out."

There was silence on the phone, then he said, "Thank you for doing that—I know you care about me and my family. I only want the best for them."

"Thank you," I said. "I think we need to talk and I would like you to come to my office tomorrow."

"I want to. By the way Brother Ron [I didn't know he was religious] from my study of the Bible she can't leave me unless I have an affair on her. From what my mom told me, Jesus said she is not to divorce me. Do you think we should study that tomorrow? Maybe she can come in and we can look at that together?"

"Oh," I said, "actually, I think she can leave you for other reasons. We'll study some of those passages if you would like." Again, silence on the phone.

I then interrupted the silence. "Todd, I know that you care about your wife but understand that God does not tolerate certain behaviors. Drugs, drunkenness, pornography, verbal humiliation, physical violence, and child neglect are all behaviors that God does not want your wife and children to experience in their home. I think that God wants them to have something better, don't you agree?" Again, silence on the phone.

"I guess you're right. Maybe we need to talk," he said.

"How about tomorrow morning? In fact why don't we have prayer right now?" I said.

Abusers are not monsters. They are trying to convince people that they are good and do not need to change. Working with them involves wisdom, compassion, and discernment.

The third major characteristic of abusers is *confusion and manipulation*. While fear is a common experience of being with an abuser, verbal and psychological abuse can confuse victims as well as those working with abusers. They may use intimidation and manipulation in situations where that works for them. They may also use self-pity and try to evoke sympathy from those around them. "I guess you really don't care about me" or "I guess you think you're perfect enough to judge me" are common statements they may make to you. Sometimes they blame, "Haven't you ever made a mistake?" Other times they can talk circles around another person in an attempt to coerce and convince that the evidence against them is slighted and one sided. Many victims tell me that their partner would be a great lawyer and can argue any point convincingly. After meeting these men, I agree. I call this the "headache syndrome" because it gives me a headache, while other intervention specialists call it "crazy making" behavior. Victims are confused by the "Jekyll and Hyde" personality and find themselves unsure of their own feelings and perception of a situation.

When an abuser denies an incident immediately after it happens, he can set his partner's head spinning. Picture a woman who arises in the morning with her stomach still tied in a knot from an ugly blowout the night before. Her partner makes a face at her in the kitchen and says, "Why are you so grumpy today?" . . . The more serious the incidents he denies, the more her grip on reality can start to slip. And if outsiders start to notice her instability, the abuser can use their observations to persuade them that her revelations of abuse by him are fantasies.[12]

Fourth, the abuser is *dominated by fear*. The abuse of power is motivated by fear and a desire to control the lives of others.[13] This may seem odd to the observer because these men appear to be in control, but they are narcissistic. They are concerned about their public image and are trying to cover up their deep-seated fears of rejection and low self-esteem. They fear being alone or abandoned. While they are trying to gain control, they are actually losing it. They are afraid of rejection by others so they try to control and manipulate. They are the heroes of their own stories because

[12]Bancroft, *Why Does He Do That?*, 72.

[13]James Newton Poling, *The Abuse of Power* (Nashville: Abingdon, 1991) 27.

they need to be honored and praised by those closest to them. They seek validation because they know that their behavior is unacceptable. I believe that they want to change but change brings discomfort and fear.

Finally, abusers are *not in touch with their true feelings*. Many males have been taught as children that the only emotion they can show is anger. They are in denial concerning their abusive behavior and justify or minimize this sin. Many motion pictures, which portray the strong silent men as peaceful until they face a crisis, reinforce this anger. The story line commonly is similar. Young man is a violent warrior. Violent warrior decides to settle down with a family. Warrior wants to retire peacefully. Man is pressured into continuing as warrior. Man resists. Man loses family. Man becomes killing machine. In *The Patriot*, Benjamin Martin, portrayed by Mel Gibson, is encouraged to use his intense "frenzied" anger to go to war. While trying to avoid this part of his nature, the political events in America, as well as his own sons, push him to use this behavior to fight the British. While this behavior horrifies his children, it is seen as justified. Benjamin Martin reacts to his environment. As with many young men, peacefulness, negotiation, and a willingness to ignore humiliation are seen as weaknesses rather than strengths. Unfortunately, some societies, including the United States, communicate to young men that there are certain behaviors associated with being a man. This message is also present in media and culture. Behaviors are deemed male or female.[14] I also find that this dichotomy of emotions is prevalent in some of the Christian marriage literature. While I believe that men and women have some physiological differences, I feel that we have much in common.

> A second myth—especially when we read popular articles or books about gender difference—lumps all men into one category and all women into the opposite category. It turns out that there is as much diversity *within* a group of women or *within* a group of men as there is *between* men and women. This has been shown to be true in studies of math skills, verbal skills, aggression, and spatial abilities. The *between-group* difference is smaller than the *within-group* difference.[15]

---

[14]Paul Kivel, *Men's Work: How to Stop the Violence that Tears Our Lives Apart* (Center City, Minn.: Hazelden, 1992) 21, 44.

[15] Alice P. Mathews, *Preaching that Speaks to Women* (Grand Rapids: Baker, 2003) 24. See also Chris Huffine, "Attention Earthlings."

In some of the popular books about males and females, men are considered the hunters and gatherers and women the homemakers.[16]

This is clear even in popular Christian literature. For example, the book *Wild At Heart: Discovering the Secret of a Man's Soul* by John Eldredge laments the fact that men have become peaceful and compassionate.

> Society at large can't make up its mind about men. Having spent the last thirty years redefining masculinity into something more sensitive, safe, manageable and, well, feminine, it now berates men for not being men. Boys will be boys, they sigh. As though if a man were to truly grow up he would forsake wilderness and wanderlust and settle down, be at home forever in Aunt Polly's parlor. "Where are all the real men?" is regular fare for talk shows and new books. You asked them to be women, I want to say. The result is a gender confusion never experienced at such a wide level in the history of the world. How can a man know he is one when his highest aim is minding his manners?[17]

Eldredge suggests that it is in the nature of men to be like God, but his view of God seems to be cultural. Men are designed to be violent, restless, and aggressive. In his mind, men are to be warriors, like God.

> Capes and swords, camouflage, bandannas and six-shooters—these are the uniforms of boyhood. Little boys yearn to know they are powerful, they are dangerous, they are someone to be reckoned with . . . If we believe that man is made in the image of God, then we would do well to remember that "the LORD is a warrior, the LORD is his name" (Exod 15:3).[18]

Alas, the author continues to suggest that our problem today is that we as men have become *feminized* or *emasculated*. We are restless because deep down we want to be daring, aggressive, tough, and heroes. We should be

---

[16]Probably the most common book is John Gray, *Men Are From Mars, Women Are From Venus: A Practical Guide for Improving Communication and Getting What You Want in Your Relationship* (New York: HarperCollins, 1992).

[17] John Eldredge, *Wild At Heart: Discovering the Secret of a Man's Soul* (Nashville: Thomas Nelson, 2001) 6–7.

[18]Ibid., 10.

warriors, not just good boys. These are the characteristics that Eldredge defines as truly masculine.

> To most men, God is either distant or he is weak—the very thing they'd report of their earthly fathers. Be honest now—what is your image of Jesus as a man? "Isn't he sort of meek and mild?" a friend remarked. "I mean the pictures I have of him show a gentle guy with children all around. Kind of like Mother Teresa." Yes, those are the pictures I've seen myself in many churches. In fact, those are the only pictures I've seen of Jesus. As I've said before, they leave me with the impression that he was the world's nicest guy. Mister Rogers with a beard. Telling me to be like him feels like telling me to go limp and passive. Be nice. Be swell. Be like Mother Teresa. I'd much rather be told to be like William Wallace.[19]

He seems to suggest that we have the feminists to blame for this problem. Instead of teaching us to model the truly great virtues of love, compassion, and mercy, Eldredge suggests that they have taken away our manhood by making us become "good boys." Yet most of the men I work with resent their fathers for being the stereotypical male. In the movie *Big Fish*, the son was angry with his father for being too involved in the adventure and telling the big story and not concerned enough about listening to his own son. Most men I know respect the dad who was home, holding the children, and being an example of a good husband.

As I read through Eldredge's book, which was given to me at a pastors' conference, I couldn't help but wonder if the author received his images of manhood from real life or the movies. His quotation of *Braveheart* suggested to me that his image of William Wallace was more from Mel Gibson than it was from history. His distaste for Mother Teresa and Mr. Rogers slaps women and compassionate men in the face.

As a minister, I appreciated the book as a gift until I read it. It is this very mindset that we are fighting in domestic violence ministry. This mindset suggests that certain behaviors are feminine or masculine. This mindset causes men to be afraid of showing qualities that others, such as Eldredge, consider feminine. One of the victim's advocates on our abuse

---

[19]Ibid., 22.

council, who is also a former victim, asked me if I had read the book. When I expressed my opinion, she agreed and said she was aggravated when she read it and would not want her son to get a copy. This has also been the sentiment of many batter intervention advocates. Eldredge suggested in the book that women want a hero, yet my wife responded with, "Girls want a hero, women want a man who is a good husband and father." Yet this is an example of how cultural and worldly thinking have crept into the church. This warps the view of God and requires Jesus to be Rambo.

I believe that labeling feelings and behavior as male or female can keep men from becoming like God. When asking men what feelings are associated with masculinity, a box is created with those emotions and feelings (Figure 6). A real man, according to many young men, is tough, strong, sexy, independent, etc.

```
┌─────────────────────────────────────────────┐
│  Tough        Vindictive      Strong         │
│                                              │
│         Quiet            Successful          │
│                                              │
│               Big                            │
│  Cool                            Powerful    │
│         Intimidating                         │
│                                  Winning     │
│                                              │
│            Real Man                          │
└─────────────────────────────────────────────┘
```

Figure 6: Definition of a Real Man?[20]

The emotions outside of the box, which are opposite those inside the box, are considered feminine (Figure 7). Thus, those who are not real men are weak, a failure, submissive, dependant, and loving.

---

[20]The following diagrams are taken from Katz, *Tough Guise.*

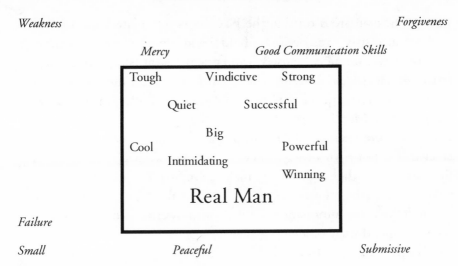

Figure 7: Behaviors Outside the Box

Our masculine culture has a way of reinforcing these "masculine emotions" by using degrading terms to force men to stay inside the box (Figure 8). Those behaviors that are opposite of a "real man's" behavior are labeled female or homosexual.

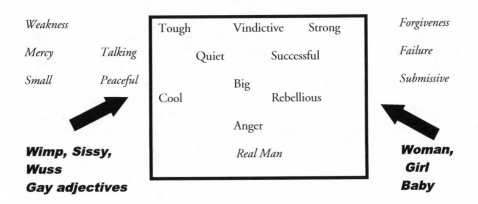

Figure 8: Staying Inside the Box

If a young man steps outside the box, he is humiliated and labeled a woman, gay, sissy, etc. Because of this, many men grow up frustrated because they cannot be themselves and practice a variety of emotions that reflect the image and glory of God. They learn to fear those who are the "opposite" of them. This is possibly the source for misogyny and homophobia. Men fear women because they practice the very emotions that men have been taught to suppress. They fear other men who are labeled "feminine" by others. They cannot express their feelings because they are taught that anger is the most culturally acceptable response to anxiety.[21] Anger is the response of "successful people" or "real men." Intimidation and humiliation result from powerful people conquering the weak in a display of anger.

Abusive people are those who do not understand that anger is a reaction to their anxiety. Anger seems to be the most prevalent emotion in their lives. This stunts the development of other emotions and gives them permission to avoid their true feelings. They do not have a resource of other feelings to process. Their experiences of life are very narrow because they have a limited number of emotions from which to draw.

Theologically, this is far removed from God. While there have been books written about God as an angry and abusive husband, I feel that these misrepresent the true nature of God.[22] While Biblical texts suggest that God is passionate and at times gets angry (Exod 32:11; Num 11:1; John 2:12-19), God grieves, relents, and is vulnerable (Gen 6:6; Exod

---

[21]"The harder we try to pin down one explanation, the more certain we are to fail. The reason, I will argue, is that anger is not a disease, with a single cause; it is a process, a transaction, a way of communicating. With the possible exception of anger caused by organic abnormalities, most angry episodes are social events: They assume meaning only in terms of the social contract between participants." Tavris, 19.

[22]Renita Weems suggests that God is the abuser in the covenant relationship with Israel. Renita Weems, *Battered Love: Marriage, Sex, and Violence in the Hebrew Prophets*, Overtures to Biblical Theology (Minneapolis: Fortress, 1995) 23. I think that the Biblical text indicates that God "hands rebellious Israel over" to the abusers. God shows love, compassion, mercy, and other relational emotions. Some of these characteristics usually are considered feminine in the ancient world. I feel that God is spirit but the emphasis in the masculine gender with God is meant to challenge men to see their nature from God, not the world. God may express anger, passion, and jealousy, but does not abuse the nation of Israel. The suffering of Israel came at the hands of others, not God. It came after decades/centuries of warning and pleading for repentance.

32:14; John 11:34). The Hebrew word for jealous (*qanah*) is a term used for a jealous husband.[23] God continues to reach out to those who would bring grief because of their disobedience, (Gen 9:9-10; Isa 65:2; Hos 2:14-20; Rom 10:21) and remains faithful. In a dialogue with Moses, *Yahweh* reveals a nature that is compassionate, gracious, slow to anger, abounding in love and faithfulness, maintaining love to thousands, and forgiving of wickedness, rebellion, and sin (Exod 34:6-7). Yet *Yahweh* does punish the guilty. *God is not a God of anger but of compassion, love, and mercy.* God may be passionate about people but this passion is shown in a desire for relationship.

In Ezekiel 16, the prophet tells the story of God and the nation of Israel. God compared Israel to a neglected and abandoned baby who was lying by the side of the road with its umbilical cord still attached and covered in the placenta. God caused the baby to live, develop, and grow to be a beautiful woman. God married the young woman and helped her become the most beautiful woman in the land. Yet she became a prostitute and chased other lovers (gods and nations). God was the victim, the abused, and the neglected one. Instead of physically abusing the woman, God handed her over to her lovers (16:39) who then raped her and destroyed her city (Israel). Then after she was humiliated, God took her back and remarried her. The text shows a passionate, angry, and hurt God. God was faithful and compassionate, but as a partner felt the pain of rejection while watching the other partner continue in spiritual affairs. So this husband turned his back on his wife and let her experience the pain of her unfaithfulness. In the end, the husband became vulnerable and remarried the unfaithful wife. God again was willing to trust, love, and become vulnerable to this unpredictable partner. The message is not how a man should treat an unfaithful wife, but how a man can forgive an unfaithful wife. The beginning of this text (Ezek 16:1-14) suggests that a man love, give, and empower a wife to be the best she can be. The husband is to be like God, one who helps the bride develop and feel as if she is the most beautiful woman in the land.

Many of these characteristics of God came to men (Exod 34:6-7; Jonah 4:2). God revealed as male is not discrimination against women but a

---

[23]David Instone-Brewer, *Divorce and Remarriage in the Bible: The Social and Literary Context* (Grand Rapids: Eerdmans, 2002) 2.

revelation to men about a God whose nature is considered feminine in other cultures. In a world that separated male and female gods, to supply the "male" and "female" emotions, *Yahweh* needed no separation. *Yahweh* is one because *Yahweh* can practice both discipline and patience. God revealed as male brought a message to men, who needed to practice the noble qualities of God's nature in their lives. God was not degrading women but was teaching men how they should behave. God as Father is simply God as a model for fathers. Jesus as a son is a model for the church of God. Jesus as a husband is a model for husbands. In a world of male violence, God reveals to men that spirituality is about patience, love, compassion, mercy, and faith. When men saw God as "He," they learned that "male" nature is grounded in God rather than in their culture.

When the faith community attempts to work with abusers, these issues need to be remembered. Abusers feel victimized, attempt to control others, are struggling with fear, and have trouble communicating their true feelings. They are not the enemy. They are not to be demonized, but loved. They are human beings who have been misguided and stunted from growing in the image of God.

> What lies at the core of reconciliation is nothing less than the enchanting and overwhelming notion that even when a human has become so distorted and disfigured by egoism, rage, despair, and fear, that person will be embraced by the Christian community. The Christian community has within its treasure trove of symbols a call for reconciliation. We are called as Christians not to demonize those who act in evil ways but rather to call them to accountability and to love them. This required that we ferret out the true insights in this message of hope. [24]

The media and society have done a good job of bringing abuse awareness into the communities. Yet there tends to be a sense of anger and vindictiveness in working with abusers. A popular musical group has written a song about a woman who kills her husband. The song mentions that, "Earl had to die." When we meet violence with anger and rage, we also become abusers. When we fail to understand the abuser's fears and

---

[24]Livingston, 65.

emotional immaturity we intimidate them and attempt to enforce compliance.

One of the greatest dangers facing those who work with abusers is the danger of being caught in the abuser's web of confusion. We should be careful that we do not enable them nor become manipulated by them. On the other hand, we need to be careful that we are not dominated by the same fear that they experience. Too often media and popular culture have chosen to meet abusers with anger and vengeance. The vigilantes become the heroes and judges of our society. This reflects our own sense of helplessness and fear. Ignorance and insecurity cannot address power and control issues. Abusers, like the victims, need love, peace, acceptance, and safety. The faith community must be innocent as doves and wise as serpents (Matt 10:16). The church must support victims by calling abusers to accountability.

> Abusive men choose when and how to be abusive. They could choose not to rape their wives anally, not to throw them down the stairs, not to threaten them verbally or emotionally. But abusive men profit from their behavior. Their partners quit jobs or take jobs, get pregnant or have abortions, cut themselves off from their friends, keep the kids quiet at times or send them away. Men who batter not only believe they have the right to use violence, but receive rewards for behaving in this manner, namely, obedience and loyalty. In addition, battering guarantees that the man wins disputes that the status quo in the relationship is maintained, and that the woman will not leave him.[25]

Children in Abusive Homes

Power and control issues also affect children who live in abusive homes. The purpose of this book is not to address child abuse but to address the effects of intimate partner violence on children. When children experience or observe verbal abuse and violence, their emotional and physical development is greatly affected. Studies have shown that children in violent

---

[25]Adams, 20.

homes suffer from a form of Post Traumatic Stress Disorder (PTSD).[26] PTSD affects children continually and can cause *hypervigilance*. Children may experience nightmares or have recurring flashbacks of violent or traumatic events that they have observed or experienced. PTSD can also cause children to behave in one of two ways.

First, children may react to trauma with *hyperarousal*. Hyperarousal is a state in which children experience high levels of anxiety. This will affect them physiologically in ways such as increased heart rate, clenched fist, standing up or pacing, intense fear, or anger. Mentally they will begin to cross the threshold of their brain activity, which causes their blood flow to increase to the outer extremities of their body. This "fight or flight" response decreases the blood flow to the rational/logical portion of the brain.[27] These children can be aroused easily and react irrationally to a perceived threat. If anger is a dominant emotion for young children, it will be used frequently. When under trauma, they become edgy and anxious. This would explain some forms of Attention Deficit Disorder (ADD) and sleep difficulties that children who witness abuse often exhibit. I have heard that small children have attacked their mother's abuser without any concern for size or their own personal harm.

Another reaction from children is *disassociation*. This is the opposite of hyperarousal in that the child retreats from the real world and experiences an isolation and denial of their emotions. They put away their feelings and go into hiding. This is more prevalent in younger children and adolescent females.[28] It is a realization that they are helpless to change the situation, so they move away from it.

---

[26]Much of this is explained on a website that discusses child trauma. See: <www.childtrauma.org> and Grant L. Martin, *Critical Problems in Children and Youth: Counseling Techniques for Problems Resulting from Attention Deficit Disorder, Sexual Abuse, Custody Battles, and Related Issues* (Waco, Tex.: Word, 1992) 143–44. See also the Boston Medical Center website which suggests that eighty to eighty-five percent of children who witnessed violence in the home suffer from mild PTSD.

[27]"When animals are threatened or perceive danger, they do respond in ways that we liken to anger: Hair (if the animal has hair) stands on end, pupils dilate, muscles tense, fins flap, warning growls or chirps or rattles sound, and the organism readies itself to fight or flee." Tavris, 34.

[28]Child Trauma.

Consequently, traumatic experiences result in people cutting themselves off emotionally and psychically from others and themselves . . . In this way, human-induced trauma naturally propels persons into a state of being radically disconnected, and also keeps them stuck in a state of social isolation from others and psychological isolation from themselves. Persons who have a history of being abused, neglected, and isolated in these ways are often prone to perpetrate similar abuse and neglect on others.[29]

Survivors of long-term childhood molestation indicate that they learned to disassociate themselves from the sexual act. They describe it as: "I was observing the act as if it wasn't really happening to me."

Children in abusive families also *experience learning and cognitive disorders* by being exposed to abusers and spousal abuse. Bancroft lists the following psychological symptoms of children exposed to domestic violence:[30]

- Attention deficits
- Hyperactivity that interferes with learning and attention
- Learning delays
- Delays in language acquisition
- Poor academic performance
- Missing school often through sickness or truancy
- Falling asleep in school
- Sibling rivalry or hierarchy

Bancroft indicates that this is not just due to witnessing domestic violence. He indicates that the exposure to an abuser has caused them to also be easily manipulated, suffer traumatic bonding, and become involved in undermining their mother.

Children are emotionally affected by living in abuse. While much work has been done to protect the women in abusive situations and provide for their safety, children many times are exposed to the abuser even after he is taken out of the house. Unsupervised visitation makes it possible for

---

[29]Means, 24.
[30]Bancroft, *When Dad Hurts Mom*, 76, 145–46.

the abuser to continue to undermine the woman and manipulate her into taking him back or letting him take the children.

Parental conflict has a destructive impact on the emotional well being of children. Parents may think that children are not aware of the abuse, but they do hear and sense the conflict that exists in the home.

> Children learn to recognize ominous tones of voice and intimidating body language. They feel sharp pains when they see their mother humiliated or degraded. They are filled with an urgent desire to rescue her, but at the same time can feel paralyzed by fear, so they are left feeling guilty standing by and not intervening. Their innocence can slip away in the process.[31]

"I hope my mom and I hope my dad, will figure out why they get so mad / I hear them scream I hear them fight, they say bad things that make me want to cry."[32] These words from a popular Portland band, *Everclear,* summarize the stress that children of abuse face in the home. Children react to trauma and stress in different ways. They may seem normal on the outside, but they internalize much of what they are witnessing.[33] Educators understand that hyperarousal and disassociation are prevalent in children from abusive and dysfunctional homes. A scene from the movie *The Breakfast Club* illustrates this point. The school troublemaker, played by Judd Nelson, experienced conflict with Dick, the teacher in charge of Saturday detention. The teacher was angry with the student and was shown pushing him to anger. At times Nelson's character would reach a point of intense anger and then seemed to emotionally and intellectually "shut down." He ran up a list of detention dates without any concern for the consequences. This happened because another adult treated him with anger, intimidation, and a lack of compassion and understanding, as his father treated him. In my experience substitute teaching students with behavior and learning disabilities, these types of children need patience

---

[31]Ibid, 13.

[32] "Wonderful," Art Alexakis/Everclear, *Songs from an American Movie, Vol. 1: Learning How to Smile* (Capitol Records, July 11, 2000).

[33]Barbara Thompson, "An Interview with James Garbarino on the Impact of Violence on Children," *World Vision* (April-May 1995) 8–9.

and clarity. The teachers and aids were a constant source of encouragement to me as I saw them quietly and calmly motivate the kids to focus and lower their level of anxiety.

Children of abuse have not developed the skills to process their experiences, as most healing adults have. As the children grow, they use only the skills that they have developed. Hyperarousal becomes hypervigilance. Fear, intimidation, and anger do not work with many of the children. Abusive parents can control smaller children through threats and violence, but adolescents who have learned to disassociate ignore these consequences.

> Various life experiences can disrupt one's developing concept of self, world, others, and God. They do this by disrupting the interpersonal environments in which the basic structures influencing one's attitudes and orientation to self and the world are formed. Experiences of human induced trauma and neglect massively distort these interpersonal relationships, damage developing mental structures, and subsequently have a continuing deleterious impact on a person's development and interactions with others.
>
> The effect of such abuse and neglect upon children is especially devastating. This is in part because a child's self-structure and defenses are weak and in the early stages of formation. Children also lack fully developed cognitive capacities, so they are even less able to understand what is happening to them than are adults in similar circumstances. Children are also more severely damaged by the tremendous power differential existing between themselves and significant adults.[34]

One should never use intimidation, fear, humiliation, shame, or threats with these children. We must practice compassion and mercy and empower children to discuss their feelings and increase their threshold of patience. Children exposed to abuse are traumatized and resist or withdraw from authority. Children must know that the church can be a place to ask any questions and share experiences with confidentiality, no matter how horrible they are. They must also know that they will be believed and heard without being judged.

---

[34]Means, 24.

Family and Friends

While many of my experiences are with victims, often family and friends seek help for those who are in violent relationships. Family and friends also face issues that cause them to be concerned about their loved ones. Many experience the same emotions that victims do.

Shock and disbelief usually are first on the list of issues. I find that most have attempted to accept the abuser into their family and have been manipulated into thinking that "he has a few rough edges but nothing serious." Others have accepted the victim into their family and are shocked that someone would ever mistreat someone they love. I think that much of this shock and disbelief happens because we demonize abusers rather than understand that they are products of a dysfunctional system.

Shame is another issue that family or friends may experience. "How could I have been so blind" is a common response. In retrospect, they believe that they ignored red flags and begin to feel responsible. Others saw it coming and feel that there was more that they should have done. Some are embarrassed that their children are having marital problems or are caught up in family violence. For dysfunctional families, this is a threat to their honor and is seen as something to be quieted. "We need to take care of our own, and it is our responsibility to set him/her straight." This type of thinking further contributes to the problem, as discussed in the next chapter.

Finally, *anger* is an issue that family and friends may face. In Genesis 34, Shechem raped Dinah, the daughter of Jacob. Shechem's father, Hamor, came to negotiate a bride price or settlement with Jacob. Shechem took over the negotiations and wanted to bargain for Dinah. Because Jacob was silent during the negotiations, Dinah's brothers decided to manipulate and take vengeance on Shechem and his village. They suggested that the Shechemites have every male circumcised before they would agree to a marriage between Dinah and Shechem. On the third day, when all of the Shechemites were sore from the surgery, the sons of Jacob slaughtered all of the men in an act of vigilantism. The brothers' anger may have been justified in their minds, but Dinah was never consulted and the Scriptures give no indication whether or not she was helped or validated.[35] Vigilantism

---

[35]For a deeper discussion of the text as well as other opinions of the "Rape of Dinah" see my article, "The Silence in Dinah's Cry: Narrative in Genesis 34 in a Context of Sexual Violence," *Journal of Religion and Abuse* 2:4 (2001) 81–98.

is a response by people who feel powerless over the fact that justice has not been achieved.

Those working with families need to remind them that the abuse is not about the family; it is about helping those directly affected by the violence. Victims need understanding, patience, peace, and safety, not vengeance. Abusers need accountability, not anger. Children need a safe place to process what is happening. While it is difficult to stay calm, not react angrily, and listen, these are what family and friends need to practice. Domestic Violence is not about them; it is about the victim, children, and abuser. The faith community must see the deeper issues in domestic violence. The faith community is not God, but a representation of God. God judges; the community empowers the family to heal. Victims must be supported, protected, and validated. Abusers must be confronted and called to see the needs of others rather than their needs. Children need a place to unwind and feel safe. Family and friends need to learn how to help the family heal as a relational and emotional system.

The faith community can become the family that is needed for healing. The abuser and victim should each have their own faith community for healing and spiritual growth. The power and control issues are so complex that a couple caught in domestic violence will have a difficult time healing in the same congregation. The couple never should be counseled together until the victim is empowered enough to confront the abuser. Each needs to experience the acceptance and care of a faith community so that they can focus on their own healing. Faith communities can work together to help abusers and victims heal, but victims must have their own place of support, protection, and safety.

If a victim is separated from her abuser, she must be able to attend church without fear of manipulation or pressure to reunite. Victims must have validation from their church in order to grow closer to God and find healing. Abusers must also have accountability and support from their church in order to develop and heal spiritually. They must be able to attend church without fear of rejection or the temptation to manipulate their partner back into a relationship. They must also be accountable not to seek another victim.[36] Since much of their self-esteem is related to an

---

[36]Bancroft, 121.

intimate relationship, they need to know that relationships with other non-abusive men are important to their healing and repentance. They have the right to belong to a community that reminds them they are not in control, challenge them to repent of sin, and encourages them to validate other victims. Churches can work with each other to see the progress of individuals. This will take patience and understanding, but it can be done to the glory of God, who calls all people to seek truth and healthy relationships.

3

The Effects of Domestic Violence on the Family System

The former chapter addressed some issues that victims face when needing help. This chapter will introduce some of the effects that domestic violence can have on families and family members. Historically little has been done to protect women in abusive relationships.[1] The burden has been placed on the victim to report the incident, press charges, find help, and survive on her own or with her family.

> Compassion for abused women is building across the continent, but we are still a society with deep habits of blaming victims. When people suffer misfortune, we jump to analyzing what they should have done differently: She should have fought back, she shouldn't have fought back;

---

[1] Excellent resources on this discussion can be found in Mary Patten Engel, "Historical Theology and Violence Against Women: Unearthing a Popular Tradition of Just Battery," 242–61 and John M. Johnson and Denise M. Bondurant, "Revisiting the 1982 Church Response Survey," 422–27, both in *Violence Against Women and Children: A Christian Theological Sourcebook*, ed. Carol J. Adams and Marie M. Fortune (New York: Continuum, 1998). For a religious discussion of violence against women globally see Kroeger and Nason-Clark, 13–37.

she was in an area where it wasn't wise to be walking; she didn't plan ahead; she didn't try hard enough or think fast enough.[2]

Even the church has failed to support victims in domestic violence.

Ultimately the blame is widespread, for Christian believers worldwide tend to ignore, minimize and deny the abuse that is rampant in families of faith. Churches provide few resources for victims of abuse. Moreover, believers are discouraged from using available community services such as shelters, counseling, abusers' groups, restraining orders and legal aid. Without such help, the abuse frequently grows more severe. The potential of emotional and spiritual healing is sacrificed to silence. Silence of the sacred. *Sacred silence.*[3]

With the increased awareness of domestic violence, availability of resources, women's rights in divorce and birth control, and the ability by the police to press charges (rather than the victim), it seems that women have more options available to them concerning abusive and dysfunctional relationships. There has also been an increase in support from abuse agencies, counselors and legal services; government funding to protect victims and hold abusers accountable; and prevention programs. The increase in resources for women may also be responsible for the decrease in the number of men murdered by their intimate partners.[4] The presence of abuse in gay and lesbian relationships and increased reports concerning male victims suggest that power and control are not limited to one gender. Intimate partner violence also has an affect on those close to the couple. Research has given us much more information on how the family is affected by this trauma and violence. Probably one of the greatest contributions to this study has come from the field of family systems theory.

---

[2]Bancroft, *When Dad Hurts Mom*, 313.
[3]Kroeger and Clark, 7–8.
[4]While the number of women murdered by their intimate partners stabilized from 1976 to 1993, the number of men murdered by their intimate partners decreased sixty percent from 1976 to 1993 and twenty-three percent from 1993 to 1997. In the past many women found that killing their abusive partner was the only way of escape. The decrease in male homicides suggests that many abused women had other options to killing their abuser. See *Intimate Partner Violence*, 3.

Family Systems Theory

Family systems theory (FST) suggests that the family is a system or group that seeks equilibrium. The family members form an emotional unit.[5] As an emotional unit each member places an emphasis on shared responsibility, reciprocity, and repetition.[6] Rather than the unit being solely biological, it is mostly emotional. Members of the family live together and try to maintain balance in the system. FST "emphasizes the function an individual's behavior has in the broader context of the relationship process."[7]

> The family-systems approach emphasizes the patterns that occur in all relationships, rather than the personality problems of the participants. Were you irritable and reserved with your first spouse, yet remarkably relaxed and open with your second? The difference is not only in you, and not even only in your spouse—the difference is in how you are together. Family-systems theory regards the family as a whole that is greater than the sum of its parts.[8]

Individuals have an effect on the health, direction, stability, and development of the emotional unit.

The environment may also have an effect on the family. Whatever the source of stress or trauma, the family seeks to maintain balance. Since the family seeks equilibrium, the members of this system may try to adapt in order to survive and exist.[9] When the family faces stress *inside the system* the members adapt or change roles. If one parent leaves, the whole family is affected and adapts. Often the oldest child will unconsciously attempt to replace the missing parent to keep the parental structure in tact. Other times a parent will seek to communicate with the child they feel closest to and thus develops a type of partnership with that child. These are both

---

[5]Michael E. Kerr and Murray Bowen, *Family Evaluation* (New York: Norton, 1988) 7.
[6]Dorothy Stroh Becvar and Raphael J. Becvar, *Family Therapy: A Systemic Integration*, 2d ed. (Boston: Allyn and Bacon, 1993) 9.
[7]Kerr and Bowen, 48–49.
[8]Tavris, 237–38.
[9]Becvar and Becvar, *Systems Theory and Family Therapy: A Primer*, 2d ed. (Lanham, Mass.: University Press of America, 1999) 71.

examples of *parentification*. This happens when a spousal relationship breaks down or ends through death or divorce.

When the family faces stress from *outside the system*, the system can adapt by closing out the source of stress and isolating itself from the environment. This is the family unit's method of protecting and coping. The family may focus inward and develop its own sense of order and standards. This will produce a controlled environment within the family system. If the family disengages from the environment, it may lose its outside perspective and nurturing ability. The members may become enmeshed and separated from society. Outsiders will become suspects and sources of distrust. An example of this is seen in Genesis 12:10-20, when Abraham deceived Pharaoh by telling him that Sarah was his sister.[10] Abraham was afraid of Pharaoh and treated him as an outsider. The Egyptian king was seen as a threat to Abraham and his family, therefore, Abraham did not owe him complete truth and sincerity.

In the ancient world the concepts of *in-group* and *out-group* are relational units that determine how people are treated. Those in the *in-group* are family, friends, kinsmen, and similar cultures. *Out-group* individuals are those who may present a threat to the purity and safety of the family or *in-group*.[11] Those outside the group are not thought worthy of the truth or blessings nor do they have any right to know the in-group. If you are the leader, you have the responsibility to protect those in your group/family and thus may keep secrets from outsiders. When something is revealed to an outsider, it suggests that they are being allowed into the group. The concepts of mystery, secrets, revelation, truth, and knowledge are reserved for those on the inside. Outsiders present a threat because

---

[10]It seems that Abraham is knowingly deceiving Pharaoh until he confesses that Sarah is his father's niece. Pharaoh was not satisfied by his explanation. Understanding that Abraham saw Pharaoh as an outsider and threat to his family is an explanation of why Abraham deceived him.

[11]For a further discussion of this concept in the ancient and Biblical world see: Bruce Malina, *The New Testament World: Insights from Cultural Anthropology*, 3d ed. (Louisville: Westminster John Knox, 2001) 58–80. For more reading see David A. deSilva, *Honor, Patronage, Kinship and Purity: Unlocking New Testament Culture* (Downer's Grove, Ill.: InterVarsity, 2000) 157–98; John T. Fitzgerald, ed. *Greco-Roman Perspectives on Friendship*, SBL Resources for Biblical Study 34 (Atlanta: Scholars, 1997); and Christopher P. Jones, *Kinship Diplomacy in the Ancient World* (Cambridge, Mass.: Harvard University Press, 1999).

they do not understand, know, or have honor worthy of the family/group. In order to enter the group, the outsider must experience an initiation or otherwise prove that they will uphold the ideals, secrets, and traditions of the family. While Christianity has an emphasis on outreach, the concepts of belief, repentance, revelation, and baptism suggest movement towards or initiation into the Christian family or in-group.[12]

Many times modern families live with this in-group and out-group concept. This is especially prevalent in immigrant families living in America. Keeping secrets and initiating or testing are important practices to preserve and maintain the honor and traditions of the family/in-group. Living in a foreign country presents a stress to the family, the family is in danger of losing its identity as a result of communicating with, being influenced by, and intermarrying with the surrounding culture.

A satisfying time in my English as a Second Language (ESL) classes is when one of the families argues in front of me. This suggests that I am part of their family and that they trust me enough to see their true side, even though I struggle to understand their language. As an insider I am bound to respect their cultures and customs. Guiding them to learn about God and practice healthy family values can only happen if they respect me and I prove to be helping them rather than hurting them. These families react to trauma and use their traditions and native language to protect and preserve their family. The pressures of living in a different culture present an outside stress that causes them to use traditions and cultural values to maintain their honor and safety. Preserving their native language and culture, even if the children speak English, is essential to their family structure. Under stress, the family leaders sometimes refuse to speak English, which forces the children to adapt by speaking their native tongue. Keeping family traditions is a method of preserving their culture and the leader, not the outsider, is the one who determines right and wrong.

---

[12]Evangelism involves sharing the good news to outsiders and including them in our *in-group*. Our *in-group* is the family of God. Just as Jesus was the friend of sinners so Christians must open the doors for their in group/families. When Jesus was questioned about his family he defined a new *in-group*. "Who are my mother, brothers? . . . Whoever does God's will is my brother, sister, and mother," (Mark 3:33, 35).

Anthropology and Family Systems

A valuable tool in understanding various family systems is the research done in cultural anthropology. This research explores not only the cultural systems of a small society, but also the family systems within that culture. In most major cultures the family is a microcosm of the larger culture. Political leaders led their cities as if they were the families, which reflected the larger culture as a whole.

Anthropologists have also suggested that when a family moved into a hostile or different culture, it attempted to enforce its own values from within rather than be transformed by the outside world. The family perceived outsiders as a threat to the growth, peace, and stability of the family system. Those in power tended to control behavior within the group by setting laws, unwritten codes and taboos and controlling marriage and procreation. It was important for the family to survive in order to leave a legacy. A system of honor and shame was enforced that provided support for those who were in leadership. Rather than penetrating the surrounding environment and trying to transform its culture, the family withdrew from the environment to keep its own sense of purity and security. Those who left or "dishonored" the family in the community were humiliated, exiled, or punished. Outsiders who entered the family were slowly absorbed and encouraged to support the existing family system of honor. To cause division within a family was seen as one of the greatest crimes (Prov 6:19).[13]

Families trying to survive in a "hostile world" view their values and system of honor as proper. Outsiders and their values are seen as a potential threat. Cultures that practice forms of misogyny, wife abuse, or harsh patriarchy influence families to hold to certain values and views of women. Missionaries and social workers have indicated that in some countries husbands challenge any discussion about being gentle with one's wife because it is not culturally acceptable. When a family has a cultural heritage that approves of spousal abuse, family members are expected to support this view. The family sees itself as a reflection of the culture and society and practices what is "normal" in their eyes.[14] Some may be challenged to

---

[13]The Proverb suggests that the seventh or last abomination, to sow discord among brothers, is the worst.

[14]Bancroft suggests that abuse may take different shapes among races and cultures. White/ Caucasian abusers may be more rigid in tolerating their spouses to argue with them,

abuse their spouse by other family members. Some communities, including the faith community, may also support abuse by not addressing or condemning it. Many of the abuse advocates have sometimes expressed frustration in working with immigrant churches that reinforce the humiliation of women and young girls. This tends to be a constant challenge to clergy training teams attempting to reach immigrant families.

When immigrant families move to the United States where spousal abuse is illegal, they may react in one of two ways. One way is to *isolate* by using language and cultural barriers. Emotional isolation may be necessary for the family to survive and preserve their culture. The outside may present a threat to the family's way of life. Learning English can be threatening to the survival of dysfunctional family values. It can also provide a means of communicating family secrets to outsiders. The dysfunctional family system must reinforce its own values by threatening isolation or expulsion from the emotional unit.

At a Russian-speaking youth conference, our city's domestic violence council presented a program concerning abuse and dating violence. Afterward, our team was presenting literature and talking with some of the youth when one of the young ladies began to ask me about how we help children who witness domestic violence in their homes. One of her friends kept trying to push her past me, but I kept talking to the young lady. The friend kept saying, "Shhhh, shhhhh, we're not supposed to talk about this." The young lady finally looked at her friend and said, "It goes on in your home, too, and we need to talk about it." My heart was heavy after they left. While these families may be living according to their family values, they now live in a country that considers abuse a crime.

The other way that immigrant families may react is to *reflect or imitate* the abusive patterns present in the culture. While the United States considers abuse a crime, we still have a problem with domestic violence.

The reality, however, is that cultural approval for partner abuse is disturbingly high in our society, even among the privileged and educated

---

whereas other cultures allow arguing but expect their spouses to keep house and perform childrearing duties in a traditional manner. Some cultures may be known for their fanatical jealousy and intolerance of spouses speaking to other men, while others may be stricter in parenting and disciplining children. One culture is not more abusive than another, but the form of abuse may be different for each culture. Bancroft, 163.

. . . and our domestic-violence statistics, while not the worst in the world, are on the high end. The United States is the only industrialized nation that has failed to ratify the UN convention on eliminating discrimination against women, which specifically refers to violence against women as a form of discrimination. Pointing fingers at other countries can be a way to ignore the serious problems in our own. [15]

Tribal cultures can develop abusive behaviors when exposed to modern societies that use power and control for survival and success.[16] The issue is not that immigrants practice abuse in a peaceful society, it is that many cultures that have power and control issues come to America where that behavior is aggravated or reinforced by our media, society, and faith communities. Or they may use our techniques to abuse and subordinate their partners/spouses.

Dysfunctional Families

Some families face dysfunction from within the system. If a parent or child begins to hurt a member inside the system, the family may adapt through isolation, reframing, keeping secrets, using language barriers, and/ or expelling those who interact with the environment or an outsider. The family unit develops its own system of ethics, wholeness, and health in order to protect its honor. The emotional unit revolves around the leader, who may be the source of the problem, and the group often sees reality through that individual's perspective. Dysfunctional families do not practice shared power, and they have an imbalance of power and emotion when the leader is abusive.

Every family member has a role to play in order for the family to grow, adapt, develop, and protect its "honor." In the case of a dysfunctional family system, the roles are played in order for the family to cope, survive, avoid humiliation, and keep a sense of peace or equilibrium.[17]

---

[15]Ibid., 164.

[16]Ibid., 166.

[17]While every family has some dysfunction, I suggest that a dysfunctional family as one that does not deal with dysfunction and a healthy family as one that is willing to confront the dysfunction in order to heal. For more information on Functional Families see Gary Chapman, *Five Signs of a Functional Family* (Chicago: Northfield, 1997).

Dysfunctional families have a different way of defining peace, honor, and normality. While one person, usually a parent, practices sinful or unhealthy behavior, the rest of the family tries to adapt to compensate for the dysfunction. They see the world through the behavior of that person. Kerr and Bowman call this *overfunctioning* and *underfunctioning*.

> The overfunctioning person is typically one who feels responsible for the emotional well-being of others and who works to compensate for perceived (real or imagined) deficits in their functioning. The underfunctioning person, on the other hand, feels dependent on the overfunctioning one to do things that he feels reluctant or unable to do himself. At the extreme, the underfunctioning one may rely on the overfunctioning one to tell him how to think, feel, and act. The overfunctioning one may not experience this degree of reliance as a burden.
>
> Following the onset of symptoms, an interesting change in this overfunctioning and underfunctioning reciprocity may occur. The wife begins to increasingly depend on her husband and perhaps other family members to accompany her and to do things for her. Her ability to function for herself becomes increasingly constrained because of her symptoms and because of the family's willingness to function for her in many areas. As the "healthy" ones increasingly function for the "sick" one in this way, an enduring type of family stability can develop, a stability that is accompanied by the presence of a chronic symptom. It is easier for family members to make accommodations that make it possible to live with the symptom than it is to address the underlying relationship process that fosters the symptom in the first place.[18]

In domestic violence, the abuser is the *underfunctioning* spouse and the rest of the family is *overfunctioning*. The family adapts to the dysfunction and lives with the problem rather than confronting the dysfunction and growing. They *make accommodation* in order to survive within this system. Sometimes the other parent plays the role of enabler (overfunctioner) by trying to cover up the dysfunction and protect the children. The children learn to keep silent and live as if everything were "normal" by an outsider's

---

[18]Kerr and Bowman, 56–57.

standards. Using the term "role playing" keeps outsiders from criticizing the family members' actions and helps outsiders focus on changing behaviors when the family begins to seek health and wholeness. Kroeger and Clark suggested that fantasy of change was one issue that kept victims from leaving their abusers.[19] This fantasy of either the abuser or victim can further reinforce this role-playing.

> The first step in breaking family patterns is to drop the fantasy of rescuing or changing one another. In family-systems language, what usually happens in the course of an ongoing difficulty is that one partner becomes overfocused on the other, and the other is underfocused on himself.[20]

When a dysfunctional family goes through change in an attempt to heal, the members are forced to change the roles that they have been playing. An example is seen when an alcoholic parent goes through detoxification and seeks to change. The family structures are challenged, even though that parent is trying to provide a healthy environment for the family. Many times the other spouse struggles with trust issues such as "Will he really continue to be trustworthy with the finances?" "Will she hold down her job and responsibilities?" "At what point do I expect him to come home drunk and break his promise to this family?" Resisting the temptation to overfunction and not trust the recovering spouse is one of the processes of healing that the family system must address in addition to the other parent's dysfunctional behavior. The children will also have trouble trusting and supporting either parent in this development.

> If we wish to understand the events of their relationship, we do not ask why something happened. Rather we ask what is going on in an effort to describe these patterns. Our perspective is holistic, and our focus is on the processes, or context, that give meaning to events instead of on the individuals or the events themselves. Our focus is also present centered: We examine here-and-now interactions rather than look to history for antecedent causes.[21]

---

[19]Kroeger and Clark, 34–35.
[20]Tavris, 240–41.
[21]Becvar and Becvar, *Family Systems Therapy*, 9–11.

The family-systems perspective is a way of thinking about people in context, of teaching people to become better observers of their own behavior and to see their own part in an unhappy pattern.[22]

Healing the dysfunctional family takes time and requires that all of the members of the family system change the roles that they have practiced in order to survive. This is difficult because those who are not "guilty" wonder why they should change their behavior. They do not see their actions as "reactions" but as normal behavior. In their mind the "guilty" party has been identified and should change to solve the problem. Yet if all change, those who underfunction can be given the *permission and freedom* to heal.

> Each person became an emotional prisoner of the way the other person functioned and neither was able to change his or her functioning enough to stop the process. Through this reciprocal interacting, the functioning of the family could then create as many problems for the patient or "problem one" as the functioning of the patient could create for the family. Family members, however, usually viewed their anxiety as being "caused" by the patient's attitudes and behavior and rarely viewed the patient's behavior as a reflection of their own anxiety-determined functioning. The patient, in turn, tended to perceive himself as an inadequate or defective person and indeed the "cause" of the family problems.[23]

In abusive families, the members adapt in order to survive. In this system, one parent usually has attempted to exercise control and power over all family members. In order to protect the children, the other spouse may try to cover up or hide the abuse from them. The term *enabler* is used for this role, but I have found that this term has a negative slant. I choose to use the term *adapt*. I think that these women are trying to survive and do whatever it takes to establish peace and avoid further abuse. While outsiders may see this as a weakness, I believe that they are valiantly adapting and surviving within a dysfunctional emotional system. Women in this position have a strong will to survive and put themselves at great

---

[22]Tavris, 240.
[23]Kerr and Bowman, 7–8.

risk. Men who are abused carry a great sense of humiliation and try to keep peace while maintaining an appearance of respect in the community. Children sometimes learn to disassociate from the system or become hyperaroused. The fight or flight response of the family causes each member of the family to adapt to the dysfunctional system.

The abuser, who is underfunctioning, is the one who determines the health of the family. He is attempting to control the family, and the members are expected to follow his wishes. The abuser is narcissistic and sees the family as supporting his best interests. It becomes the family's responsibility to honor, submit to, and serve him. This person has found a way to determine the direction of the family. He is underfunctioning and expects others in the family to be overfunctioning. This produces a sense of isolation, fear, guilt, and loyalty that keeps the family overly focused on the abuser in an attempt to change him. This also keeps the family quiet, under control, and confused. I have met women who work a full-time job, take care of the children, and keep the house clean while their abusive husband fails to find or keep a job, clean the house, or share in the parenting. She doesn't know what he does all day at home and wonders why he constantly sleeps, spends money, and creates debt for the family. Yet he has convinced his wife that it is everyone else's fault that he can't work and that it is her responsibility to keep the family together by her work and service to him. On top of this, he demands sex when he desires it. These women still communicate to me that God expects them to serve and support their husband no matter how they feel about the relationship. She overfunctions not because she desires to do so, but because her husband (and many times her church) has convinced her that she is responsible for the stability of the marriage. In this dysfunction, the family has a different sense of honor and wholeness. The one in control (underfunctioner) determines what is honorable or normal. The family does not become healthy or honorable on their own; these are reserved for the abuser. The center of power is to be respected, obeyed, and served. All behavior is seen through the eyes of the abuser. The safety and health of the family members is determined by their willingness to honor the "head of the family" and live in such a way that his/her decisions are respected both at home and in the outside world.

The abuser also determines spoken and unspoken rules of conduct. Family members learn, by trial and error, what is acceptable and what is unacceptable. Those outside the family have no bearing on what is normal. While outsiders may see who underfunctions and manipulates, they are considered to have a warped view of family. The one in power makes decisions concerning what is normal. Those behaviors that serve and show respect to the head of the family are honorable. Those that do not are punishable through violence, verbal abuse, or threat of expulsion from the family.

One of the greatest fears that I hear from victims involves being cut off and disengaged from their families. I have seen adult survivors of molestation point the finger at their abuser only to be criticized and isolated from siblings and the other parent even if they also have been victimized. I have seen wives take a stand against their husbands for abuse only to later be pressured by in-laws to take him back. I have known of preachers who *excommunicate or disfellowship* abused wives for filing restraining orders against their husbands, who are "fellow brothers." Isolation, disengagement, and expulsion are used to shame and humiliate victims who oppose the honor of the abusive dysfunctional family. The one in control dominates the emotional unit and manipulates those outside the family to support and honor his wishes. Only those outsiders considered worthy by the underfunctioning individual (which means that they agree with him) can enter into the unit.

In domestic violence trainings there seems to be a criticism of the FST in how counselors committed to this model address victims and abusers. While therapists may indicate that the victims are part of a system, they in no way justify the abusers' actions nor do they suggest that the victims wish to be abused.

> Some people object to the systems approach precisely because it does not seek to apportion blame, and because it describes each participant's role in an interconnected network. This idea implies, critics say, that a woman who is beaten by her husband is as much to "blame" for his behavior as he is. It reinforces the view of woman as masochist: If she stays in a bad relationship, she must enjoy its pain. And it obscures the critical moral line between victimizer and victim.
>
> I know of no systems therapist who would endorse any of these inferences. On the contrary, systems therapists want victims to become empowered enough to break away from the psychological and physical

bullying that victimizers apply so freely. They want victims to understand the essential fact about any relationship pattern: that they have choices, and that they have the power to break out of the pattern. Far from blaming victims, I think, the systems approach helps them correctly identify solutions. It is not masochisms that keeps women (or men) trapped in destructive patterns, but the fear of greater pain or loss if they change the pattern or leave . . . Once "victims" understand why they are so overfocused on the relationship, even at the expense of their own happiness and self-esteem, they can begin to take the steps to free themselves.[24]

On the other hand, it in no way excuses the behavior of the spouse who is abusive to observe that the abused spouse plays a role in the pattern. In many couples, an episode of verbal or physical violence is followed by tearful and remorseful apologies, and loving concern. The abused spouse forgives, and the cycle starts over again. And it surely will start over, because the violent episode has been rewarded with the affection that the couple should have been giving one another to start with.[25]

Tavris suggests that the abuser is only reacting to their environment and trying to control the family members. While the abuser is at fault for the choice to abuse, victims can only break free by *choosing to leave.*

It is difficult for a man who punches a woman or throws her into a wall to not know that he is an abuser. It is equally difficult for a woman who sustains a black eye and body bruises not to know she has been abuse, although both of them find rationales to avoid reality. However, the subtle manifestations of nonphysical abuse usually escape acknowledgment—at least for a long period of time. Although a man can't help being consciously aware of depriving a woman of money or social contacts or of drumming into her that she is stupid and crazy, he can be consciously unaware that what he is doing is legally abusive. Similarly, a woman, cognizant that she is systematically being made miserable, may not recognize what is happening as abuse. The

---

[24]Tavris, 245.
[25]Ibid., 246.

netherworld environment in which they both live, therefore, keeps abuse alive and thriving until—and it—the woman steps into the reality of the real world by demanding a halt.[26]

Therapists must understand how this cycle works rather than blaming the victim for staying in the relationship. Likewise, the counselor must also understand that the longer the victim stays in the relationship, the harder it will be for the abuser to change their behavior. Victims and children should be empowered and supported to choose to be loved, respected, and safe. Tavris suggests the following:

- Abuse is a mutual problem, part of the family system.
- Abuse is learned.
- Abuse is an effort to solve a problem.[27]

Outsiders are usually viewed as a threat to the family caught in abuse. Outsiders bring the threat of exposure, and family members are groomed to keep the honor of the family. When a member marries, it brings great danger to the abuser and the dysfunctional system. According to the abuser, honor must be maintained. Many times the abuser will manipulate the outsider and gain his or her respect and favor.

> They had been attending church for almost a year. Karen and her second husband, Scott, had been friends with us for a long time and we knew their children well. They had been married eight years. While we visiting in their home one evening, Karen shared with us why she did not believe in God. Her stepfather had molested her until she turned 12. She had asked God for help but it never came. It broke our hearts to hear the words she spoke and to see Scott's frustration. Scott had been told this after they had been married for three years. He couldn't say anything to the stepfather. They lived next door to him, Karen worked for him, and they spent a lot of family time together. Yet Scott, the outsider, was given a "gag" order. Karen felt sorry for her stepfather and believed he had changed, or at least she hoped he had because their children spent

---

[26]Miller, 4.
[27]Ibid.

the night at "grandma and grandpa's" often. Day after day Scott faced the man who caused his wife such pain, and through clenched teeth he had to be cordial and *act as if he did not know or suspect anything*. He had to, because the man had given them their home!

This is an example of the code of silence in abusive families. It is a method of control and manipulation in order to honor and serve the abuser. It keeps the family and in-laws "in line." This seems foreign to an outsider but is a normal way of life to those groomed and manipulated to keep the peace.

The times my wife and I visited with Karen's stepfather were difficult. We went to our kids' sporting events together and spent time sitting with their family. We knew what he had done, yet he was very charming, attentive, and encouraging. They had the appearance of one big happy family. From the outside, the family members were lucky to have such a caring stepfather. From the inside, the family was hiding a dark secret. Our biggest concern was the children. When discussing this with Scott and Karen, we asked if they felt that leaving the kids at "grandma and grandpa's" was best. We asked if it was possible that he might molest their daughter and sons. Karen's response was, "I hope not."

Outsiders do not understand that the family subjected to violence lives in a world dictated by an individual who is self-serving. Outsiders do not understand that in the victim's view, justice brings pain and suffering, truth means humiliation, silence is golden, and wholeness means not being hurt. Their self-esteem is not grounded in individual pride; it is grounded in favors and blessings given by a person of power and control. It is not the victim's esteem that matters but the abuser's. The abuser can still control the victim and their family even after the victim has left home!

Abusive Families as Distinct Cultures

The abusive family can become a system that is similar to the immigrant family, which attempts to preserve its system of honor and traditional roles. When existing in a society that considers abuse a crime, it may become isolated from the environment or reflect the power and control issues of the culture. This "anti-cultural" dysfunction immediately throws the family into a "strangers in the world" context, where the outside community is perceived as a threat to the existence of the family. The abuser perceives the threat because they are living counterculturally. Yet their desire for control and manipulation causes them to react to their environment. The abusers control their families through three methods.

First, they communicate the *perception of threat* to their family. The family is warned that a system of honor exists that they must uphold. This honor centers on the abuser and is interpreted through him. Truth telling and honesty are only acceptable within the context of the dysfunctional family. The family is to be honest with each other, but outsiders are not trusted because they bring a sense of threat. Abraham and Isaac both deceived a king who presented a threat to their wives (Gen 12:10-20; 26:1-11). Outsiders, abusers claim, will not understand their system of honor and will not accept their way of life. It is imperative for each family member to uphold this code of conduct and silence in order for the family to survive. Keeping the abuser protected and safe is seen as a noble quality of the family. Lying, covering up, and manipulating others are seen as noble qualities in each member because they protect the honor and secrecy of the family.

> The shame-bound family has many ways to keep the feelings of unworthiness in place. It's not that family members consciously want to feel ashamed, but the feelings of shame keep the secrets secret. The shame keeps one bound to the family out of loyalty, by not talking about what goes on or by playing a role like the joker or the fix-it person. In a family with many generations of unspoken incest, the shame factor keeps each generation tied to the system. A client finds herself ostracized from the family by refusing to let her children go to family events where the males who commit incest will be drinking and partying over the holidays. She faces the family dynamic that in the shame-bound system, even when she is away from the family, the blame falls on her. If she tells the truth, she is punished. She is also discouraged from getting an education or leaving the town in which these generations have perpetuated the lies of incest.[28]

---

[28]Karen A. McClintock, *Sexual Shame: An Urgent Call to Healing* (Minneapolis: Fortress, 2001) 24.

Second, there is a *code of silence*. To communicate with outsiders the truths about the family is taboo. Police, shelter advocates, counselors, school officials, and others present a perceived threat to the stability of the family. The abuser has manipulated the members of the family to believe that outsiders are a threat to the peace and safety of the household. The family members are to reinforce this code by keeping silent or pressuring others to be silent. To speak out against the sins of the abuser is a violation of the honor of the dysfunctional family. If a member is not silent, they will be given the "silent treatment." All other family members are to "shun" the one who dishonored them by breaking the silence. One woman had kicked her husband out because of his abusive behavior and alcoholism, and his family supported her in this. Once the man went to rehabilitation and said he was sorry, they began to pressure her to take him back. She felt he hadn't changed but they felt she should take him back anyway. As she resisted they began to ignore her and distance themselves from her and the children emotionally and physically.

Third, *fear and humiliation* are tactics used to control the members of the family. The fear of rejection or punishment from the abuser and other family members are concerns of the victims and children. Those who break the rules are humiliated and shamed into submission. Even those who marry are expected to keep the secrets intact. Sometimes an outsider is brought into the system only to be manipulated by the family. The son-in-law keeps quiet because he believes that otherwise he will lose his children and his wife may divorce him for breaking the silence. The daughter-in-law may see that the son acts like his father but believes she is powerless to do anything.

This dysfunctional family system is dangerous and harmful to the members existing within it. Healthy families empower the members to grow, develop, and mature. Empowering involves faith, trust, respect, love, and encouragement of the benefit of others. The dysfunctional family system does not encourage family members to be what they can be—it encourages them to be what the person in power and control wants them to be. The healthy family cannot be open and live freely within the culture of the dysfunctional family system. God's world is good, but human culture may not be so good. The children of God are to transform evil in the world by empowering others through love, respect, accountability, truth, justice, and compassion. Since the abuser is dominated by fear, shame, and narcissism, he presents a danger for the family. He also sees faith and hope as weaknesses. The abuser exercises power over people rather than empowering others. The abuser extinguishes the motivation to change within the family because change can be dangerous to this family system.

Dysfunction, Abuse, and Family Members

Understanding the dysfunctional family system in abuse is helpful in order to understand how it affects the members of the family. It is important that outsiders who attempt to intervene understand how complex this system is and how difficult it is for the family to achieve change and true wholeness. It is also important for outsiders to understand why those inside the system must be silent.

Victims

First, victims are struggling with a *code of silence*. For them to speak out brings great anxiety and fear. They fear punishment through further abuse, neglect, isolation, or humiliation. They also are concerned about confidentiality. This not only includes keeping what they say confidential but also acting as if one is not aware that the abuser is controlling their family. Victims must keep silent in order to maintain the harmony and integrity of the abuser and family. Women who have been abused share with me that they believe no one will understand them, they are powerless, and they are completely dependent upon the abusive partner. While this seems illogical to the listener, it seems rational and clear to the victim. Remember, they receive much of their information from the abuser. The abuser has been selective in what he has revealed to them, and the victim believes that she is at fault. The abuser many times has foreseen the threat of the victim speaking out and creates fear in the family.

Some victims experience times when the abuser constantly calls, stalks, or appears when they do not expect them. This can give the illusion that the abuser is somewhat omniscient or all-knowing. The victim is under the impression that the abuser knows their every move, action, and conversation. Adult survivors of childhood abuse also share with me that they were groomed to believe that no one would help them. To the victim, silence is necessary to self-esteem and survival.

Second, victims struggle with *self-respect*. Studies have been done concerning the *Stockholm Syndrome*.[29] This syndrome creates a type of traumatic bonding that can occur between the victim and their oppressor. When separated from the abuser, the victim and children can sense guilt and a longing for the abuser. Victims are told that their sense of self-worth, love, and respect comes from the abuser. When separated, they experience isolation, guilt, and loneliness. The abuser has conditioned them to depend upon him.

An example of this can be found in the story of the Jewish exodus from Egypt. *Yahweh* brought the Jews out of slavery yet after a short while they had a strong desire to return to Egypt. They returned to the Egyptian worship of Anubis the calf (Exod 32), tested the Lord (Exod 17:7), and desired to be back in Egypt (Exod 16:1-4). The Egyptians had so brutalized the Jews that they had lost their ability to shepherd and live as nomads (Gen 47:3). The Jews had become dependent upon the brutal Pharaoh to the point that they were afraid to trust another leader.[30]

It is difficult to rescue victims because they are attached to a dysfunctional system. Many times their view of the world comes from the abuser. The one who underfunctions needs them to overfunction. Their behavior must support the abuser. Victims who leave when the abuse starts may break the cycle in their lives and the lives of their children. Yet long-term exposure to this dysfunctional system can alter their view of reality to the point that they view an abusive and dysfunctional system as normal. To change is a scary concept that may keep many women from going public with the abuse. Many women will only share their years of emotional, verbal, and physical abuse after their husband has died. Some women even feel a need to respect their deceased husband and grit their teeth or bite their tongue when those in church praise these men.

---

[29]Dugan and Hock, 15. This study was performed on victims who were held captive during a bank robbery in Stockholm, Sweden. After the victims were freed, they tended to display a dependence upon their captors a few days after they were released. This dependence was an emotional bond called traumatic bonding.

[30]To read more about how God worked with the Jews in the Exodus as a parallel to working with domestic violence see my article "Open Your Eyes," *Journal of Religion and Abuse* 4:1 (2002) 27–36.

Third, *victims need to be empowered* to develop healthy relationship boundaries. I find that many who have suffered abuse or trauma either tend to have a strong barrier or no barrier at all when it comes to relationships. This happens due to the codependency and trust issues. We help abuse survivors see human relationships like a yard surrounding a home. In the beginning they may want to put up a privacy fence or brick wall. As time progresses and they begin to trust their neighbors they may use a chain link fence. They should always have a gate, the type of which depends on their comfort zone. Whenever they are hurt, they can close the gate. The idea is that they choose what type of fence to have and that those close to them should understand that their yard and home are private and in their comfort zone.

Victims can, however, be empowered to see themselves as powerful individuals. In the Exodus from Egypt, God did not lead the Jews through Philistia. They were led the long way. Why? God did not want them to get discouraged and turn back (Exod 13:17-18). They were slaves, not warriors, and God knew that they would struggle in war and become afraid. So God led them the long way. The people resisted, complained, were indecisive, and worshipped idols. When confronted, they repented. Yet God also gave them small victories in battle. Why? God wanted to build their confidence and let them know that they were not alone. When the nation went to Jericho, they were ready to fight battles. They were confident and empowered. God patiently guided the nation and gave them chances for small victories so that they could be empowered to grow and have peace in their new freedom.

Victims need to be empowered and patiently guided out of abuse. In cases of extreme violence whether there is a threat to the victim's and children's safety, we must work with our legal system to protect the families. Victims must be encouraged to speak out against abuse in their lives. They can be encouraged to listen to that inner voice that they have been told to ignore and silence. They can be empowered to stand and leave the situation and provide for themselves and their children. They can be encouraged to know that God loves them and that there is a community that will accept them. Acceptance means that the community needs to patiently work by providing them with opportunities for small victories to strengthen them enough to one day confront their abuser. Providing for themselves, training in a vocation, and having a stable home are great victories for those leaving an abusive relationship.

Abusers

Abusers are struggling with *control and manipulation* in the family system. Kerr and Bowman call them underfunctioning because their behavior is less than that expected for healthy individuals. This brings a sense of shame and humiliation. While drugs and alcohol have been blamed for much of the domestic violence today, they often anesthetize the abuser's pain of abuse.[31] The abuser may feel guilty about his behavior and try to escape by using alcohol or drugs. Abuse is about power and control, and the abuser uses control to get results. Abusers choose to control others. The community of faith has an opportunity to challenge the abuser to serve others rather than to control them. In the past, this concept of service and self-sacrifice has been placed upon the victims rather than the abusers.

It is equally as ludicrous to have advised the Kosovo Muslims to submit to the Serb, Milosovich, in hopes that their submission would have overcome his violence and hatred of Muslims. Could we imagine going to the victims in Kuwait and telling them that they should have continued to submit to Saddam Hussein with the hope that their submission would have changed his heart? It is the abuser who must be challenged to serve and repent in order to heal. There must be a balance of power, and many times victims need help in the power struggle.

Second, abusers are struggling with a *lack or fear of intimacy*. They seek to control others because they struggle with low self-esteem. While this seems odd for abusers to be narcissistic and have low self-esteem, it

---

[31]I do have people suggest to me that abusers tend to be involved with alcohol. The abuser does not abuse because he is intoxicated. Alcohol lowers one's inhibitions. If the individual uses power and control over their spouse, then they will be less inhibited to use control tactics or physical violence on their spouse after a few drinks. Once they have become intoxicated, they lose much of their physical control and are not as likely to abuse another individual. This explains why the police may be called to a domestic violence incident and find that the abuser has been drinking. Instead of drawing a correlation between abuse and alcohol, we must understand that power and control exist but may be intensified in the early stages of alcohol and drug use.

suggests that they feel a need to be praised and loved. They control others because they need others in their lives. They feel that it is important to be praised because they fear rejection. They feel that intimacy has to be forced because they are not comfortable with themselves. Most of the men I have helped have few, if any, male friends. Those with high anxiety and fears of isolation usually have difficulty differentiating themselves from their emotions.[32] They fear intimacy because they fear being alone. They control others because they need to feel good about themselves. They are narcissistic and seek their own praise over the praise of God.

Churches must not only call abusers to accountability, they must also love them and help them develop spiritually. This does not mean that churches allow themselves to be manipulated by these abusers nor does it mean that churches become marriage counselors between the abuser and victim. Churches must take hold of these men and stand by them. Just as God called a violent man by the name of Saul of Tarsus to accountability, the church must confront and arrange an encounter with abusers. Just as Barnabas accepted Saul, even though the apostles hesitated, so the church must offer the chance of hope and spiritual reconciliation to abusers. Just as Saul suffered for and became an advocate for those who were his victims (Christians), so abusers must face the emotional suffering of repentance, reciprocity, and accountability with those whom they have victimized. Their repentance is not lip service—it is a life of service and sacrifice.

Engaging this Abusive Culture

Working with families in domestic violence is both dangerous and risky. One should understand that they will be intervening into a culture that is vastly different from their own as well as one that distrusts anyone seeking to change the family. I have heard others pass judgment on these families, assuming that they like living in this culture or that they are doomed to be products of their culture. This is similar to saying that a child from a non-English speaking home will never learn to speak English. Exposure

---

[32]Ron Richardson, *Creating a Healthier Church: Family Systems Theory, Leadership, and Congregational Life,* Creative Pastoral Care and Counseling Series (Minneapolis: Fortress, 1996) 58–59, 63, 86–87.

to school, teachers, coaches, and friends will develop a generation that can redefine its language and culture. This same exposure can help those in dysfunctional families break the cycle. We must intervene and not give up hope.

First, intervention involves *understanding and respecting the cultural and family values that are presented by the family*. The family must see that the outsider is trying to help rather than hurt the family. Getting help disrupts the family, and it can only happen when a member wants to leave of her own accord. Those working within this system must gain the trust and respect of key people in the family. The outsider cannot be seen as a threat to the family, but as an ally to the health and development of the emotional unit. Hostility, pity, and criticism of dysfunctional families who experience violence can further distance them from getting help from many churches. When outsiders present a threat to these families, they are in danger of causing the system to isolate even further. While outsiders and intervention providers may not approve of what happens in these families, it is important to understand and guide the families to health and safety. All actions must be in the best interest of the family. An outsider with a "hero" or "Messiah" mentality will only cause the family to protect its members and the abuser to respond with more power and control. The family seeks equilibrium. Healing takes time and patience, and it is important to help the family move in that direction. Years of dysfunction move a family toward greater problems. The family cannot change overnight. Rome was not built in a day, neither is a healthy family. The members of a family cannot be coerced, but with patience they should be persuaded to change.

Second, intervention involves *empowering the family members to change*. Trying to rescue a victim may only further manipulate them and cause increased guilt. Often, an outsider gets an adrenaline rush persuading a woman to leave an abusive relationship. The outsider can then go home with a sigh of relief, believing that the situation is over. To his or her surprise, though, the woman does not call the next day. This does not empower the woman—it controls her. It may be easy to persuade a victim because he or she is used to being controlled and treated that way. While attempting to help, an outsider may lack the patience and endurance needed to help a victim acknowledge that she does not deserve to be abused. The victim becomes overwhelmed and moves from one system to another. The only system where the victim had learned to survive and had a sense of control was at home. Now the victim is placed into an environment where he or she is respected and people are nice. Many had learned from their abuser that these *outsiders* want to manipulate and take advantage of them.

One victim stated that the shelter had become a place of tension. "Why are these people nice to me?" "Why was everyone doing things for my children?" "When will they turn and attack me?" While the environment was safe, these women were mentally reliving the tension phase of the abuse cycle. Shelter advocates have shared with me that this is a time when conflicts develop within the shelters. Often shelters are a place where there is overcrowding, other residents are harshly disciplining their children, children are subjected to changing schools, there is little privacy, people are scared, angry, and tense, and adult women are given curfews or restrictions. The children ask, "When is dad coming back?" or "Are you and dad getting a divorce?" What is often worse is that the man with which they have an emotional bond cannot talk to them or receive their calls. Is it any surprise that many times women prefer to return home? At least there they have a sense of order, control, and privacy.

This is why it is important for the woman to be supported rather than controlled by outsiders. *The woman should leave only when she is ready.* A common statistic given at abuse workshops suggests that an abused woman leaves and returns to her partner an average of seven times before finally ending the relationship. Whether this is accurate or not, it illustrates that women commonly leave and return more than once. Those who are victims of abuse must be encouraged to become independent and confront their abuser. This may take years of patience, and it involves various stages. The stages occur as follows:

1. Leaving the abuser.
2. Learning to love themselves.
3. Ending the relationship if the abuser does not change.
4. Becoming independent and avoiding abusive personalities by setting up boundaries.
5. Developing their behavior and that of their children to prevent future codependency.
6. Confronting those who have abused them in the past.

Victims must be empowered to heal by accepting that they are precious in God's sight and are worthy of love and respect. They must love themselves enough to expect to be loved. They cannot love their neighbor unless they love themselves.

Abusers also should be empowered to change. While court-mandated counseling is the most common form of batterer intervention, abusers must choose to change. Current research on batterer intervention suggests that the more forms of intervention that are involved in an abuser's healing, the better chance he has of not returning to abusive behavior.[33] Studies concerning batterer treatment programs indicate that those who complete these programs are less likely to be abusive to an intimate partner than those who drop out or never enter the treatment program.[34] Currently, the problems that face batterer groups are the high dropout rate (fifty percent only attend the first meeting and sixty to seventy-five percent drop out during the program), alcohol and drug abuse, mental health issues that are not determined in the intake session, and culturally specific programs or acculturation.[35]

Minimally, abusers must complete the treatment programs required by their state in order to heal and break the cycle of violence and high anxiety that dominates their behavior. The programs are tough and challenging, and individuals will only complete the sessions if they desire to change. Effective programs may involve months or even an entire year of attendance for an abuser to experience change. Batterer intervention programs are most effective if a combination of confrontation,

---

[33]These forms include arrests with convictions, treatments, and severe sentences. Julia C. Babcock and Ramalina Steiner, "The Relationship Between Treatment, Incarceration, and Recidivism of Battering: A Program Evaluation of Seattle's Coordinated Community Response to Domestic Violence," *Journal of Family Psychology* 13:1 (1999) 46–59; R. C. Davis, B. G. Taylor, and C. D. Maxwell, "Does Batterer Treatment Reduce Violence? A Randomized Experiment in Brooklyn," *Report of the National Institute of Justice* (2000); and J. L. Edleson and M. Syers, "The Effects of Group Treatment for Men Who Batter: An 18 Month Follow-up Study," *Research on Social Work Practice* 1 (3) 227–43.

[34]R. C. Davis, Julia C. Babcock, S. E. Palmer, R. A. Brown, and M. E. Barrera, "Group Treatment for Abusive Husbands: Long-term Evaluation," *American Journal of Orthopsychiatry* 62 (1992) 276–83.

[35]Courtenay S. Silvergleid, "Research on the Effectiveness of Intervention Programs for Abusive Men," presented at *Fundamentals of Working With Abusive Men* workshop, Portland State University, Portland, Oregon, January 2001.

accountability, and support is used. The spiritual community equally can provide support to form a system of encouragement and accountability for the abuser.

Outsiders must love the abuser enough to hold him accountable for his acts of violence and humiliation. While some would prefer to respond to violent men with violence, this will not prompt change in the violent man. To act with compassion and firmness is an attempt to understand why the abuser behaves as he does.

I sat in the hospital room and visited with Vernon. He was recovering from surgery and it looked as if the cancer was continuing to grow. He was a man in his sixties who had been estranged from church. My first visit with him and his wife was a few years previous. My wife and I had decided to visit all former church members in this small Missouri town in order to encourage them to return to the congregation. We had been in town two months and were excited to make a difference. Vernon always had a reason why he was not at church that had to do with his unfair treatment from the congregation.

His son, Mike, was also in the room. He was a man I had disliked for a year. I helped Sharon, his wife, leave him, and our church had encouraged her and the kids to leave and be safe. He blamed his abusive behavior on alcohol, lack of a job, and Sharon. He manipulated me into letting him see Sharon and I thought he was going to kill her. I vowed never to allow myself to trust him. He was charming and manipulative—just as I had learned in the abuse trainings. He always claimed to be the victim, and now I had to sit in the same room with him.

Mike was silent while Vernon and I spoke. "Good," I thought, "he probably ought to be ashamed of what he did to his family, God, and, of course, me." It was a struggle to smile at him and act cordial. I thought of the conversations I had had with his children at church camp and how he had treated them and their mom.

At least I could talk to Vernon. He knew what Mike was like. It seemed that every statement Vernon made was prefaced with, "Now Ron, you and I understand spiritual matters but, Mike, you won't understand this . . . " or "Mike, you probably can't relate to this because you don't care about God . . ." Over and over again I heard Vernon bring up Mike's failures, faults, and sins. Mike was "stupid," "insensitive," or "lacked true knowledge." I began to wonder how Vernon, who was equally as sinful, could be so hard on his son. This was his flesh and blood. Who could Mike turn to for help? In fact, isn't Vernon a little responsible for how his son sees life, the world, and even God? Yet Mike sat there with his head down and said nothing.

As I left, my heart ached for Mike. I realized I had made an emotional connection with a man I had vowed to hate. I realized that maybe God was teaching me that all humans need love and compassion.

This is an example of the compassion that needs to be expressed for abusers. Abusers are human beings, in the image of God, who are broken and need to be accepted and held accountable. The community of faith can do great good for violent men and women if we are willing to invest our emotions to call them to accountability.

> Equally important is the need for watchful and supportive relationships with the batterers who feel that they are being abandoned one more time. When a woman leaves her abusive partner, the church community should have a group of men and women, trained in the dynamics of intimate violence, who will, for example, stop by to have lunch or dinner with the man. It is important to encourage the man not to stalk his ex-partner. If the man feels that he has other people who care about his well-being and understand the difficulty of losing his partner and children, he may be more likely to succeed in his journey toward nonviolence. The church community has a primary responsibility to assure the batterer that he remains connected to a caring community of support.[36]

Abusers can be empowered to change if they have a group that accepts them and holds them accountable for their actions. Court-mandated batterer intervention is most effective, but it can also be coupled with church-mandated spiritual growth. The faith community has the authority to require abusers to attend counseling and meet for spiritual accountability. I have set up regular meetings and prayer sessions with abusive men and

---

[36]Livingston, 23.

have seen a change in their spirituality. I have found them willing to give me permission to contact their batter intervention leader, parole officer, or other counselor in order to form a network of support and accountability. As with all ministries, this involves risk and trust, as does *agape* love. It also involves the realization that as a man, raised in a dysfunctional family, I too could easily become abusive and controlling.

Finally, empowering families of domestic violence involves *balancing power in the relationships*. Healthy relationships are about shared power. People should not use relationships to manipulate, humiliate, or control nor to allow their spouse to do so. In intimate partner relationships there should never be a care-taking role (with the exception of severe physical or mental trauma or age-related illness of a spouse). Both partners should share power and respect each other's rights and dignity. In marriage, being a good husband involves empowering his wife to be the best she can be and being a good wife means empowering her husband to be the best he can be. Marriage is about both spouses fulfilling their responsibilities. This is the meaning of love and honor in a marriage. Couples are not to try to gain power over another but to empower each other in order to work as a team.

The Community of Faith

In domestic violence, one person has attempted to control or has gained control over the other. They have done this not to better the other person but to better themselves. This control smacks of selfishness rather than respect. It is grounded in conceit rather than in love and empowerment. The victim becomes the one who is controlled and manipulated and begins to see only the needs of the other rather than themselves. Unfortunately, Christianity's emphasis on self-sacrifice becomes a tool in the behavior of the abuser to further control the other partner. Gill-Austern wrote that self-sacrifice and self-denial have the following negative effects on women:[37]

---

[37]Brita L. Gill-Austern, "Love Understood as Self-Sacrifice and Self-Denial: What Does It Do to Women?" in *Through the Eyes of Women: Insights for Pastoral Care*, ed. by Jeanne Stevenson Moessner (Minneapolis: Fortress, 1996) 310–15.

- It causes women to lose touch with their own needs and desires.
- It can lead to a loss of a sense of self and loss of voice.
- It can create a reservoir of resentment as women are victimized.
- It can lead to overfunctioning on behalf of others and underfunctioning on behalf of self, which contributes to a loss of self-esteem and an individual's own direction.
- It can undermine the capacity for genuine mutuality and intimacy.
- It creates great stress and strain.
- It can lead women to abdicate their responsibility to use their God-given gifts for God.
- It can contribute to exploitation and domination of relationships by a more powerful party.

When victims hear sermons, songs, or classes on emptying themselves, they apply it to themselves. They begin to feel guilty if they have not been what God has called them to be. Since self-blame is a natural defense for abuse victims, they feel guilty and feel as if it is their fault that the marriage suffers.

Faith communities have a great opportunity to help families caught in domestic violence. This begins with the willingness to accept all people and help them to heal. This healing comes as an empowerment for any human to stand before their creator and praise God for the Spirit of life. When working with domestic violence, this means that the church must be diligent in protecting victims from abusers. Counseling victims separately is the best way to validate them and to remove the temptation for the abuser to control the partner and the church. It is also important that a congregation only work with one of the individuals and refer the other to a strong community that will accept them. Each individual has the right to come to worship without being distracted by the other. Each individual has the right to develop their faith before God without the other affecting their spiritual formation. Faith communities should not allow themselves to be manipulated into the cycle of abuse. They should be supportive but differentiated in the healing process of both people.

For victims, faith communities must be supportive, protective, and empowering for the family. This will demand patience and understanding. Understanding that victims have played a role in an emotional system will be valuable in guiding them to be strong and confident in their faith.

Validating their pain and suffering is necessary for them to grow in Christ. The community of faith must validate their suffering by letting them know that what has happened to them is wrong and unjust. Their abusers must validate them by confessing that they have been abusive, that they have sinned, and that they will do whatever it takes to change and give back to their intimate partners. When Moses told the Israelites that God knew their pain, they worshipped *Yahweh* (Exod 4:16). Victims cannot truly be free until they are validated and able to confront their abuser. Jesus teaches that victims must be able to confront the abusers in order for the relationship to be healed (Matthew 18). God is relational and confronts the children when they sin. Why? God wants relationships to be restored. God wants to be respected and honored. I believe that victims cannot truly heal until they are able to confront their abuser or the memory of their deceased abuser. I will address this in chapter nine.

The abusers, on the other hand, cannot see the needs of their spouse because they are focused on their own needs. They believe that the wife has been insubordinate and that she is the cause of stress in the marriage. This relationship then becomes one of humiliation, and the wife is reprimanded for thinking of herself. She is to be giving and serving much like the horse in George Orwell's *Animal Farm*. The hard-working servant (horse) never questioned the leaders and ended up in the slaughterhouse because he needed to be cared for. I am careful about the marriage literature I encourage dysfunctional and abusive families to read. For better or worse does not include abuse. Making lemonade out of lemons does not sanctify dysfunction and sin. Blooming where you are planted does not justify abuse.

Both spouses are to support, strengthen, and encourage each other. This involves romance, honesty, forgiveness, accountability, and confronting wrong behavior. Each should feel comfortable holding the other to standards of holiness and honor within the family. This creates a respect between two people who are in a balanced relationship. If there is an imbalance of power, the victim must be protected immediately. God is a God who hears the cries of the victims and demands that they be protected. Victims first must be encouraged to be safe, and then the process that strengthens them to confront abuse can begin.

I do not believe that people will truly heal until they can stand against those who have hurt them. When victims are safe, they can begin the process of looking within themselves and discerning that they are to be loved and treated with respect. Because victims have been manipulated or humiliated, many have learned to mistrust anything that makes them feel worthy, especially when it comes from outsiders. This is a tactic used by abusers, and it causes the victim to see themselves through the eyes of others. They will do what pleases others before they do what makes them happy. They will put themselves at risk in order to serve others. Churches should be aware of this and help them heal by encouraging them to begin looking inward. King David looked inward and knew that he was a beautiful creation of *Yahweh* "I praise you because I am fearfully and wonderfully made" (Ps 139:11).

When the relationship is unbalanced, the abuser also needs to be held accountable for his actions and selfish attitudes. This means that outsiders need to confront abusers and challenge them to change their behavior. Those confronting them must be careful that they are not causing another imbalance of power. Outsiders should not side with the abusers or allow themselves to be manipulated into becoming another servant of the abuser. Outsiders should also refrain from condemning and humiliating the abuser. The community of faith can work with trained professionals to provide a safe place for abusers to heal and learn to practice shared power in their relationships.

> The most productive strategy is for churches to work together with other social service providers to support the existing batterer's treatment program. I believe that every community should recognize the importance of reconciling the violent offenders in its midst to the larger community, but this goal is only possible with an extended and rigorous program of responsibility. Where there is already a batterers' treatment program working within the community, the ecclesial community should be sure that part of the process of satisfaction involves attending these meetings.[38]

The community must also love and empower the abusers. This is a sacrifice and a risk, but it is what God calls the community to do. Abusers

---

[38]Ibid., 83.

can be guided and challenged to repent, but it must come from a community that has invested time, patience, and passion into helping them heal. Abusers are to be empowered to heal and repent to their families.

The community of faith can also promote shared power between couples. The church has the right and responsibility to empower victims to heal and to confront those who violate them. Helping former victims set healthy relational boundaries gives them the chance to feel a sense of power. The community has the right and responsibility to call abusers to submission, accountability, and self-control. When Jesus healed the demon-possessed man (Luke 8:26-39), he did not allow him to accompany him until he returned to his community and told them about God. What reaction would this man have faced when walking into the town? People would have remembered him as the "crazy flasher," the violent man, and the howling maniac that could not be controlled. Yet his task was to face those he had hurt and tell them, as well as show them about his transformation through Jesus.

Likewise, every abuser should be called to face those that they have hurt and hear their pain and cries. In order to heal, they have to acknowledge their sinfulness and the effects that their abuse has had on others. The community of faith has a great opportunity to send abusers back into their community to heal and allow others to heal. It also has the responsibility to protect and validate victims so that they can see that they are in God's image and worthy of love and respect.

The community of faith can also prevent abuse by teaching men to model the nature of God. Men's classes and fellowships can keep men in accountable relationships with other men. Abusive men usually do not have many male friends. Men's groups can hold men accountable and provide the opportunity to develop friendships that many men tend to resist. We must also redefine masculinity by the nature of Yahweh, Jesus, and the Holy Spirit. Masculinity is not as narrowly defined as in our culture, but rather it is as diverse as God. God *is one* and practices behavior that is valid for both male and female. Masculinity is not seen in opposition to women; it is seen in complement with women.

Faith communities can help families caught in violence by understanding the dysfunctional family system, empowering members to change, and helping each member balance power in the relationship. While this takes an emotional investment by members of the community, it is an act of love and compassion for families seeking help and strength in a world that seeks God. God expects the faith community to model divine characteristics to all people. Humans caught in violence are humans, in the image of God, who are broken and need to be loved. God extends compassion and justice to all people and calls the community of faith to do the same. This involves embracing people, holding them accountable for their actions, and providing opportunities for them to change.

Churches can focus on identifying power and control issues in marriage classes, pre-marital counseling, and youth groups. Family classes can help families develop healthy relationship skills. Youth ministers can work with teens to address dating violence, family violence, and the need to hold each other accountable for abusive behavior.

Domestic violence affects everyone. But does everyone affect domestic violence?

Part 2
A Christian Theology for Domestic Violence

God has called us to peace . . .
—Paul the Apostle

4
God, Theology, and Abuse

What is Theology?

Theology can be a frightening word. It seems that when we hear *theology* we think of something abstract, something distant from common concerns, or an academic exercise. Many people seem apprehensive about theology, but it is not a word meant to distance the study of religion from the common man nor is it an academic exercise or discipline. Theology is meant to make a complex message about God relevant to people. When Jesus spoke in parables, he was practicing theology. When the Apostle Paul explained Jewish texts to common Gentiles, he was practicing theology. When the writers of Proverbs made life applications from animals and daily events, they were practicing theology. When the prophets spoke God's message in metaphors and stories, they were practicing theology.

A Study or Discussion About God

Theology means *a study or discussion about God*.[1] This means that it begins with God. While Christians have many issues, discussions, and doctrines that can exhaust their time, these issues are futile if they do not begin with a discussion about God. Whenever we are asked, "What does God have to say about . . . " or "What does the Bible say about . . . ," we are being forced to begin with God. God is our authority and the nature, actions, and heart of God are where we begin.

Christian theology also suggests that the words and actions of Jesus reflect the nature and heart of God. We believe that the Bible is a revelation of God's character, actions, and desire for all creation, therefore Jesus is also the revelation of God. When discussing domestic violence and abuse, one must begin with the question: "How does God feel about the issue and how is this manifest in Jesus?" Many churches and ministers try to address or dismiss domestic violence without even consulting God, the Bible, or God's revelation in nature. Other Christians give their opinions on domestic violence by stating, "I know that God doesn't want people to be treated this way but . . . ," as if they have permission to dismiss or ignore God's view of the matter. A theology of domestic violence begins with God and addresses the Creator's feelings about this issue.

Human Discussion and Interaction

Second, theology *involves human discussion and interaction*. A study that begins with God must eventually extend to human beings. We call this *theological reflection*. Once we learn something about God, we must share what we have learned. While Western culture is very individualistic, Eastern culture has a desire to dialogue, discuss, share, and learn with or from others. Western people tend to individually reflect on what they have learned. Eastern people tend to share ideas and look for a consensus. Since the Biblical culture came from the ancient Near Eastern world, it seems

---

[1] Theology is from two Greek words. *Theos* means "God" and *logos* means "word" or "study." A simple definition of theology is the *study of God* or *sharing of words about God*.

logical that theological reflection, dialogue, and consensus are part of the Judeo-Christian culture.

> With no direction/guidance the people fall,
> but there is safety with many advisors. (Prov 11:14)

> The way of a fool seems correct in their eyes,
> but a wise person listens to advice. (Prov 12:15)

> Plans fail for lack of counsel,
> but with many advisers they succeed. (Prov 15:22)

> The heart of the righteous meditates on an answer,
> but the mouth of the wicked pours (blurts out) evil things. (Prov 15:28)

> Whoever answers before listening
> is foolish and should be ashamed. (Prov 18:13)

> One who remains stiff-necked after many rebukes
> will suddenly be broken and will not heal (Prov 29:1).

> Therefore my dear friends, as you have always obeyed in my presence, much more now in my absence continue to work out your (plural) salvation with fear and trembling because it is God who works among you . . . . (Phil 2:12)

> I encourage Eudoia and I encourage Syntyche to agree with each other in the Lord. I also ask you, loyal co-workers, to receive these women together . . . . (Phil 4:2-3)

The purpose of writing texts was to allow future readers to join into a discussion. While "Westerners" may read the Biblical text to learn how to be saved, the biblical writers intended for us to read the text so that we might share and work with others. Theological reflection is not an individual process; it is a group process. Why? The center of theology is faith in God. In order to learn and understand theology, one must believe that God exists (Heb 11:1-3, 6). One must also believe that God rewards seekers. This is a foundational belief that Anselm called *faith seeking understanding*.[2] When people want to understand spiritual issues, they come together to share ideas. Therefore, theology involves studying, seeking, and sharing.

> Wherever and whenever it occurs, theological reflection is not only a personal but also an interactive, dialogical, and community-related process. The voices of others are heard. Some of these voices, like those of the biblical writers, come from texts of centuries past. Others are those of our contemporaries. Still others are our own. These voices offer us food for thought to be heeded or debated or improved upon or set aside as unhelpful. To engage in theological reflection is to join in an ongoing conversation with others that began long before we ever came along and will continue long after we have passed away.[3]

Theology is of great value when discussed with others. Yet this discussion must be one that seeks to know rather than to condemn.

> No theologian can know about everyone and everything. To learn more than we already know is one good reason to enter into conversation with others. Limiting the circle of conversation partners in advance, whether due to prejudice or ignorance, is always the theologian's loss. That makes it the church's loss as well.[4]

If we know how God feels about domestic violence, then we must discuss this with others. There are those who are passionate about protecting victims and batterers, holding batterers and victims accountable, protecting children, preserving marriages, and correcting dysfunction in families. There are also those who are passionate about God. When we come together, we force each other to reflect theologically on God, domestic

---

[2]David Clark indicates that faith can be a foundational or properly basic belief, which is strengthened by later arguments for the existence of God. David K. Clark, "Faith and Foundationalism," in *The Rationality of Theism*, ed. Paul Copan and Paul K. Moser (New York: Routledge, 2003) 35–36.

[3]Howard W. Stone and James O. Duke, *How to Think Theologically* (Minneapolis: Fortress, 1996) 4.

[4]Ibid., 6.

violence, victims, and abusers. For me, this process has been a wonderful time of growth spiritually, socially, and as a husband. For others, the process becomes a time to renew their faith in God and the value of Christianity in the world. It is encouraging to see the eyes of domestic violence advocates light up when it is suggested that God expects Christians to help them.

An Articulation of Faith

Finally, theology is an *articulation of a faith that seeks to learn.*[5] As we seek to know more about God and we discuss and reflect upon our understanding with others, it is important that we have a statement of what we believe. Stanley Grenz suggests that this articulation comes from the church's desire to define our beliefs, instruct others, and summarize our statements of faith.[6] Theology has a purpose in mind. It is to be a guide to help people draw closer to the Creator and better understand the nature and heart of God. We study to learn, dialogue to reflect, and share to inform others about this God. Much of the work in domestic violence involves becoming aware of and discussing God's view of victims and abusers. While a study of God leads to a conviction, the practice of theology can develop relationships with others and strengthen this *faith seeking understanding.* Thus, it is important to speak with victims or abusers about God and domestic violence.

Christian theology suggests that God is revealed in nature, scripture, and the words and actions of Jesus Christ. While nature cannot reveal the personal character of God, Jesus reveals how God feels about children, women, the oppressed, and humanity.[7] Jesus is the reflection of God, representing the nature and heart of the Creator for all humans (Col 1:15; Heb 1:1-2). Jesus' ministry is the model for our obedience to God and our practicing the works of God.

---

[5]Stanley J. Grenz, *Theology for the Community of God* (Grand Rapids: Eerdmans, 2000) 1.

[6]Ibid., 4.

[7]Millard J. Erickson, *Christian Theology*, 2d ed. (Grand Rapids: Baker, 1999) 715; Grenz, 245.

> Even though he was a son he learned obedience from what he suffered
> and when he finished, all of those who obey him have a way for eternal
> salvation . . . . (Heb 5:18)

The Spirit also reflects the nature and heart of God. God has placed the
Spirit within humans not only as a testimony to God's existence but as a
source of power to help Christians become like Jesus.

> When the encourager comes, whom I send from the Father, the Spirit
> of truth, which goes from the Father, that one will testify about me.
> (John 15:26)

> Those who live according to the sinful nature think fleshly but those
> who live according to the Spirit are spiritual. To think fleshly brings
> death but to think spiritually brings life and peace. Therefore to think
> fleshly makes one an enemy of God, because they are not able and cannot
> submit to the law of God. They are not able to and cannot please God.
> But you are not fleshly! You are spiritual, since the Spirit of God lives in
> you. (Rom 8:5-9)

As Paul Moser suggested, Jesus and the Spirit are powerful witnesses to
the nature and character of God.

> What else could God supply as salient evidence of divine reality, besides
> his Spirit and his unique Son? They provide the best evidence imaginable,
> the only evidence worthy of full commitment to God.[8]

Theology and Domestic Violence: God's Nature and Abuse

If we wish to address domestic violence, we must begin with God. How
does God feel about abuse? How does God feel about victims and batterers?
What does the Bible teach about domestic violence and the nature of
God's people? Are power and control characteristics of God? When talking

---

[8]Paul K. Moser, "Cognitive Inspiration and Knowledge of God," *Rationality of Theism*,
63.

why the discussion on God as angry and violent?

with batterer intervention providers and victims' advocates, a discussion about God usually tends to focus on Joshua and the violent wars of the Hebrew Scriptures. While these are issues of violence, power, and control, this only represents a small portion of the nature of God. We must acknowledge that God does punish and allows the use of violence on individuals and nations that continually resist the Creator. We must also remember that God warned the nation to repent for decades and sometimes centuries before enacting punishment. It is fair to believe that this represents a small portion of God's actions.

When people talk about their faith, many suggest that the God of the Old Testament was an angry ogre; Jesus was the nice loving Savior, and the Spirit was/is a feel-good force in their lives. It appears that somewhere between the Old and New Testaments,[9] God decided to become nice and realized that we all sin and need a break. Jesus was sent to show that God had been through "therapy" and came to realize that people aren't going to change so maybe the Creator should. The Spirit is the force that groans to God and reminds the Creator that we can't do anything right and that's why Jesus died. Jesus took the brunt of God's anger. Then God looked upon the suffering Son and saw that "this was not good." God sent Jesus and the Spirit to give us a break and to help God remember that getting angry doesn't solve anything. They continually persuade God not to act out in vengeance. By this theology, it seems that the Trinity is actually an accountability group where the Son and Spirit exist to pacify the Father who tends to "snap" when provoked to anger. This thinking is flawed. For some reason we have missed whole texts that tell us God has always been merciful and compassionate. Maybe that is why so many do not read the Old Testament! What a shame!

Overwhelmingly, *God practices mercy, forgiveness, and patience.* Violence is usually a final act after years, decades, or centuries of patience. In Exod 34:6-7, God was revealed as one who is compassionate, gracious, slow to anger, abounding in love and faithfulness, maintaining love to thousands, and forgiving wickedness, rebellion, and sin. God punishes the wicked for three or four generations, but extends forgiveness to a thousand

---

[9]I usually try to avoid the terms *Old Testament* and *New Testament* by using Hebrew and Greek Scriptures since these terms are more correct. In this book I have chosen to keep the "traditional" terms since most readers are familiar with this terminology.

generations (Deut 7:9). Forgiveness, patience, and mercy are major characteristics of God's nature. When God forgave the Ninevites, Jonah replied with, "I knew that you are a gracious and merciful God, slow to anger and full of faithfulness, a God who feels sorry for the evil ones" (Jonah 4:2). In the Old Testament, God is shown as one who forgives an unfaithful wife, renews a covenant with a sinful nation, gives life to a people who will turn away, and enters a covenant with a people knowing that "their heart is inclined to do evil from their youth" (Gen 8:21). God's nature is not one of violence and anger but one of love, mercy, and compassion. To focus on God's anger is to have a limited perspective of the divine nature. The Bible describes the nature of God as merciful and compassionate.

In the incarnation, the nature of God is seen in Jesus. The Gospel writers described Jesus as someone who was meek, was patient, cried, listened to women, held children, and encouraged the oppressed. Early Christian writers described Jesus as patient, loving, and compassionate. The Bible tells us that Jesus is the reflection and image of *Yahweh* (Col 1:15; Heb 1:4). Yet, as the risen Lord, Jesus has put his enemies under his feet (Acts 2:35). The risen Lord acts in vengeance and repays those who do evil, yet we tend to remember him as a forgiving, loving, and compassionate Messiah. Jesus came to explain God's nature and character, not redefine it. He came to show us the compassion, justice, and character of God (John 1:18; Heb 1:3). The Spirit also reflects the nature of God. The Spirit does bring the conviction and judgment of God (Acts 5:1-11), yet it overwhelmingly represents the peace of God.

> But the fruit of the Spirit is love, joy, peace, endurance, kindness, goodness, faithfulness, meekness, and self control . . . If we live by the Spirit we must be in order with the Spirit. (Gal 5:22-25)

God's nature is shown in the scriptures, the incarnation, and the Spirit as one of compassion, peace, and patience.

Power and control are issues that must be addressed by the nature of God. Does God control human beings? Are children of God forced or coerced into submission and worship? Do we have free will? Can we make our own choices? Is our future already set? Theology calls us to study the nature of God and reflect on the divine presence in Jesus and the Spirit. Since God's nature is one of gentleness, mercy, and compassion, then how does God feel about abuse? More importantly, how does God feel about those who physically, emotionally, verbally, and sexually abuse or humiliate others? If mercy is part of God's nature, then what do we do with power and control? A study of God and domestic violence challenges us to ask these questions and seek answers.

Since God seeks relationship with humans, we can believe that God is relational. In the Garden of Eden, God said that it was not good for the man to be alone (Gen 2:18). Humans are created in God's image or "our image" (Gen 1:26). The Hebrew word for "our" is plural and suggests that God is a plurality, or community, as are humans. The early church writers used this to suggest that God existed as a trinity (Father, Son, and Holy Spirit). God seeks relationship because God exists in relationship and initiates covenant.

> The doctrine of the Trinity reminds us that the God who loves the world is a God who draws near to people in intimate communion, where both giving and receiving are the aim of love, in order that persons might have life and have it in all its abundance.[10]

Regardless of how wicked, sinful, rebellious, or disobedient humans have proven to be, God continues to call humans to repentance and to establish covenants with the creation. In covenant, God proved to be faithful and honorable by providing for the needs of humans. When humans break or transgress the covenant, God is dishonored in the world (Mal 1:6). God then has two options in order to restore or maintain honor in the presence of creation—punishment or forgiveness. Forgiveness is an option, but it involves repentance by the sinner.[11] Punishment is another option, and it involves no action by the transgressor. Therefore, God

---

[10]Gill-Austern, 319.

[11]In any discussion of forgiveness and repentance, some suggest that Jesus' words on the cross ("Father forgive them because they do not know what they are doing," Luke 23:34) indicate that forgiveness was given without repentance. While this seems tempting to use in order to justify this belief, the following would suggest that those at the cross were not forgiven at that point. First, the thief on the cross, rather than the other criminal, was later promised Paradise *because of his confession of Jesus.* Second, Acts 2:36-38 and 3:13, 19, 26 suggest that those who rejected Jesus, even at the cross, needed to repent to receive forgiveness. Third, Luke 24:47 also suggests that repentance and forgiveness of

maintains honor by providing for those in the covenant and practicing justice. Humans have the responsibility to honor God by obeying the covenant. God honors us by blessing us and being faithful.[12]

In the covenant there is always the option of unfaithfulness. God *chooses* to uphold the terms of the covenant. God is faithful, cannot lie, and keeps promises (Deut 7:7-9; Titus 1:4). The wonderful news is that God is faithful (*chesed*) and *chooses* to uphold the terms of the relationship. The bad news is that over the years humans have *chosen* to be unfaithful to the covenant. Therefore, in order to be honorable God must *choose* punishment or forgiveness. At times, God punished transgressors (Isa 54:6; Jer 3:8). Sometimes when sinners prayed, God *chose* not to hear them, as in the case of the Babylonian captivity (Jer 11:9-14; 14:11-12; Ezek 8:18). Most of the time when sinners appealed to God, they were forgiven (Jonah 3:10; 1 Kgs 21:28-29). In every example, God made a *choice*. Whether it was forgiveness or punishment, God was exercising a *choice*. In every example the transgressors also made a *choice*. In covenant there exists *choice*, free will, honor, and mutual respect. God does not force humans into a decision. God gives humans the ability to choose good or evil in the world and while in covenant.

> The covenant knows not only of a demand, but also of a promise: "You shall be my people and I will be your God." In this way it provides life with a goal and history with a meaning . . . With this God men know exactly where they stand; *an atmosphere of trust and security* is created, in which they find both the strength for a willing surrender to the will of God and joyful courage to grapple with the problems of life.[13]

---

sins work together. Fourth, Jesus was making a request on the cross, showing his desire to mediate between God and man rather than granting forgiveness to all. Finally, while the crucifixion may have illustrated that God was extending forgiveness to all humans (Rom 5:8-10) we all must repent and die to sin in baptism (Rom 6:1-7).

[12]Faith and faithfulness are the same word in Greek and Hebrew. The Hebrew *chesed* is usually translated "loving kindness" but has the meaning of faithful or loyal when discussed in the context of covenant. God's *chesed* suggests that God is faithful to the covenant. For humans, this suggests loyalty and obedience in the covenant.

[13]Walther Eichrodt, *Theology of the Old Testament*, 2 vols., trans. J. A. Baker, Old Testament Library (Philadelphia: Westminster, 1961) 1.38. I have tried to avoid gender-specific language when referring to God in order to be sensitive to all readers. I do, however, allow other authors the respect they deserve when quoting them. I have chosen to leave their quotes as is regardless of their use of gender-specific language when referring to God.

This clear dissociation from any naturalistic idea of the relationship with the divinity is buttressed by yet another consequence of the covenant concept, namely that this is something on which God has entered freely and which on his side may dissolve at any time. Any compulsive linking of God to his people is thus utterly denied. He existed long before the nation, he is by nature independent of their existence and can abandon them whenever they refuse to be conformed to his will.[14]

The covenant with *Yahweh* depends on God's faithfulness, but it also requires the same choice from humans.

Power and control involve coercion, manipulation, and abuse. God does not engage in relationships in this way. When people continue to choose to sin, God allows Satan, a ruler, an army, or the events of life to affect them. God does not force people to make a certain choice. God persuades through the preaching by others and pleads for people to choose the truth. Because of this choice, God's method of outreach is not by coercion but by persuasion.

> Stand in the courtyard of *Yahweh*'s house and speak to all the people of the towns of Judah who come to worship in the house of *Yahweh*. Tell them everything I command you to speak; do not omit a word. Perhaps they will listen and each will turn from their evil way. *Then I will feel sorry and not bring evil on them* because of the evil they have done. (Jer 26:2-3)

> *I do not delight in the death of anyone*, declares the Lord *Yahweh*. Repent and live! (Ezek 18:32)

God empowers those in covenant to see the truth and make right choices. One example is 1 Cor 10:13.

> You have not received any temptation except what is common to man. God is faithful and will not permit you be tempted beyond what you are able to do, but with the temptation you will have a way out so that you can bear it.

---

[14]Ibid., 44.

The passage tells us that God empowers us to overcome sin and temptation. First, God protects us from excessive evil and *does not allow* more than we can handle. The Creator keeps Satan at bay and allows the devil only limited power over individuals (Job 1–2). Second, God still *allows us* to have a choice. We have the potential and ability to choose evil or good, and God knows this. Third, *God has faith that we can make the right choice.* God hopes in us, even though we are weak, and believes that we have the right and ability to resist sin.

> God's greatness is most fundamentally about love. God created the world out of love and for the purpose of love. And this requires that he created free agents. There can be no love without risk. The possibility of war, therefore, is built into the possibility of love.[15]

> God created the world out of love and for the purpose of love. But as all emotionally healthy people intuitively know, love must be chosen. And choice means that a person can say no. Unless people can choose not to love, they can't genuinely choose to love. The possibility of the one is built into the possibility of the other. Love simply cannot be coerced or programmed into people. Up to the time of Augustine the church understood and emphasized this point. The church fathers repeatedly stressed that love and virtue require morally responsible choice. Thus they taught that God's mode of operation in running the world is not coercion but persuasion.[16]

This is empowerment. God persuades, protects, and empowers us so that we can make a right choice. The fact that we choose evil is not a reflection upon God but it brings a sense of shame. The shame is not upon us but God. Our choosing evil may grieve God, but it does not discredit the divine nature. God can not be blamed for the choices of others, yet choosing that which is good provides a great sense of joy to God. Within covenant there is always the ability to choose good or evil. The choices, not the control, bring honor or shame to God.

---

[15]Gregory A. Boyd, *Is God to Blame?: Beyond Pat Answers to the Problem of Suffering* (Downer's Grove, Ill.: InterVarsity, 2003) 76.
[16]Ibid., 63.

Some of my atheist friends feel this suggests a weak god. They ask, "If God were all-powerful, wouldn't he or she protect everyone from evil and keep him or her from making bad choices?" Yet none of them practice this type of control in their parenting. They feel that parents should train children to make right choices. They also try not to control their children, yet when I tell them that God also does this, they feel God is weak. Instead of forcing us into a mold, God provides hope that we can and will live lives that bring honor and glory to our Creator.

> This central scriptural theme, however, presupposes that evil exists for God as well as for humans, that God does not will it, and thus that some beings (those who are evil) have the ability to act against God's will. It requires the understanding that it is possible for some beings (angels and humans at least) genuinely to resist, and even to thwart, whatever blueprint God might wish their lives to follow. It requires accepting the view that God, for whatever reasons, designed the cosmos such that he does not necessarily always get his way, and may in fact detest the way some things are turning out. It requires the view that God does not monopolize power, and hence that omnipotence cannot be equated with meticulous omnicontrol.[17]

God *empowers* people to make right choices with the possibility that they may also make bad choices. If God could intervene, humans would not have free will and free choice.[18]

This was evident in Jesus' ministry. Jesus mentioned that Judas was a devil and was going to betray him (John 6:70; 13:10, 18). After washing Judas' feet, Jesus almost persuaded Judas to make a good choice.[19] Jesus told the Father that he had protected all of his disciples from Satan except Judas (17:12). Judas made a *choice* to leave, and Jesus could not change his heart. Peter, after denying Jesus, made a choice to turn and strengthen

---

[17]Boyd, *God At War: The Bible and Spiritual Conflict* (Downer's Grove, Ill.: InterVarsity Press, 1997) 47.

[18]Boyd, *Is God to Blame?*, 63.

[19]Notice in John 13:1 that Satan entered Judas' heart. After Jesus handed the bread to Judas Satan had to again enter him (13:27). It seems that Judas had to make a choice both times. It seems to me that Jesus' act of washing feet may have given Judas a change of heart.

others (Luke 22:31-32; Acts 1:18-26). Jesus *empowered* the disciples to stand on their own feet and be faithful. The Spirit also *empowers* others by dwelling within them. Yet the Spirit can be quenched (1 Thess 5:18), grieved (Eph 4:29) and is submissive to prophets (1 Cor 14:32). Morally, Christians can live in such a way that they either walk with the Spirit or drive it out. The Spirit *empowers* the people of God to live holy lives, but it does not control or overpower them. This is why preaching and persuading are important tasks in the ministry of Christ and the Spirit.

God does exhibit power over evil. While Satan and evil are allowed to exist, God punishes and judges evil and those who practice it. God is a God of justice and evil has limited power, but at the end of its time, God wins. Throughout the Bible God displays judgment at various times. Because humans have free choice, they are given the opportunity to choose between good and evil. Yet at God's decided time (usually called *Yom Yahweh* or the "day of the LORD"), judgment happens and the wicked are punished. Pagan nations punish the unfaithful, and those nations that refuse to humble themselves before *Yahweh* are punished. God allows humans to choose and face the blessings or consequences of those choices.

This is illustrated in the prophets. Three prophets that show this well are Nahum, Zephaniah, and Habakkuk. In Zephaniah, the Jewish king Josiah administered God's punishment on Judah for its unfaithfulness (Zeph 1:2, 4, 8). God was vindicating the oppressed (3:1) and dispensing justice upon the arrogant Jewish leaders (3:2-5). God was acting as a judge because they had chosen evil. In Nahum, God judged Assyria (Ninevah was its capital) for bloodshed and idolatry. God also acted as a judge who wished to protect and vindicate the oppressed children of Israel (Nah 1:7; 2:2). In these texts, the victims cried out for justice and God heard them. While decades of oppression passed, God was not blind and had chosen a day for judgment. God had even given both nations one last chance.

> Seek *Yahweh* all the humble of the land, you who do what God commands. Seek righteousness, seek humility, perhaps you will be sheltered on the day of Yahweh's anger. (Zeph 2:3)

In Habakkuk, however, the justice of God overwhelmed the prophet. Habakkuk wondered how God could send the Babylonians to ruthlessly destroy the Jews. The Jewish leaders were violent (Hab 2:12, 17), practiced extortion (2:9), and murdered innocent people (2:12,17). This day would be a day of punishment. Habakkuk cried out for vengeance, but he was overwhelmed by God's response.

> Why do you make me see sin and trouble? You watch while looting and trouble are before me; there is strife and conflict happens because of this. The Torah is ineffective (slack) and there is no justice. The wicked hem in the righteous and therefore justice is perverted. (Hab 1:3-4)

Carol Dempsey suggests that this violence of God creates more questions than solutions in the issue of violence, power, and control.

> From a hermeneutical perspective, the book of Habakkuk raises questions about the use and abuse of power, a topic that could engender and invigorate further scholarly discussions on the text.[20]

> What a frightening picture readers are presented with in [Habakkuk chapter 1] vv. 5-11. The use of power for oppression and devastation is obvious. The text confronts readers about God: what kind of a God would use an empire, especially a violent and unjust one, to deal with another kingdom's injustices? In this text, God is someone who can control the fiercest of countries to incur punitive justice on the unrighteous.[21]

Concerning the violence in Zephaniah, Dempsey writes:

> One sees in these texts an ethnocentric view of God, who comes with power to defend Israel by overpowering those countries who have taunted and conquered "God's people." Here, power is used to overpower, and violence gives birth to more violence.[22]

---

[20]Carol Dempsey, *The Prophets: A Liberation-Critical Reading* (Minneapolis: Augsburg Fortress, 2000) 78.
[21]Ibid., 80.
[22]Ibid., 89.

While Dempsey has a valid observation and question concerning God's use of power, Zephaniah suggests that God sent prophets to warn people and call them to repentance. After warning about the day of the LORD, God pled with Israel to repent.

> Gather together, gather shameful nation, before the appointed decree as that day sweeps by like chaff, before the fierce anger of *Yahweh* comes upon you, before the day of *Yahweh*'s wrath comes upon you. Seek *Yahweh*, all you oppressed (humble) of the land, you who do justice. Seek righteousness, seek humility; perhaps you will be protected in the day of *Yahweh*'s anger (Zeph 2:1-3)

God is a God of justice. God uses force to balance power and vindicate or protect victims. Those who use power over others must be confronted.

I am amazed at how many individuals feel that God is unjust for punishing the wicked, but if a neighbor were attacking his wife and beating her, wouldn't they expect the police to go to the home, armed, to confront the neighbor? Wouldn't they expect the law enforcement officials to reason with the abuser? Possibly. Wouldn't they also expect these officials to protect themselves as well as the victim and reserve the right to use lethal force if necessary? Law enforcement officials acknowledge that domestic disturbances are the most dangerous calls that officers receive. We accept that our police officers should be prepared to use force or power in order to protect victims and themselves. If the abuser refuses to act reasonably or cooperate with officials, the police are justified in using force. Yet God practices this form of justice and is criticized for it. After decades or centuries of pleading, warning, and challenging the oppressors to stop, God finally acts and is criticized for doing so.

Victims would suggest that at times violence is necessary for their safety. From a Biblical perspective, Nahum and Zephaniah suggest that God is just because the oppressors are defeated and judged. Habakkuk would agree, but he was overwhelmed by the violence that happens. I tell my college students that Habakkuk is similar to the batterer intervention counselor who pleads for compassion and a chance to help the batterer through the fire while Zephaniah sees the suffering of the victims and calls for justice. In both cases neither is happy to see this violence, but both realize that it is just and many times necessary. God is a God of justice and acts because the Creator knows the hearts of all men and women and seeks to protect victims and judge abusers.

In all of this, God is still a God of vengeance. Solomon Schimmel suggests that many victims suffer because they are told that vengeance or the desire for revenge/justice is wrong. Yet God brings revenge on the wicked through objective institutions. Schimmel indicates that those who are hurt may not be able to dispense proper judgment on their abuser. The purpose of legal systems is to properly weigh out the evidence and the nature of the criminal and call them to repentance while validating the victim.[23] This is evident in Paul's challenge to let God take care of revenge (Rom 12:19) followed by the statement that authorities are God's method of punishing evil workers (Rom 13:4). This tells Christians that God will use human institutions to punish those who oppress and victimize others. While this seems violent, it is God's way of providing impartial judgment on criminals.

A third issue concerning the nature of God is the *fate of the oppressed*. God is the defender of the oppressed (Exod 22:22-24; Ps 9:9; Prov 17:5). Oppression makes God angry.

> Do not mistreat a widow or an orphan. If you do and they cry out to me, I will certainly hear their cry. My anger will be aroused, and I will kill you by the sword; your wives will become widows and your children fatherless. (Exod 22:22-24)

God commanded the Israelites to protect and defend the oppressed. The oppressed included widows, orphans, the poor, aliens, and any others who are victims in society.[24] God led the Israelites out of Egypt and protected them because they were oppressed (Exod 22:21). They were also expected to show this same concern for the oppressed. Throughout the Hebrew Scriptures, God became angry when nations abused and oppressed the weak of society. Women, children, and aliens were among

---

[23]Solomon Schimmel, *Wounds Not Healed by Time: The Power of Repentance and Forgiveness* (New York: Oxford University Press, 2002) 21–23.

[24]The Hebrew word for oppressed is *'aniy*. This word is translated later by the Greek word *tapeinos,* which is used for humble. The humble are those humiliated and oppressed in society. Do victims of domestic violence fit into this category?

this category. It is God's nature to protect and defend the cause of the weak and oppressed.[25]

> The one who oppresses the poor despises their maker,
> but whoever is kind to the needy honors God. (Prov 14:31)

> Do not move an ancient boundary stone or encroach on the fields of the orphans for their defender (redeemer or kinsman) is strong and will take up their case against you. (Prov 23:10-11)

Jesus also reflects the nature of God in his ministry. The Gospel of Luke illustrates God's passion for the weak and oppressed. Luke 4:16-19 is a story about Jesus proclaiming in the synagogue that his mission involved freeing the captives, helping the blind see, releasing the oppressed, and preaching good news to the poor. As John the Baptist was dying, he sent two men to inquire if Jesus were the awaited Messiah. While ministering to the oppressed, Jesus answered:

> Go back and report to John what you have seen and heard; the blind receive sight, the lame walk, those who have leprosy are cured, the deaf hear, the dead are raised, and the good news is preached to the poor. Blessed is the one who is not offended[26] by me. (Luke 7:22-23)

Jesus showed the same passion for the oppressed that God displayed in the Old Testament. The two judgment scenes in the Gospels (Matt 25:31-46; Luke 16:19-31) involve people who had neglected the needs of the poor and oppressed. They were rejected and condemned by Jesus. The Holy Spirit in Acts also displayed this nature. The Spirit sent the early church to the Gentiles, poor, widows, and outcasts. The Spirit condemned Ananias and Sapphira concerning an issue of money distributed to the

---

[25]Harold V. Bennett, *Injustice Made Legal: Deuteronomic Law and the Plight of Widows, Strangers, and Orphans in Ancient Israel* (Grand Rapids: Eerdmans, 2002) 1–2.
[26]The Greek word is *skandalon*, which has been translated stumbling block, stumble, or fall away. It carries the sense of offense or repulse. It seems that Jesus is reminding John's messengers that his ministry is offensive to others because he worked with the oppressed (Luke 7:34). They were called to a choice—ministry to the poor or ministry like the Pharisees.

poor (Acts 5:1-10) and sent Paul and Barnabas to the Gentiles (Acts 13:1-3, 52). Paul saw this as a way to remember the poor (Gal 2:10).

Finally, the nature of God is seen in a *relationship with humanity*. As mentioned earlier, God seeks relationship with humans. The covenant became a major event in the various stages of human history. God made covenants with Noah and the earth (Gen 9:1-17), Abraham (Gen 15:1), David (2 Sam 7:5-16), Judah as they returned home from exile (Jer 31:31-34), and us through Jesus (Luke 22:20-22). God was the initiator of these covenants. It has always been God's desire to establish and maintain a relationship with humans. Yet God does not encourage or tolerate a dysfunctional relationship in covenant. God does not turn a deaf ear when abused or dishonored. God divorced Israel for being unfaithful to the covenant (Isa 54:9; Jer 3:8). God does not establish a relationship that ignores sin and transgression. God seeks a healthy, compassionate, and supportive relationship with humans. God is not a doormat and is not interested in having a relationship that requires control, manipulation, or overfunctioning from either partner. God desires to be known, respected, and honored by the creation.

> I will now bring the tribe of Jacob back from captivity and will have compassion on all the family of Israel, and I will be jealous for my holy name. They will forget their shame and all the unfaithfulness they did against me when they lived in safety in their land and without trouble. When I have brought them back from the Gentiles and have gathered them from the countries of their enemies, I will show myself holy through them in the sight of the Gentiles. Then they will know that I am *Yahweh* their God, for though I sent them into exile to the Gentiles, I will gather them to their own land, and not leave anyone behind. I will not hide my face from them, I will pour out my Spirit on the house of Israel, declares the Lord *Yahweh*. (Ezek 39:25-29)

God's vision for humans involves mutual respect, honor, and blessing. God deserves to be respected, honored, loved, and obeyed. God should have someone who is faithful. The relational God grieves, rejoices, and forgives. This is not a weak God; it is a passionate God. Our God is good and desires a relationship with others.

Jesus displayed this same passion in his ministry. He wept, drove sinners out of the temple, challenged the disciples, rebuked the Pharisees, held children, encouraged widows and parents of deceased children, and rejoiced. Jesus initiated a relationship with humans and called the disciples "friends" (John 15:12). Jesus asked Peter, James, and John to accompany him in a time of grief (Mark 14:34), and he watched a friend betray him (Luke 22:61). Jesus became close to humans so that he could experience the joy of relationship and the pain of betrayal and abuse. The Spirit, likewise, lives among humans to guide and intercede for them (Rom 8:5-16). Yet a life of sin can grieve or quench the Spirit (1 Thess 5:18; Eph 4:29). A relational God is not a weak God but a passionate one. To risk rejection and/or joy are powerful characteristics of the nature of God. The very God who initiates love is a God who risks rejection or acceptance.

Theology is a study of the nature of God. Theology tells us that God is not a God of wrath and anger but one of peace, mercy, and compassion. God is faithful and chooses to forgive and love human beings. Theology also tells us that God empowers us to choose good. God does not control humans but guides us and believes that we can choose good over evil. God stands for the weak and oppressed and is angry when victims are abused or oppressed. Yet God continues to seek healthy relationships with humans. But what does theological reflection tell us about God and abuse?

Theological Reflection and Abuse

If God is opposed to the abuse and oppression of others, then what role do we have in theological reflection? If theological reflection is faith seeking understanding among others who seek the nature of God, then what should we do? Domestic violence ministry's greatest impact on our theology must be that it drives us to the Scriptures. It should cause us to reflect on the nature of God. Christians must address abuse not just because it is a social justice issue but because it is a theological issue. It is not only a crime against humanity, it is a sin against God. We know that it angers and grieves God because of the divine nature that is illustrated in the Scriptures.

How did my wife and I come to this conclusion? We began to work with victims of domestic violence advocates, we went to workshops, and then we began to help victims. Throughout this process, we talked with advocates and counselors and heard their opinions about churches. Apathy from churches concerning this issue drives us forward. The bad advice, or bad theology, that ministers have given women who left their husbands over abuse disturbs me. The more we learned, the more we searched the scriptures. The more we listened, the more we reflected. The more we faced apathy, the bolder we became.

The email from a victim's advocate (Figure 1, pp. xxii–xxiii) suggested that ministers had failed to address abuse. Do you remember the last few sentences? "We look for any resources . . . " Could this be faith seeking understanding? Then notice: "The faith community is slowly becoming more of a hindrance than a resource." Have these faith communities honored or dishonored God? The advocate's email moves me to return to the Scriptures. I believe that if the church wants to practice *good theology* concerning domestic violence and abuse we must dialogue with those who work in abuse.

> I have also had a few dozen clients over the years who belong to fundamentalist religious groups, usually Christian or Islamic fundamentalist or Orthodox Judaic. Abusive men from these groups tend to openly espouse a system in which women have next to no rights and a man is entitled to be the unquestioned ruler of the home. To make matters worse, these religious sects have greatly increased their political power around the globe over the past two decades . . . Women who live within these religous groups may feel especially trapped by abuse, since their reistance to domination is likely to be viewed as evil and the surrounding community may support or even revere the abuser.[27]

Abuse advocates consistently indicate a sense of distrust toward churches and ministers. My wife and I have worked hard to earn their respect and prove to them that we will protect victims of abuse. This has taken much time, energy, and discussion. We sit at the table with victims, abusers, and counselors and talk openly about what we know of God. It is the responsibility of faith communities to draw the oppressed into our sermons, classes, and discussions in order to accurately talk about the nature of

---

[27]Bancroft, 166.

God. Social justice must be part of our theological reflection. Ray Anderson has said it best.

> Christians cannot turn away from any form of inhumanity without separating themselves from the humanity of God. Most Christians would be scandalized to be told that abandoning the homeless, overlooking the deep injustice of poverty and systematically excluding the socially unacceptable is the moral and spiritual equivalent of apartheid.[28]

> Social justice is not an abstract principle, nor is it an ideal to be pursued. Social justice is the core of human experience. It is the bread and water; it is blood and bones; it is brothers and sisters who unlearn the knowledge of how to hurt and how to kill and who learn to live in power, the freedom and the hope with which God intended that we should live. If there is any basis for social justice, it lies between us, within our humanity; it is anthropological. Social justice is a divinely ordained order of human existence. Humanity is essentially cohumanity.[29]

The church must deal with social justice because the church is supposed to be the representation of God and the incarnation. In 1917 Walter Rauschenbusch addressed a group of theologians and stated, "The social gospel needs a theology to make it effective but theology needs the social gospel to vitalize it."[30] Rauschenbusch had spent years ministering to German immigrants and had been criticized for focusing on social issues rather than "theological issues."

> The dogmas and theological ideas of the early church were those ideas which at that time were needed to hold the church together, to rally its forces and to give it victorious energy against antagonistic powers. Today many of those ideas are without present significance. Our reverence for them is a kind of ancestor worship. The social gospel gets hold of our heart now—as the Nicene Creed did in the fourth century.[31]

---

[28]Ray S. Anderson, *The Shape of Practical Theology: Empowering Ministry with Theological Praxis* (Downer's Grove, Ill.: InterVarsity, 2001) 179.
[29]Ibid., 312.
[30]Walter Rauschenbusch, *A Theology for the Social Gospel* (Nashville: Abingdon, 1917) 1.
[31]Ibid., 13.

Rauschenbusch could have said today what he said then. If we looked at the table of contents of modern theology books, they would contain topics that seem irrelevant to the common reader. They are theoretical but not practical.

Domestic violence is an issue that forces us to the Scriptures and causes us to ask questions. Domestic violence workers, victims, and batterers are a great resource for theological reflection. If we want to grow in this area, we must invite the oppressed and those who work with the oppressed to the table.

> Many voices declare that the church has either caused men to be violent toward their wives or at least provided fertile soil for men's mistreatment of power within their families. They argue that since the church is part of the problem, it cannot be part of the solution. Thus when violence against women is being discussed, God's people are seldom consulted. Since we speak out so infrequently about violence, our collective voice is never heard on this issue. Generally speaking, leaders in religious organizations and those involved in community pastoral care are never even invited to participate at the secular consultation table. The silence of our churches and our leaders is often interpreted in the public square as complicity with violent acts.[32]

Those who work with abuse will ask questions and challenge us to reflect and review many of our doctrines. They will send us back to the Scriptures to reexamine much of our past traditions and theology. To dismiss divorce, dysfunctional family issues, and all forms of abuse as non traditional is theologically hiding our head in the sand.

> Theological repentance is demanded of the church when it offers flavored water to those who come expecting the new wine and stale bread to those expecting a nourishing meal . . . Spiritual repentance is demanded of the church when it is found opposing the mission of God for the sake of preserving its own institutional and traditional forms.[33]

---

[32]Kroeger and Clark, 16.
[33]Anderson, 182.

An Articulation of Faith

The result of this reflection will cause us to rearticulate our faith in a different manner. What issues become important to the Christian community? How do we view hot topics such as marriage, family, divorce, dating, and male-female relationships? How does the attitude of entitlement fit into male and female theology? Suddenly, we who are called by God have to take off our rose-colored glasses and see the plight of the oppressed. Our focus on spiritual growth, faith, mercy, and peace must be seen in a new light.

Personally, I have changed my preaching concerning marriage and divorce. Our church is becoming more effective at divorce recovery. Our view of healthy families and our family ministry are changing. The emphasis of premarital and marital counseling has changed. When we talk about husbands and wives, we talk about respect and encouragement. Our men's classes and our youth group teachings are different. People who are rude, verbally abusive, and intimidating are no longer people with *personality quirks*; they are people with *spiritual issues*. Being led by the Spirit has more to do with the way we treat people than how much Bible we know or how many church services we attend.

The Christian view of evangelism must also change. Evangelism means that the church has a prophetic voice in the community. Evangelism means that we go to the oppressed (Luke 4:16-19) rather than wait for them to come into the building. If they do come to us, we must believe that God has sent them so that they can receive help. Sometimes evangelism and a prophetic voice are a response we give when we see injustice and are provoked to action. We are known in our community by what we stand for and what we stand against. *The congregation is not a consumer in the community, it is a resource for the community*. We not only minister to our own, we minister to our neighbors and the world. Evangelism is compassion rather than an intellectual assent to Jesus. Evangelism is love rather than selfishness.

The church cannot hide from these issues. In the introduction to this book, it was suggested that this is a major problem in our country. A minister who had been a missionary in Zimbabwe for many decades once lectured that we need to get out of our offices and be in the community. During the question and answer session, I asked him how the church was responding to abuse in Zimbabwe. "We don't have a problem with abuse," he replied. The statistics concerning abuse in third-world countries is staggering, how can someone say that his area does not have a problem with abuse? Theology forces us to open our eyes, reflect, and articulate a theology for the common man. Our theology and their theology must become one. Why? Because their God and our God must be one!

5

The Nature of God and Masculinity

One of our older members shared with me that her father, Marvin, was pretty cruel to her mother, Mildred, while they were growing up. When Mildred was a single young woman she provided child care for a family. The husband and wife, Charles and Mary, had hired her to care for their children. Things seemed to work well for a while. After months of employment, Charles became attracted to Mildred and forced himself on her. She became pregnant, and to save the family honor, Charles' younger brother, Marvin, was coerced into marrying her. Marvin neglected the first born son, Randolph. Even though Randolph grew up thinking that Marvin was his father, he struggled with the pain and rejection he felt from Marvin. More children were born to this marriage, including the woman telling me the story. She shared with me that her dad was a bitter man and cruel to Mildred, yet they went to church faithfully and were involved in many church activities. Mildred died, and eventually so did Marvin. When the children were going through his possessions, they found out about the parentage of the oldest son, Randolph. He had suffered emotional scars because of the bitterness of his supposed "father" Marvin. Marvin's cruelty to Mildred also affected the family. The woman telling me the story told me that, after the funeral, the adult children found many religious books in Marvin's library. What I heard next sent chills down my spine. "Ron," she said, "in dad's books he had highlighted every passage that talked about women submitting to their husbands or that women were to be obedient." She then said, "He never highlighted the passages or commentaries about men and about being a good husband and father. How could a man be that cruel and go to church?"

Male privilege is the attitude that suggests that men have a right to demand honor, respect, and submission from women and children. Male privilege suggests that men rule and women say, "Yes, sir!" Male privilege is seen on *The Honeymooners* when Jackie Gleason would threaten to hit his wife, Alice, and send her "to the moon!" Male privilege is shown when Archie Bunker calls his wife a "dingbat" and when Edith seems to crave this type of attention. Male privilege is seen when rock musicians have scantily clad women sexually and erotically bowing. Male privilege exists when pornographic magazines, websites, media, and advertisements suggest that women should be seen as sex objects *for* men. Male privilege happens when men degrade women for money, attention, or publicity. Male privilege suggests that women need to be "good girls" in order to attract a man and that maternity gives a woman worth.[1] Male privilege does not always originate with men; women can also encourage it. Women who turn their heads from incidents of male privilege, or allow their sons to abuse are pushing the male privilege agenda. *The Best Little Whore House in Texas* showed women who encouraged other women to be treated as sex objects and who justified male privilege as a "service" to men.

A movie that illustrates this battle among women is *The Color Purple*. In the movie, the mother, played by Whoopie Goldberg, encouraged her son to beat his "strong-willed wife," played by Oprah Winfrey. Goldberg's character was an abused wife, and she felt that this was good advice for her son. Later, an angry Winfrey came to confront the mother-in-law and indicated that she had given wrong advice to her son (both Winfrey and her movie husband had black eyes). This was an excellent illustration of

---

[1]Mary John Mananzan, "Feminine Socialization: Women as Victims and Collaborators," *Violence Against Women*, ed. Elisabeth Schüssler Fiorenza and M. Shawn Copeland (Maryknoll, N.Y.: Orbis, 1994) 47–49.

how women have become a part of the male privilege problem in America.[2] Winfrey, the strong woman, would not allow herself to be disrespected. Goldberg's character, through time, became an equally strong woman and left her abusive husband, played by Danny Glover. The movie communicates a message that Jackson Katz has stated often: "Strong men are attracted to strong women, weak men are intimidated by strong women."[3]

God, however, does not practice male privilege. God practices creator privilege. God practices compassion, leadership, mercy, forgiveness, and justice. *Yahweh* has created us male and female, and both are in the image of God (Gen 1:27). Only God has the right to ask for submission. The book of Job shows us a wonderful account of a man who wished to question God. *Yahweh*'s response is found in Job 38–41. God asked Job if he was able to do all the things that the Creator must do in the universe. When looking at the awesome responsibilities of a creator Job replied, "My ears had heard of you but now my eyes have seen you. Therefore I despise myself and repent in dust and ashes" (Job 42:6). Humans submit and humble themselves to God because we realize that only God can handle the tasks ahead. God, however, did not force submission.

For centuries humans have thought that they are the masters of their own destinies; yet when we fail, we turn to God. Submission is a willingness to let God lead our lives. This is why I have chosen to submit to God. I tried being my own master and realized my inabilities and failures in doing so. In my belief system, I found that Satan was controlling and coercive and after serving in that kingdom I chose to leave. It was a tough transition, but it was driven by my desire to let God lead and change my life. I decided to make Jesus Lord of my life. God has not forced me into submission. I gave the reins to God because the Creator can deal with problems that I cannot handle. I always have the option to stay or leave just as others have the choice to follow whomever they wish. All of us have the chance to submit to God or Satan.

---

[2]Even though the movie took place in the early part of twentieth-century America, the message is still relevant today. This was the first movie about abuse that I had ever watched, and the characters' roles are played out even today.

[3]Jackson Katz, "More Than a Few Good Men: American Manhood and Violence Against Women," keynote address given at the Justice and Hope Domestic Violence Conference, March 21, 2003, Kelso, Washington.

As the Creator, God is willing to lead those who wish to submit and fight the battle between good and evil. Creator privilege is not based on fear or control; it is based on respect, love, and a willingness to yield. God calls for willing submission and obedience rather than forced respect. While this seems manipulative to some, we must remember that God always initiates covenant, promises to be faithful, and carries the burden of the relationship.

> God's disclosure of himself is not grasped speculatively, not expounded in the form of a lesson; it is as [if] he breaks in on the life of his people in his dealings with them and moulds them according to his will that he grants them knowledge of his being.[4]

God's love was conditional, expecting faithfulness and loyalty by the people, but it was unconditional since God was always willing to restore the sinful nation to a relationship.[5]

> The use of the covenant concept in secular life argues that the religious *berit* too was always regarded as a bilateral relationship; for even though the burden is most unequally distributed between the two contracting parties, this makes no difference to the fact that the relationship is still essentially two sided.[6]

In the ancient world covenants between those of higher status and those of lower status were necessary to provide aid to the poor, needy, and afflicted. Kings would initiate covenants with other cities, peoples, or cultures to provide for their needs.[7] In the Roman Empire this was also called a "patron/client" relationship. Texts have been written that describe

---

[4]Eichrodt, 37.

[5]Ibid., 37. Weems discusses the unfaithful wife metaphor in the prophets as a relationship between God and Israel that was marked by mutual obligations and mutual responsibilities. Weems, 17.

[6]Eichrodt, 37. *Berit* is the Hebrew word for covenant.

[7]T. R. Hobbs, "Reflections on Honor, Shame, and Covenant Relations," *Journal of Biblical Literature* 116 (1997) 501–3; Saul M. Olyan, "Honor, Shame, and Covenant Relations in Ancient Israel and Its Environment," *Journal of Biblical Literature* 115 (1996) 201–18.

the roles of the initiator, or patron.[8] The responsibilities of the patron were to carry the burden of the relationship and provide for the clients. Benefactors were those who were wealthy enough to financially support clients and give liberally so that cities, communities, and farms could continue to exist.

> The world of the author and readers of the New Testament, however, was one in which personal patronage was an essential means of acquiring access to goods, protection or opportunities for employment and advancement. Not only was it essential—it was expected and publicized! The giving and receiving of favors was, according to a first-century participant, the "practice that constitutes the chief bond of human society."[9]

In Luke 7:5, a Roman centurion made it possible for a Jewish synagogue to continue because he financially supported the group. When Israel made a covenant with the Gibeonites (Joshua 9–10), Israel had a responsibility to protect them from invading armies. When Rome made peace with other cities, it was Rome's job to provide them with military support. When *Yahweh* made a covenant with Abraham, the responsibility to bless, provide, protect, and lead the family rested on God's shoulders (Gen 12:1-3).

What were the responsibilities of the clients or receptors of the covenant? Their tasks were to listen, to obey, and to support the other party. If called to help in war, they sent soldiers. If financial support was needed, they sent money. If given a law from *Yahweh*, they were expected to obey.

> For when I brought your fathers out of Egypt I did not just give them commands about burnt offerings and sacrifices, but I gave them this command: I said, "Obey me, and I will be your God and you will be my

---

[8]"He who gives benefits imitates the gods, he who seeks a return, money-lenders" (Seneca, *Ben.* 3.15.4). For more written information on this see *Ben.* 4.26.1; 4.28.1; and Sirach 12:1.

[9]Seneca, *Ben.* 1.4.2, quoted in deSilva, 96; Malina, 93–97; and Halvor Moxnes, "Patron-Client Relations and the New Community in Luke-Acts," *The Social World of Luke-Acts*, ed. Jerome H. Neyrey (Peabody: Hendrickson, 1991) 241–68.

people. Walk in all the ways I command you, so that it may go well with you." (Jer 7:22-23)

The responsibilities of the weaker client party were to support, respect, and submit. While this seems offensive to most Americans, it is a part of life in other countries. The strong are expected to help the weak. In our country we do practice this, although we call it a donation or tax write-off. Wealthy businesses support sports teams, community projects, and environmental issues. Employers give raises, insurance, or vacations to employees. Schools give retirements to teachers and offer sports programs that do not always benefit the school financially but provide recreation for students. When employees face financial difficulties, we call upon the business to carry the financial burden for their "clients." Why? Deep down we believe that those who have should provide for those who need help. Yet we as clients also see our responsibility to support these institutions and provide them with a sense of loyalty and security.

This is an example of covenant. Both parties work together to bless or mutually benefit each other. Can this covenant or patron/client relationship be misused? Yes. Both sides can misuse the relationship. We see this when the employee treats his job and company only as a "stepping stone," or when the company fires the long-time employee because she is a "liability." We see this when the company leaders embezzle money, and the employees lose their retirement benefits. We see this when the company closes because of employee theft. We see this often, and yet forget that the relationship is not the problem, nor is the patron the one we should fear. The relationship between greater and lesser is not always wrong. It is the *misuse* of that relationship that is wrong. An evil heart can damage many people. When the patron provides for us, we support, serve, respect, and sometimes submit. We have no problem entering a contract with those who help us and wish to act in our best interest.

This is what I mean by Creator privilege. We submit to God not because we are forced to do so but because we yield to the Creator's ability to handle our lives. Submission is never forced; otherwise, there would be no atheists around today.[10] Male privilege *expects* and *demands* submission.

---

[10]I do not say this to attack atheists. My father was an atheist, and I have a lot of respect for him as well as atheists with whom I have had debates and discussions in Portland. If

Creator privilege *earns* respect and willing submission. Male privilege uses *manipulation and coercion* to gain power over a wife or female partner. Creator privilege *seeks to persuade and empower* humans to work with God to fight evil. Creator privilege also carries greater responsibility to empower and provide for others.

Marriage is about shared power within a covenant relationship. One spouse may be given *leadership, but this means that they carry the greater responsibility for the health of the relationship*. Just as the family breadwinner willingly works and provides financially for the family, so the Creator handles the battle with Satan and the demons. Just as the parent selflessly gives money to the family, God provides for the children. Just as a stay-at-home spouse understands and respects the partner's time at work, so God's children submit and respect God.

My counseling is very limited, but I rarely meet a woman who is not willing to support her husband emotionally as provider for the family, even if it means staying home with the children. I also find more husbands willing to stay home with the children if they know that their wives are able to provide a better income for the family. I see that husbands and wives can work together in a covenant relationship where one carries the financial burden and the other supports and respects the spouse for that sacrifice. Yet I feel it is equally important for the working spouse to validate the spouse who takes responsibility for child care and house maintenance. In a healthy marriage, both spouses work together to provide for the financial and emotional needs of the family. I find that many women "submit" to their husbands because they choose to, not because they are forced. I also find that many husbands equally respect and "submit" to their wives in decisions and issues within the family. This type of relationship practices shared power and mutual respect. It means acting as a team.

God truly forced submission then what would happen to those who did not submit? Would they still be alive today? The existence of unbelievers and atheists suggests to me that God allows people to exercise free choice. The existence of those who do evil also suggests that God allows free will.

God the Father/Husband

I have attempted to be sensitive to the use of gender language in my description of God throughout this book. Jesus' statement, "God is Spirit," suggests to me that God is neither male nor female (John 4:24). Both male and female are created in God's image (Gen 1:27-28). Yet Israel, like their neighbors, continually tried to worship male and female gods (Jer 44:19). The Assyrian goddess Asherah seemed to be placed next to *Yahweh* (2 Kgs 23:13; Ezek 8:5) in their places of worship and cities. The ancient world needed to distinguish male and female natures in their theology, but *Yahweh* claimed to be warrior, father, mother, and gentle healer (Isa 66:13).[11] *Yahweh* was neither male nor female, but both genders can reflect God's nature.

Jesus, according to Greco-Roman culture, also exhibited "feminine" characteristics in his ministry.

> For Jesus to present himself without a house, in a no-place, was therefore to be deprived of a role either as a householder, which given his age would have been his normal position, or as a son in a household. Thus, his masculinity was threatened. He did not behave as a "real man." He was "out of place." And when we looked at Jesus' call sayings and sayings about leaving the house or about conflicts in the household, most of them were explicitly or implicitly addressed to men.[12]

The emphasis on mercy, compassion, and peace; the presence of women and children in his ministry; and the choice to be single would have all been suspect to male honor in the ancient world. The solution is not to call God "she" or to overemphasize the male references to God and the Spirit. We should understand that God is spirit and that men and women reflect God's nature. But male references about God, Jesus, and the Spirit have a much greater message to men than women.

First, the revelation of God is meant to *teach men something about the divine nature*. When God is revealed it suggests that something new was

---

[11] *Yahweh* also claims to "beget" or give birth to the children of Israel.

[12] Halvor Moxnes, *Putting Jesus in His Place: A Radical Vision of Household and Kingdom* (Louisville: Westminster John Knox, 2003) 96.

being taught. Second, the revelation of God as male *suggests to men something different*. What was the new message that God as male revealed? God is showing men how they should behave. While God is Spirit, it seems that men have proven to be a big problem in the history of God's world. The sins of adultery; idolatry; drunkenness; violence; social injustice; oppression of widows, orphans, and aliens; and poor leadership were problems for Israel. While we have stories of sinful females in the Scriptures, the majority of stories involve men disobeying God and being violent to others. God was trying to teach men how to submit and how to act in their community. This is why there was such an emphasis on the mercy, compassion, peace, forgiveness, and love of God. God was identifying the "new world man." What was being said was, "Men, this is how you should act!" In fact, it seems to have been the women and children who understood submission, loyalty, and faithfulness better than the men.

God's Revelation in a Dysfunctional Culture

This is best seen by some of the texts that illustrate the culture where Jesus was revealed. There are a couple of texts found in the New Testament that may illustrate this point. First, men had failed to be effective leaders at the time of Christ. The prophecy of Malachi that predicts the coming of the *Yahweh* and the preaching of Elijah is found in Malachi 4:5-6.

> I will send you the prophet Elijah before that great and dreadful day of *Yahweh* comes. He will turn the *hearts of the fathers to their children, and the hearts of the children to their fathers*; or else I will come and strike the land with a curse.

This quote is from the Hebrew text of Malachi. The Jews had returned from Babylon/Persian captivity in 538/535 BC and were neglecting the temple. By the time Malachi preached to Judah the nation was heading back to the sins of their past. They were neglecting God by giving cheap sacrifices (1:8, 12), dishonoring *Yahweh* (1:6), and practicing injustice (2:9, 17; 3:5, 15). God warned them at the end of Malachi to repent or else "I will come down for judgment" (4:1-6). The way to prepare for judgment and mercy was to call families together. The text called them to remember the Law of Moses (4:4). Before God came to judge the earth, families needed to be restored.

This text is different in two other places where it is quoted. First, the Greek text of Malachi, written possibly around 200 BC, reads:

> He will turn the *hearts of the fathers to their children,*
> *and a man to his neighbor.*

When the text is quoted again in Luke 1:17 concerning John the Baptist, the text reads:

> He will turn the *hearts of the fathers to their children and the disobedient to*
> *the wisdom of the righteous* to make ready a people prepared for the Lord.

Why the differences? The phrases hearts for the children to their fathers, a man to his neighbor, and the disobedient to the wisdom of the righteous all suggest that the community is being affected by the fathers. All three have the phrase *hearts of the fathers to their children* in common. Is it possible that the fathers were still a problem? Is it possible that the fathers were still the cause of the sins of the community? Or, is it possible that there was a need for good fathers in faith community?[13]

By the time Jesus came to earth, the family and society of Palestine were undergoing tremendous change. The Jews were scattered throughout the Roman Empire. The development of a unified world culture (which Alexander the Great called the *oikomene*) and the increase in divorce and blended families had an impact on how individuals saw themselves in the world. People in the Greco-Roman culture began to desire salvation, monotheism, associations and clubs, and a sense of connectedness to their world, spirituality, and each other.[14] They longed for family connections,

---

[13]While many commentators do not discuss in detail the differences between the Septuagint and Hebrew texts of Malachi, Fitzmyer suggests that Luke places an emphasis on the fathers. "The conversion is to remedy a paternal neglect of the young in Israel; Luke is hinting, in adopting this phrase, at the neglect shown by Israel of old toward those who are to become Abraham's children," in Joseph A. Fitzmyer, *The Gospel According to Luke I–IX*, Anchor Bible 28 (New York: Doubleday, 1981) 320.

[14]"The unsettling conditions of the time led people to long and search for *soteria*, salvation, a release from the burdens of finitude, the misery and failure of human life . . . The

which were provided by the clubs, synagogues, and congregations.[15] Christianity's emphasis on family terms such as home, called out (the term for church [*ekklesia*]), chosen, brothers and sisters, father, fellowship, and children were a response to experiences sought by people of the time. Paul's use of the verb for reconciliation (*apokatallasso*) and his introduction of a compound form of this verb suggest that Paul made a popular Greek word become a common term in Christianity.[16] Reconciliation became a popular term in Christianity even though it was seldom used in pagan Greco-Roman culture. The world that received the incarnation longed to have the hearts of the fathers turned to the children and each other. The Hebrew concept of covenant and God's faithfulness was illustrated by the word reconciliation. This reconciliation and the family were important truths that God and Christianity supplied to a lonely world in the first century.

Jesus' use of Father and Son terminology suggested that he was modeling a relationship needed in the ancient world. His use of the Aramaic word *abba* with Father also suggests that he was revealing a relationship that people desired from their God. While the Old Testament used the family as a way to see God, the New Testament used the family to illustrate a loving God in a dysfunctional family society.[17] Rather than view God through the family, the early church sought to redefine the family through God and Jesus.

> Here are my mother and my brothers! Whoever does the will of God is
> my brother and sister and mother. (Mark 3:34-35)

Hellenistic-Roman age was a religious age, with a tendency toward monotheism and a common longing for salvation," in Antonia Tripolitis, *Religions of the Hellenistic Roman Age* (Grand Rapids: Eerdmans, 2002) 2, 6.

[15]Joseph H. Hellerman, *The Ancient Church as Family* (Minneapolis: Fortress, 2001) 3–4. Harland suggests that the types of associations most common were groups by 1) household, 2) ethnicity, 3) neighborhoods, 4) occupation, and 5) cult or temple connections. Philip A. Harland, *Associations, Synagogues, and Congregations: Claiming a Place in Ancient Mediterranean Society* (Minneapolis: Fortress, 2003) 29.

[16]Stanley E. Porter, *Katallasso in Ancient Greek Literature: With Reference to the Pauline Writings*, Estudios de Filología Neotestamentaria 5 (Cordoba: El Almendro, 1994) 16.

[17]Leo G. Perdue, *Families in Ancient Israel* (Louisville: Westminster John Knox, 1993) 135.

Husbands, love your wives just as Christ loved the church. (Eph 5:25)

As apostles of Christ we could have been a burden to you, but we were gentle among you, like a nurse caring for her little children . . . For you know that we dealt with each of you as a father deals with his own children, encouraging, comforting, and urging you to live lives worthy of God, who calls you into his kingdom and glory. (1 Thess 2:6-7, 11-12)

God and the ministry of the church were the models for the family. In a dysfunctional family system, the place to begin was God. Therefore, the church called people out of their dysfunctional families into a new family. The church also called fathers and husbands to a new model of family and marriage.

The Dysfunctional Family World in the First Century

Recent studies on the Roman family have provided valuable information concerning the roles of fathers in the development and leadership of the home.[18] Fathers had complete power over their children, and this has led interpreters to view the family head, *paterfamilias,* as harsh and cruel.[19]

---

[18]Suzanne Dixon, "The Sentimental Ideal of the Roman Family," in *Marriage, Divorce, and Children in Ancient Rome*, ed. Beryl Rawson (Oxford: Clarendon, 1991) 99–113; Emiel Eyben, "Fathers and Sons," in *Marriage, Divorce, and Children in Ancient Rome*, ed. Beryl Rawson (Oxford: Clarendon, 1991) 114–43; James S. Jeffers, "Jewish and Christian Families in First-Century Rome," in *Judaism and Christianity in First-Century Rome*, ed. Karl P. Donfried and Peter Richardson (Grand Rapids: Eerdmans, 1998) 128–50; W. K. Lacey, "Patria Potestas," in *Family in Ancient Rome*, ed. Beryl Rawson (Ithaca, N.Y.: Cornell University Press, 1986) 121–44; Eva Marie Lassen, "The Roman Family: Ideal and Metaphor," in *Constructing Early Christian Families: Family as Social Reality and Metaphor*, ed. Halvor Moxnes (London: Routledge, 1997) 103–20; Moxnes, "What is Family: Problems in Constructing Early Christian Families," in *Constructing Early Christian Families: Family as Social Reality and Metaphor*, ed. Halvor Moxnes (London: Routledge, 1997) 13–41; Thomas Wiedemann, *Adults and Children in the Roman Empire* (New Haven: Yale University Press, 1989); and O. Larry Yarbrough, "Parents and Children in the Jewish Family of Antiquity," in *The Jewish Family in Antiquity*, ed. Shaye J. D. Cohen (Atlanta: Scholars, 1993).

[19]Seneca *De Providentia* 2:5 says that fathers showed love by ordering the sons to work and toil and that through sweat and tears they began the pursuits of the day. Eyben also indicates that the father's right to expose infants, scourge, sell, pawn, and imprison or

The view of the Roman father as cruel and abusive has been drawn from texts that speak out against the abuse of children, but the texts do not necessarily indicate that most parents practiced this behavior.[20]

There are hardly any people who wield as much power over their sons as we do. (Gaius, *Institutes* 557)

The rule of a father over his children is royal, for he receives both love and the respect due to age, exercising a kind of royal power. (Aristotle, *Politics,* 1.12)

There seems to be more evidence that fathers were not as cruel at the time of Paul as had been previously assumed.[21] Children were needed to pass on one's legacy; thus, they were not as mistreated and abused as were the slaves.[22] There was, however, an attitude of indifference rather than harshness toward children.

On the whole, the young child seems to have been of minor interest to the Roman literary classes. Childhood is occasionally invoked in a detached and general way by adult authors as a symbol of the uneducated or innocent human, but literary references to children and childhood are relatively few and often vague, revealing little interest in the activities of young children for their own sake

It could be the oddities of survival that leave the modern reader with the impression that Roman parents and Roman society were more

---

kill his son at any time has led to the belief that fathers were cruel and harsh. Yet many fathers did not practice these rights. Eyben, 115.

[20]Wiedeman points out that the stories of royal childhood abuse were not common. The monstrous stories were written because they were abnormal (Weidman, 40–83). Bartchy claims that believing that abuse was common is due to a narrow reading of Roman literature. There was strong condemnation of abusing or over-disciplining children. S. Scott Bartchy, "Families in the Greco-Roman World," in *The Family Handbook*, ed. Herbert Anderson et al. (Louisville: Westminster John Knox, 1998) 284.

[21]Eyben also mentions that strict love from the *paterfamilias* was driven by a desire to have children respect and honor them as well as other authority figures. Later in Roman history, parenting became more compassionate. Eyben, 116,19.

[22]Richard Saller, "Corporal Punishment, Authority, and Obedience in the Roman Household," in *Marriage, Divorce, and Children in Ancient Rome*, ed. Beryl Rawson (Oxford: Clarendon, 1991) 161–62.

concerned with the moral and practical training of children than in their cognitive, physical, and emotional development, but the surviving literature does support the conclusion that educators and medical writers were not as interested in the young child as their modern equivalents are.[23]

Children were treated better than slaves, but the high infant mortality rate and indifference toward small children indicates that children were not treated as well as they are in modern times.[24]

This indifference toward children may have contributed to a view that children were unimportant in the father's pursuits of the state. Suzanne Dixon claims that the purpose of the family was for progeneration, economic and emotional support, inheritance, and socialization.[25] Children were considered part of the irrational, vulnerable, and helpless segments of society.[26]

> For the slave has no deliberative faculty at all; the woman has, but it is without authority, **and the child has, but it is immature.** (Aristotle, *Politics,* 1.13)

Burial customs confirm that children and adolescents did not have a full place in the community.[27] It is possible that the high infant mortality rate caused parents to maintain an emotional distance from their children. This would explain the delegation of their care to professional caregivers, which seemed common in the Greco-Roman world. *Pedagogues* were slaves hired to instruct children of upper-class families. They were slaves who were chosen to train, develop, and instruct children for their fathers. These *pedagogues* tended to be harsh. Much of the development of children was left to babysitters, nurses, pedagogues, and other slaves. Evidence from

---

[23]Dixon, *The Roman Family* (Baltimore: Johns Hopkins University Press, 1992) 100, 116.

[24]Ibid., 116, 118, 130.

[25]Ibid., 24–27.

[26]The child occurs in association with animals, women, and tyrants—all four symbolize behavior opposite to that of the adult male citizen. Weideman, 8.; Moxnes, *Putting Jesus in His Place,* 92–93; and James L. Resseguie, *Spiritual Landscape: Images of the Spiritual Life in the Gospel of Luke* (Peabody, Mass.: Hendrickson, 2004) 54.

[27]Dixon, *Roman Family,* 179.

inscriptions indicates that a strong bond, lasting into adulthood, existed between these slaves and the children.[28] It seems that in upper-class families, fathers played more of a delegating role and entrusted the major tasks of child development to slaves, schools, and sometimes their wives.[29] While some fathers were concerned about the development of their children, the majority of the work was done by others.[30]

In some homes women became supervisors of their households and put up with their husbands' affairs.[31] The wife was to be submissive and accept her husband's gods and lifestyle. She was not to bring shame upon the home by dishonoring her husband. In Roman culture divorce had become a common practice.[32] This may have been due to arranged marriages, emerging trends of impermanence of the marriage bond, the dissolution of upper-class families, and the view that marriage and procreation were Roman duty rather than choice.[33] Divorce had become easier by the first century; marriage could be dissolved by the statement "take your things and go," a note of divorce, or the announcement of a divorce by a messenger.[34] Susan Treggiari also mentions that infertility in a couple was just cause for a divorce.[35]

Children were expected to uphold the father's honor by submitting, showing respect, and maintaining public honor.[36] Fathers may have been

---

[28]See Keith R. Bradley's chapter, "Child Care at Rome: The Role of Men," in *Discovering the Roman Family* (New York: Oxford University Press, 1991) 37–75.

[29]"It was clearly usual for elite children to grow up surrounded by a variety of such caregivers, especially in early childhood." Dixon, 119.

[30]Ibid., 116–17, 131.

[31] Jeffers, 141; and David C. Verner, *The Household of God: The Social World of the Pastoral Epistles*, SBL Dissertation Series 71 (Chico, Calif.: Scholars, 1983) 31, 68–70.

[32]Bradley, "Remarriage and the Structure of the Upper-Class Roman Family," in *Marriage, Divorce, and Children in Ancient Rome*, ed. Beryl Rawson (Oxford: Clarendon, 1991), 85.

[33]Ibid., 96–97.

[34]Susan Treggiari, "Divorce Roman Style: How Easy and How Frequent Was It?" in *Marriage, Divorce, and Children in Ancient Rome*, ed. Beryl Rawson (Oxford: Clarendon, 1991) 35.

[35]Ibid., 38; Yarbrough, 41,43; and *m. Yeb.* 6:6.

[36]"The male householder, then, functioned both as the representative of his *domus/oikos* . . . and as the agent of his household's subordination to the loftier goals of the city." Bartchy also writes that the honor of the *paterfamilias* was dependent upon his ability to protect his *domus* (Bartchy, 16). Submission and respect in the *domus/oikos* was necessary for the father to maintain honor and prove to be effective in ruling in the city/*polis*. Moxnes, 28.

strict, but they were preparing their children to carry the honor of the family as well as that of the state. The family was culturally and socio-economically driven. The *paterfamilias* was concerned with politics in both his home and the city. [37]

Palestinian homes were more vocationally structured.[38] The family needed to work together to exist as a self-supporting unit. This caused fathers to be involved in apprenticing and teaching (Sir 30:3; 4 Macc 18:6-19; Jdt 8:2; 16:6; 19:4; Prov 13:24). Mothers were also involved in educating their children. As time passed, though, the Palestinian homes were influenced by Greco-Roman culture.

Jewish marriages and families were affected by divorce.[39] Jesus' warning about divorce (Matt 5:31-32; 19:3-9) indicates that the religious leaders were allowing this common practice to affect the Jewish community. The *Mishnah* (a collection of the Jewish Rabbi's traditions from 200 BC–200 AD) and its interpretation of legal divorce were heavily affected by the changes in Greco-Roman culture.[40] It began to influence the Jewish family in the first century. In the Jewish culture highly influenced by Greek culture, a father was not to play or laugh with children.

> Pamper a child and he will terrorize you, play with him and he will grieve you. Do not laugh with him or you will have sorrow with him, and in the end you will gnash your teeth. Give him no freedom in his youth and do not ignore his errors. Bow down his neck in his youth and beat his sides while he is young or else he will become stubborn and disobey you, and you will have sorrow of soul from him. Discipline your son and make his yoke heavy so that you may not be offended by his shamelessness. (Sirach 30:7-13)

Hellenistic Jewish homes were influenced by the delegation, indifference, and controlling methods of the *paterfamilias*. Jesus' use of

---

[37]Ibid., 20.

[38]Ibid., 36.

[39] Santiago Guijarro, "The Family in First-Century Galilee," in *Constructing Early Christian Families: Family as Social Reality and Metaphor*, ed. Halvor Moxnes (London: Routledge, 1997) 46.

[40]It is interesting to note that Gittin allows divorce by messenger, dismissal, and a note thrown or given to the spouse, usually the woman.

manager/steward in parables indicates that many Jewish homes were *Hellenized.* The *manager/steward* was the slave in charge of accounts (Matt 13:27; Luke 16:1-3; 12:42). He, rather than the father, became the manager of the house affairs.

Christian marriage and parenting, however, involved compassion (Luke 11:1-12) and gentleness (Col 3:21). Husbands were to love and initiate faithfulness to their wives (Eph 5:33-47). Fathers, rather than the *pedagogues*, were to discipline and instruct their own children. Fathers were also challenged to train their children by nurturing them in the instruction and warning of the Lord as part of the Christian household rather than delegating it to child minders and wet nurses (Eph 6:4). Paul called fathers to be involved in disciplining, instructing, and nurturing their children (1 Thess 2:10-12). *One way that Christianity brought a sense of stability, love, and compassion to the family was through male spiritual leadership.*

Male Privilege or Male Modeling?

The Biblical texts do not give men permission to command, expect, or force respect and submission from females and children in the community. The use of masculine terminology for God and comparisons of fathers and husbands with Jesus suggest male *role-modeling*. In a world of family dysfunction, families were not the models for God. God/Jesus was the model for families. The Biblical texts suggest that men model their lives after God/Jesus rather than see themselves as a god. How does God model male leadership?

God Maintains Relationship

First, *God is a God who maintains relationships.* I find that in domestic violence, the victim, usually the woman, is blamed for causing the marriage to fail. We generally attack the victim because we feel the burden falls on her. This is a misunderstanding of covenant. The burden falls on the husband. One passage that illustrates this is Eph 5:21-33, which is built around this fundamental principle: "Submit to one another out of fear/

136

respect for Christ" (5:21). Christian marriage is shared power. Both partners respect and submit to one another because they have a deep love for each other. Paul wrote this verse before he gave instructions to the wife and the husband. Before reading the rest of the text, men must acknowledge that a marriage is mutual submission and each must work with their spouse for the health and development of their relationship and family.

> Wives, submit to your husbands as to the Lord. For the husband is the head of the wife as Christ is the head of the church, his body, of which he is the Savior. Now as the church submits to Christ, so also wives should submit to their husbands in everything. (Eph 5:22-24)

This was not written for husbands; therefore, it should not be quoted by husbands toward their wives. It is likely that this is a short section because women in the first century were probably already submitting to their husbands. However, in light of evidence concerning Roman women, the plea only suggests that the wives continue to respect their husbands.[41]

Submission was a military term that meant to step down and let someone else lead. It says nothing about status; it is only his or her willingness to let someone lead and support them. The church can only submit to Jesus because Jesus has earned the right to be respected and loved. Women should expect their husbands to be model men for their families. This does not teach that women are doormats; it teaches that women can submit to a man who is godly and who submits to her (5:21).

Additionally, the Spirit (1 Cor 14:32) is submissive to the prophets. God's Spirit can be controlled and silenced by human beings. Does this indicate that the Spirit or God is less than human beings? Submission says nothing about status; it is only an act of giving, support, and encouragement. Women and men submit to each other (Eph 5:21) in the ways God has shown them through love, peace, compassion, and joy.

---

[41]For more information on the New Roman Wives, their rebellion in the Roman culture, and Paul's encouragement for the female Christian community see Bruce Winter, *Roman Wives, Roman Widows: The Appearance of New Women and the Pauline Communities* (Grand Rapids: Eerdmans, 2003) 17–30.

Husbands love your wives as Christ loved the church and gave himself up for her to make her holy, cleansing her by the washing with water through the word, and to present her to himself as a radiant church, without stain or wrinkle or any other blemish but holy and blameless. In this same way, husbands ought to love their wives as their own bodies. He who loves his wife loves himself. After all, no one ever hated his own body, but he feeds and cares for it, just as Christ does the church—for we are members of his body. For this reason a man will leave his father and mother and be united to his wife, and the two will become one flesh. This is a profound mystery—but I am talking about Christ and the church. However, each one of you also must love his wife as he loves himself, and the wife must respect her husband. (5:25-33)

This longer section was written to husbands. Why so long? Is it possible that these men needed to change? Notice the model that Paul used. Jesus is the model of compassion, love, concern, care, and gentleness. When I describe a husband in these terms, in counseling, I never have a female state that they would not respect a man like this. Many times women state that their husband thinks he's God. What "god" are they referring to? What would happen if their husband acted like the real God?

In domestic violence the problem is that husbands do not act like Jesus or God. A man, who hits, humiliates, rapes, or verbally abuses his wife is acting contrary to the God who created him. When talking with men, we go through this passage of scripture and talk about their behavior compared to Jesus. In the early church, God/Jesus was the model for husbands and fathers. It should be the same today. Husbands should initiate love and practice compassion toward their wives. Since God initiates covenant and seeks to bless those in covenant, husbands must reflect this nature in their covenants, marriages, and relationships. The church needs to call these men to repentance and accountability. We have both the right and responsibility, but do we have the courage? God does not maintain a relationship through force, coercion, or control but by love, persuasion, and forgiveness. Men must practice love, compassion, honor, and mercy in their relationships with others, including women.

Maintaining a relationship means that men and husbands should act righteously. To oppress the poor and weak is a sign of unrighteousness. To defend and support the "weaker" one is a reflection of God's nature. A relationship with our wives should lift them up and bless them. If they feel worse by being in a relationship with us, it is our issue rather than theirs. Marriage should help both partners become better and feel better about themselves.

> If mutuality is one of the aims of love between adults, then people need to ask themselves how their own acts of self-sacrificing love either further mutuality or reinforce roles and structures of domination and subordination.[42]

God Displays Mercy and Compassion

Second, *God is a God who expects leaders to practice mercy and compassion.* There has been much discussion about male headship, but it comes from a lack of understanding concerning leadership. For the husband to be the head means that he provides leadership. What style of leadership? The husband must lead as God leads. In the Ephesian text, quoted above, two issues of leadership are discussed.

The man leaves his parents in order to cleave to his wife (Gen. 2; Eph. 5:32-33). This cleaving is a covenant. His parents led him in covenant; now it is time for him to do the same with another woman.[43] As one who cleaves, he has responsibilities to her as a husband. He is to provide her with support, mercy, love, and compassion. He is to help her develop so that she might be blameless before God. If her emotional, sexual, spiritual, or other needs are not being met, he should be listening to her to help her. With him in her life, she is to grow closer to God, not farther away.

> Karen had been referred to me by a church. Her husband was in a local seminary, and she had left because she claimed that he had been verbally and at times physically abusive to her. As she told me the story, she would, at times, question herself. The seminary seemed to support Thomas and communicated to Karen that she was wrong for leaving him.

---

[42]Gill-Austern, 317–18.
[43]Notice that how his parents love him influences how he loves his wife.

"Maybe it is me. Maybe it is not as bad as I think," she said.

"Do you think the marriage is bad?" I asked.

"Yes, I guess so," she said. "But Thomas doesn't think it is that bad."

"What does Thomas say?" I asked.

"He thinks that I am causing the problems in the marriage. He says it is me. We have tried counseling but I seem to blow up and get mad. Then the counselor takes his side," She blurted out.

"Does the counselor take his side or is that what Thomas tells you?" I questioned.

"Maybe a little of both," she sighed.

"Karen, I have a question for you. You have been separated from Thomas for three months. Do you feel better about yourself?"

"Yes," she immediately said.

"If you went back to him, how would you feel then?" I said.

"I would feel bad about who I am and would feel depressed," she responded.

"And does your relationship with Jesus make you feel better about who you are?"

"Yes, if I left Jesus I would feel worse," she said.

"That's interesting, Karen. If marriage is a reflection of Jesus' covenant with the church then why do you feel better being away from Thomas? Shouldn't it be the other way around?" I asked.

"I see your point," Karen said as she nodded her head.

A healthy relationship should make us feel better about who we are.

Many spiritual women come to church alone or with their children because their husbands fail to lead as God expects. If these men are "heads of the family," then what type of "head" are they? If these men are "leaders," then what type of "leaders" are they? Leadership carries responsibility. Doesn't God call the church to go to them and challenge them? In Ezek 34:1-20, God sent the prophet to call the leaders of the community to repentance. They were lazy, selfish, and abusive to the flock. When leaders ignore their responsibilities, God calls them to repentance through the prophets of God. If husbands ignore the needs of those they love then those in the kingdom should challenge them. Instead, we confront the victim!

Two other passages also discuss leadership and husbands. In 1 Pet 3:7, Peter wrote to the Jewish Christians scattered in the Roman Empire:

> Husbands, in the same way be *considerate* as you live with your wives, and treat them with respect as the *weaker partner* as heirs with you of the gracious gift of life, *so that nothing will hinder your prayers.*

Peter told the husbands to be *considerate* or gentle with their wives. This has to do with the covenant issues discussed earlier. The husband is the initiator/patron and the wife is the recipient/client in this covenant. When Peter calls her *the weaker partner* he is not criticizing women; rather, he is making a statement to men. Just as God has a responsibility to humans, so the husband has a responsibility to his wife.

In the ancient world women had few rights and were dependent upon men. While this may seem degrading to modern women, Peter is challenging the men to be responsible and loving rather than harsh. He wants men to provide love and compassion in the relationship. Since men in the ancient world were the breadwinners, warriors, and public members of the family, they needed to shoulder the responsibility of strengthening the marriage (unlike what was happening in the world). To fail to do this would mean that he was not considerate to his wife. To be inconsiderate, or selfish, would hinder their prayers. Just as God ignores the pleas of those who oppress the poor, so *God will ignore the prayers of a husband who emotionally, physically, and spiritually starves or abuses his wife.*

> If a man shuts his ears to the cry of the poor
> he too will cry out and not be answered. (Prov 21:13)

> Husbands love your wives and do not be harsh with them. (Col 3:19)

Husbands must realize that the way they treat their wives, children, and others around them has a direct effect on how God will treat them (Eph 6:9; Col 4:1). Physically, verbally, and emotionally abusive men are in direct violation of what God has called them to be. While they may claim that they have not committed adultery, they are still in violation of their wedding covenant and need to be held accountable.[44] Theologically, a man who abuses his wife is in danger of being, or has already been, cut off from God. God does not answer the prayers of oppressors and abusers. God does not model this type of relationship.

Male Privilege and Christian Theology

Male privilege is not a right for men. Male privilege is a result of dysfunction and abuse. Male responsibilities are what spiritual men are called to fulfill. As husbands we must initiate love and compassion in our marriages. Our role as "leaders" is to provide the emotional, spiritual, and physical needs of our wives and families. For centuries wives have carried the weight of their marriages and children alone. They have wrestled with their children in church and then come home to be greeted by their husbands with "what are you fixing for dinner." They have covered scars, bruises, black eyes, and tears and have patiently suffered at the hands of men who felt it was their right to control them. Wives have given their hearts and lives to a Savior who, in their eyes, is a man. They have prayed to a God who is a father even though many have had earthly fathers who were tyrants.

It is time that men become like the man Jesus proved to be. It is time that men become the spiritual ones that God has proven to be. It is time that men listen to God who shows men how they ought to live. It is time that husbands love their wives as Jesus loves the church. It is time that men treat women as spiritual people, in the image of God. It is time that men grow up and provide for the spiritual, emotional, and psychological needs of those who trust them.

---

[44]Traditionally, we have limited the cause for divorce in the Christian life to adultery and sexual immorality. In the following chapters, I will discuss how abuse violates the covenant. For further reading on this see Yonder Moynihan Gillihan, "Jewish Laws on Illicit Marriage, the Defilement of Offspring, and the Holiness of the Temple: A New Halakic Interpretation of 1 Corinthians 7:14," *Journal of Biblical Literature* 121 (2002) 711–44.

6

Marriage and Divorce Issues

It is easy for someone who is not abused to pass judgment on victims. Victims do not stay in their relationships because they enjoy being abused. They do not return to their husbands because they prefer the violence and humiliation. Victims are caught in a web of control, power, and violence, and for them to break free involves personal, emotional, and psychological risk. As mentioned in the first section, the dynamics of abuse and family dysfunction are hard to understand unless you have lived in that environment.

Imagine what it is like to leave your abusive partner. You wrestle the kids into the car and flee for your life. Your adrenaline is pumping, and you hope that you made the right choice. You are still shaking from the yelling and hitting, but you know you must stay calm for the kids. You call a shelter, and there is no room. If you are lucky, you have a friend who will let you stay. If not, you may go to your parents' home, where you have seen your mother abused for years. You've tried to leave before, and your parents were mad at you for going back to him. In the past they have told you that the man you love is a bum, therefore, you decide to keep the details from your family. "We just had a fight," you say. Everyone tells you that it will blow over and you can go home tomorrow. It is crowded and the kids want to go home; this is not a good visit to grandma's house. Maybe this was a bad idea.

If you called the police, they may have taken him away in handcuffs. He was both cussing and threatening you or he was crying and saying he loves you and it will never happen again. Your emotions of fear, confusion, and anger have been bottled up inside. The officer is a big man, pretty intimidating but nice, and he cannot get emotionally connected to you at this time. The domestic violence advocate cannot come because the city has cut out the program and left it on the shoulders of the already overworked detectives. The officer tells you that since you live in Oregon your husband will be prosecuted for this crime (if you live somewhere else, you may have to file charges yourself) and suggests you get a restraining order to keep him away.

The flashing lights from the police car have drawn the attention of the neighborhood, so you try to hide your face and smile as if it were just a little incident. You go inside the house where the children are screaming, crying, and wondering when daddy will come home. Your oldest daughter is in the corner, and she tells you that if he sets foot in the house again she is leaving. Your son is in another corner with a knife in his hand and says, "If he comes back I swear to God I'll kill him!" The other children are asking why you had the bad policeman come and take daddy to jail. After a few hours you manage to get the kids in bed and lay your head down. Maybe it will be better in the morning. Maybe you don't need to file the restraining order. Maybe he'll come home tomorrow and we'll forget the whole thing happened.

If you are brave enough to get a restraining order, at City Hall, you will try to call in sick from work. You'll resurrect the emotionally drained children and drop them off at school or the sitter's house saying, "I can't pay you now. Can I pay you later?" You will fight the traffic, and if you are in Portland, you'll try to find a parking place. If you can find one, the meter is one dollar per hour and only good for three hours. Now you will have to walk three blocks to city hall. You will go through the metal detectors, climb the stairs, and find the small room with the ten page restraining order applications. This application is complicated, and it will take at least an hour to complete, assuming you didn't bring children with you. The advocate is very nice, but she is bilingual and in demand from others. She does a great job of helping you as well as the other five women in the room. The form is confusing. You need to know what is in your home, what guns he owns, and how many times he has hit and threatened you in the past few months. It's all running together in your mind, but you have to get the papers done by noon so that you can go before the judge at 1:00. "Great, the parking meter—I am going to have to come up with more money!" The advocate is helpful and supportive but cannot tell you what to write.

Then you wait for a few hours. There is no place to get lunch so you skip it. At 1:00, you go before the judge. "I hope the judge is not a man. I am afraid of men in power," you sigh. Your prayers are answered, and the female judge finally gets to you. "So many women are in here for restraining orders. Am I one among many today?" The judge is compassionate and kind and explains everything to you. It is nice not to be talked down to! She has the clerk stamp the restraining order, and you are asked to go downstairs to talk to the Sheriff's deputies.

The Sheriff's employees are nice, but they are behind so they quickly read the rules to you. You don't want to be a bother so you only ask one question, "When can I go home?" They inform you that the restraining order will be served tomorrow (it may take longer in other states). "If he answers the door he will be served. If not, we keep trying until he is home," they inform you. "You might want to stay with a friend until he is served." You think, "Why did I ask such a dumb question, there are a million others I should have asked." You stay with a friend but feel that you are an imposition. This time you tell your friend that you won't go back to him like you did last time. Your children are angry and emotional and they wonder when dad will be home and ask you out of fear, not concern. Your friend is struggling to pay the bills and is strapped emotionally, so the next three days will be tense and confusing.

You go home to a house that your husband has trashed. Your favorite pictures have been broken, and he left a note over the old wedding picture, "Please forgive me!" The deputy who accompanied you suggests that you change the locks and notify the neighbors so you can be safe. ("That's great," you say, "now everyone knows we can't keep our family together and I can't even change a light bulb, much less a lock.") You go to church on that Sunday, hoping that God and the church will help you and the kids in this horrible time of your life. Will you hear an encouraging sermon about how God and the church take a stand to protect victims? Will you see children with their dads playing and laughing? Will anyone recognize you or notice the bruises? Or will you hear that divorce is bad, all marriages have ups and downs, forgiveness is a virtue, or your church's evangelism team is targeting two-parent homes with children?

I met someone once who felt good about leaving her husband until she went to church.

I came to the shelter to visit Cecilia and see how she was doing. Two weeks earlier I had been involved in mediation between her counselors and the men who were counseling her husband (which I discussed earlier in chapter 1). She had been strong in her refusal to return to Robert or give him conjugal visits. She shared with me that throughout her life and marriage some person always seemed to be there to invite her to church, listen to her, or encourage her to leave her abusive relationships.

"Do you believe that God sends people to help us?" I asked.

"Yes, I do. Do you think these men and women were from God?" she responded.

"It wouldn't surprise me," I said.

"But they tried to get me out of the house and away from family," she said.

"Were you being abused during these times?"

"Sometimes, but usually it was when bad things were happening to me," Cecilia replied.

"Do you think that God was trying to get you out and help you to be safe?" I probed.

"I am very confused," she said, "and I need your advice. Last Sunday I went to church and the minister said that Satan is breaking up families. Satan is causing families to divorce. Maybe I should go back to my husband. It seems that Satan wants me to be away from my husband."

I took her to Matthew 10:34-36 and showed the verses to her.

Do not suppose that I have come to bring peace to the earth. I did not come to bring peace, but a sword. For I have come to turn a man against his father, a daughter against her mother, a daughter-in-law against her mother-in-law. One's enemies will be those of their own family.

"Do you think that Jesus will split up a family if one person is devoted to God and the other opposes God?" I asked.

"I see your point," she said. "I guess I was just feeling guilty because I had left my husband and I saw so many church women sitting with theirs that Sunday morning. I guess the sermon also made me feel a little guilty."

This is all too common when we encourage abuse victims to attend church. They sit in the pews and see healthy families (or those that appear to be healthy) and hear sermons about how bad divorce is and how Satan is causing the breakdown of the family. They hear how Jesus overcame evil by submission and endurance. They hear that marriage is not about happiness but commitment. They hear how we are victims of the wickedness of society and that hope, prayer, and endurance will bring us victory. Of all the people in the congregation, they are probably listening most intently to what is being preached. They return home with feelings of guilt because they have taken a stand for themselves, their children, and the truth only to find it unwelcome in our worship services. Our government has empowered our civil servants to confront evil, yet we tell them to endure evil. Enduring evil can cause victims to stay victims. The person caught in abuse seems to feel that they have no alternative and are not able to leave or get help. Because they feel that they have no alternatives, they face barriers on the road to recovery. I call these barriers theological roadblocks on the road to healing.

Why Are There Roadblocks?

Those who face the threat of physical and emotional abuse in the home do so because they love their families. I remember a *Roseanne* episode where she stated, "Our kids may be messed up but at least they're our kids." None of the victims I have helped want to break up their family. They just want to be safe. They just want the abuse to stop. Children who are abused also want the pain to stop. "I just want him to stop hitting me." "I just want him to be nice to me." "I want her to love me." "I want things to be the way they used to be." These are common statements that I hear from victims of abuse. No one wants to go through the trauma of separation and divorce. As stated in chapter 1, fear for their safety, finances, and fear of change hinder women from leaving their abuser. For these reasons so many are reluctant to leave, call the authorities, or tell the church. This is why so much abuse is unnoticed or unreported.

I believe that our cultural values and spiritual doctrines play a major role in preventing women from leaving their husbands. The cultural issues of male power also prevent men whom their intimate female partners have abused from going public. There is a sense of shame in getting outsiders involved as well as the authorities. The emphasis from awareness groups and the media have helped us to see the need to address domestic violence, but the shame for families in abuse still remains. No one wants others to believe that they cannot "manage their families."

One director of a children's home suggested to me that they no longer use the term *orphan's home* because many of their children are taken from abusive homes. He told me, "The breakup of the family is forcing us to deal less with orphans and more with kids from troubled homes." "I don't know if that's it," I said. "I think it is due to the permission that our government has given to remove children from dysfunctional homes. I think that this is a blessing from God because now we can't turn our heads."

While many of us might cringe at the thought of the government agencies being authorized by God, it is a biblical concept (Rom 13:1-6). We live in a time when child services and abuse shelters can work with law enforcement officials to determine the difference between a healthy environment and a dysfunctional environment. Eschatology (the study of the end times) is a popular topic filled with stories about government persecution of Christians. These stories seem to cause a distrust of government agencies. Dysfunctional families see the government as an enemy rather than an ally. Yet

God has given our government this right because the community of faith has failed to do the job of protecting women and children from abuse and oppression. Statistically, victims of abuse who want protection from an abuser seek help from family, friends, and the spiritual community rather than the police.[1] Victims seek help from those with whom they have a

---

[1] In Australia sixty-seven percent of ministers were sought out by victims of domestic violence and child abuse from their congregation and strangers. Cynthia Dixon, "Clergy as Carers: A Response to the Pastoral Concern of Violence in the Family," *Journal of Psychology and Christianity* 16:2 (1997) 126. I would also like to add that population studies from 1993 to 1999 throughout the world indicate that abuse victims, when

relationship. Yet in Figure 1 (pp. xxi–xxiii), many domestic violence advocates feel that churches and family are some of the most ineffective at providing services for victims. We have failed to empower victims as our government agencies have done. Is it possible that the government agencies are God's tool to protect the oppressed who cry out for justice? Is it possible that the effectiveness of these government agencies is a reflection of our inadequacies? Is it possible that they are a judgment to the faith community? Has the faith community empowered abusers to continue to abuse?

How does the faith community become an enabler in the abuse cycle? We hold to spiritual doctrines that further victimize victims and keep abusers abusing. We turn our heads to the cries of the oppressed. We confront victims rather than abusers and call for submission rather than justice. We place the roadblocks of *marriage and divorce issues, parenting issues,* and *issues of victimization* in front of the victims and unknowingly prevent them from leaving. In the rest of this chapter we will discuss the first of these issues: marriage and divorce.

Issues of Marriage and Divorce

Marriage and family teachings in our spiritual communities are filled with presuppositions, false allegations, and warped perceptions of what a healthy family is meant to be. Much of this stems from our lack of understanding of covenant and its responsibilities to marriage and family. I have heard ministers teach that victims are bound to a covenant even when the partner is unfaithful. I have heard churches tell victims that being divorced is a sin and more damaging to children than being in a dysfunctional relationship. At an *I Still Do* conference I heard a speaker tell the group that he had a "normal, dysfunctional family." He proceeded to suggest that those of us from a divorced home would have felt better if our parents would have stayed together. To this my response was, "No!" I remember the fighting

---

given the chance to speak out about their abuse, talk to family and friends rather than the police. Their other response is to keep silent. Obviously victims fear telling law enforcement officials instead of their friends. *Population Report Series L: Number 11*; Table 3.

and dysfunction in my parents' marriage, mostly due to my father, and the divorce actually brought a sense of peace. Is a dysfunctional marriage relationship pleasing to God and in honor of the covenant? Is a dysfunctional marriage beneficial to couples and their children?

The Marriage Covenant

God and the Covenant

The marriage covenant is a reflection of the covenant between God and the creation. The covenant is holy and calls for faithfulness from both partners. The covenant is a "contract" with stipulations and obligations. God expects loyalty from the "bride." The Hebrew term, *berit,* was a contract and agreement between two parties.[2] I have found that many ministers and Christians believe that God carries the burden in the covenant with humans and expects little in return. They believe that God's covenant is not conditional and that God keeps the relationship with humans regardless of their actions. Bowman would define this as an overfunctioning partner in the relationship. The biblical texts suggest that in covenant humans have a responsibility to honor and respect their God.

> The ancient biblical people came to understand, then, that covenant was central to life, it sustained life, preserved it, and ensured its future. For them, covenant was relationship—God in relationship with creation, creation in relationship with God, God in relationship with human beings, human beings in relationship with God; human beings in relationship with the natural world, the natural world in relationship with human beings; and God, human beings, and the natural world all in relationship together with all creation, and all creation in relationship with God. Additionally, the ancient biblical people came to understand

---

[2]Moshe Weinfeld, *"Berith,"* in *Theological Dictionary of the Old Testament,* ed. Johannes G. Botterweck, Helmer Ringgren, and Heinz-Josef Fabry, vol. 2 (Grand Rapids: Eerdmans, 1974) 278. For a fuller discussion of covenant and marriage see Instone-Brewer, 1–19.

that to be in covenant was to be interdependent. When covenant was preserved, life flourished. When covenant was broken, life suffered.[3]

The prophets heralded this expectation, railed against their people when they broke covenant, and offered them a vision of hope that was contingent on their repentance and God's initiative at making a new covenant with them. From the prophetic texts, one sees that when the Israelites break covenant with God, not only does their relationship with God and with one another suffer but the land and the natural world also suffer.[4]

As originally written, there was no distinction between "covenant" and "contract." There is only one word for both . . . and there is no reason to believe that this one word represented more than one type of agreement. This applies not only to the OT [Old Testament] use of the term "covenant" but also to its use in the NT [New Testament] and beyond into the Church Fathers. Throughout this period, the term "covenant" meant a contract that could be broken if either side reneged on their half of the agreement.[5]

As Eichrodt, Dempsey, and Instone-Brewer suggest, covenant has always been two-sided. God promises to be faithful to humanity and expects the same loyalty from the creation. Since marriage is a reflection of a covenant between God and humans and Christ and the church, then loyalty within the covenant should reflect shared faithfulness.

Know that *Yahweh* your God is God; a faithful God, who keeps the covenant of love to a thousand generations with those who love [God] and keep [God's] covenant. (Deut 7:7-11)

The covenant can be broken. God is faithful and loyal to the covenant and the children (Deut 7:9-11; Titus 1:4). But man, historically, has

---

[3]Dempsey, *Hope Amid the Ruins: The Ethics of Israel's Prophets* (St. Louis: Chalice, 2000) 20.
[4]Ibid., 32.
[5]Instone-Brewer, 17.

violated this holy relationship (Jer 11:8; Heb 8:7-13). When the covenant is broken or violated, the offended party has two options: punish or forgive. In the Bible, God displays both options in the covenant. God can punish the people (captivity and divorce) or forgive them.

> *Yahweh* will call you back as if you were a wife deserted and spiritually distressed, a young wife, rejected, says your God. For a little while I *abandoned* you, but with compassion I will bring you back. In a surge of anger I turned my face from you, for a moment, but with faithfulness I will have compassion on you says *Yahweh* your redeemer. (Isa 54:6-7)

> I gave faithless Israel her *certificate of divorce* and sent her away because of all her adulteries. (Jer 3:8)

> This is what *Yahweh* says: "Where is your mother's *certificate of divorce* with which I sent her away? Which creditor did I sell you to? You were sold because of your sins; because of your transgressions your mother was sent away." (Isa 50:1)

The Babylonian and Assyrian captivities were strong examples of God's punishment of those who broke the covenant. *Yahweh* described these events as an abandoning or divorce of the nation. God refused to show compassion and protect the Jews when they had violated the covenant.

> Therefore this is what *Yahweh* says, "I will bring on them a disaster they cannot escape. *Although they cry out to me I will not listen* . . . Do not pray for this people nor petition for them, *because I will not listen when they call to me* in the time of their distress." (Jer 11:12)

> "They greatly love to wander; they do not restrain their feet. So *Yahweh* does not accept them; and will now remember their wickedness and *punish them for their sins.*" Then *Yahweh* said to me, "Do not pray for this people. Although they fast, *I will not listen to their cry,* though they offer burnt offerings and grain offerings, *I will not accept them.* Instead, *I will destroy them* with the sword, famine, and plagues." (Jer 14:9)

Why was God so harsh? God had warned the Jews and called them to repentance. The covenant required faithfulness from both parties. God had been faithful to the nation of Israel, however, Israel had not been faithful to their vows to the covenant. Yet, the prophetic books illustrate that God confronted Israel concerning their profaning in the covenant.

Stand in the courtyard of *Yahweh's* house and speak to all the people of the towns of Judah who come to worship in the house of *Yahweh*. Tell them everything I command you; do not omit a word. Perhaps they will listen and each will turn from his evil way. Then I will have mercy and not bring on them the disaster I was planning because of the evil they have done. (Jer 26:2-3)

Therefore, house of Israel, I will judge you, each one according to your ways, declares *Yahweh*. Repent! Turn away from all your sins, then sin will not be your destruction. Get rid of the sins you have committed and get a new heart and new spirit. Why will you die, house of Israel? I do not take pleasure in anyone's death, declares *Yahweh*, so repent and live! (Ezek 18:30-32)

Israel and Judah had been warned concerning their unfaithfulness to the covenant. They were acting as a husband who ignores his wife, abuses her, and is sexually, emotionally, and psychologically unfaithful to her. They were acting as a wife who humiliates her husband and is unfaithful to him. The covenant relationship had become a dysfunctional relationship. *God's practice of divorce was an aggressive action to protect the sanctity and purity of covenant.* The covenant relationship became dysfunctional because of humans. Hebrews 8:7-8 suggests that God found fault with the people, not the covenant. The sin of the people profaned and destroyed the covenant. *Yahweh* had to become *overfunctioning* to keep the covenant, while Israel continued to *underfunction* due to sin and neglect. God could not tolerate this type of relationship and had to divorce Israel for the sake of the holy nature of *berit*. God punished them for the sake of honor. Divorce, likewise, is an aggressive action to maintain the honor of covenant relationship.

Just as the covenant is a contract, marriage also is also a contract with stipulations and obligations.[6] Just as the covenant is not one-sided and requires loyalty from both sides, so marriage also requires loyalty from both individuals. By loyalty I am not only referring to sexual faithfulness but also to issues of respect and shared power. Marriage is likened to God's covenant and relationship to Israel (Jer 3:8; Ezek 16:1-10) and Jesus' relationship to the church (Eph 5:25; Rev 21:2). When we fail to love, honor, and respect God/Jesus, we violate the covenant. When one spouse fails to love, honor, and respect the other, they (not the victim) violate the covenant. The victim, as does God, has the option to call the other to repentance and challenge them to holiness.

God the Faithful?

Christians and ministers may question these concepts from the prophets and wonder how God could punish people and abandon them. There tends to be a strong reaction to any thought of God punishing even the wickedest of people and allowing them to perish. Our perspective on what it means to be God is sometimes a lose/lose situation. If God condemns my loved ones, God is unjust. If God forgives my enemies, God is a monster. If God punishes, God is abusive. If God does not act, God is nonexistent. It seems that our concept of covenant is tied into this perspective of God. God is to be faithful, so we believe, regardless of my actions. We believe that covenant cannot be a two-way street, because we are too weak for that. We believe that covenant is a one-sided relationship, where God *overfunctions* for those of us who *underfunction*.

Humans make mistakes. We are weak and only God is perfect. Yet the sanctity of covenant is profaned when there is unfaithfulness. We have the ability to resist the temptation to sin, and we are never tempted with more than we can resist (1 Cor 10:13)! Therefore, living in covenant is a marriage with God. God promises to be faithful and expects us to be faithful. In covenant there is always an understanding of shared responsibility. One example is found in the story of Joshua and the battle of Ai (Josh 7). God

---

[6]Instone-Brewer, 1–19. This chapter discusses marriage covenants, covenant in the ancient Near East, and its application to biblical studies.

promised to never leave or forsake Israel (Deut 31:6, 8, 23; Josh 1:3, 9). Is this an unconditional statement? Read what happened when Achan disobeyed God by stealing loot from Jericho (Joshua 7). Israel lost the battle to the small town of Ai. After that Joshua cried to the Lord.

> *Yahweh*, why did you bring us across the Jordan; to deliver us into the hands of the Amorites, to destroy us? If only we had been content to stay on the other side of the Jordan. (Josh 7:7)

Joshua and the nation of Israel felt abandoned. God had promised to be with them and never forsake them. A phrase that occurred frequently reminded them that God would be faithful: "Be strong and courageous, do not be terrified; do not be discouraged, for *Yahweh* your God is with you wherever you go," (Josh 1:9; Deut 31:6, 8, 23; 20:1-4). Why did they lose the battle? Notice God's reply.

> *Yahweh* said to Joshua, "Stand up! What are you doing down on your face? Israel has sinned; *they have violated my covenant, which I commanded them to keep.* They have taken some of the devoted things; they have stolen, they have lied, they have put them with their own possessions. That is why the Israelites cannot stand against their enemies; they turn their backs and run because they have been made liable to destruction. *I will not be with you anymore unless* you destroy whatever among you is devoted to destruction." (Josh 7:10-12)

God's reply was that the covenant had been violated and was in danger of being broken. God's loyalty to the covenant required their obedience and faithfulness.

The same scenario is found with Samson (Judg 13-16). Samson was to be a Nazirite and set apart to God from birth to death (Judg 13:7). Yet much of Samson's life was dedicated to acting like anything but a Nazirite. He ate honey from a dead animal carcass (14:18), married a Philistine (14:1-20), killed men (14:19), touched a dead donkey's carcass (15:16), slept with a prostitute (16:1), and became romantically involved with another Philistine woman (16:4). Samson's life was not only in violation of his Nazirite covenant; it was in violation of his covenant with *Yahweh*. Finally, Samson gave away the secret of his strength by telling Delilah that a razor had not shaved his head. She cut his hair and told him the Philistines had come to get him (16:19). Thinking that he could fight these men, "he did not realize that *Yahweh* had left him" (16:20). This is a sad story of one who demanded God's faithfulness but refused to return the favor. God left Samson to suffer alone. The one "set apart for God" became "set apart from God." While the biblical text indicates that Samson later repented, it is a strong reminder that God may abandon those who wish to practice sin and disobedience in their covenant. We cannot live in a dysfunctional relationship with God where we expect God to overfunction while we do not attempt to give back.

> The Old Testament speaks of marriage as a "covenant" . . . which was the ancient Near Eastern term for any kind of binding agreement or contract. The correct phrase for a marriage agreement in the Old Testament is therefore a "marriage contract." Like any other contract, this contained an agreement and penalties for breaking the agreement. The penalty for breaking the marriage contract was divorce with loss of the dowry.[7]

I find that people have trouble understanding that covenant is a contract which carries responsibility and faithfulness from both partners. We have emphasized God's faithfulness but have neglected our responsibilities. Americans tend to expect loyalty from others—because we enter into contracts for our benefit—and are quick to point out how others violate contracts (the American frontier was built on broken promises and treaties with Native Americans). We worry about clauses and stipulations in our contracts that free us from responsibility. Sometimes we believe that giving must be with "no strings attached." This is evident in our unwillingness to take gifts if the giver has any ulterior motive for giving to us. The belief that God gives without expecting anything in return is extremely popular. One example is the application of the term "free gift" when we talk about the doctrine of grace through Christ. The view that God has given Jesus as a free gift (as opposed to a gift with reciprocity) or that God's grace is free indicates to us that God gives without expecting anything in return.

---

[7]Instone-Brewer, 19.

This is contrary to the Eastern concept of reciprocity. A gift in the ancient Near East meant that something was expected in return. There were no *free gifts*! Reciprocity is found in the ancient world's views of covenant, patronage, and gift giving. Nothing is given without expecting a return. The parable of the ten coins (Luke 19:11-27) suggests that the wealthy noble was within his cultural and theological rights to expect the servants to give a return on his investment. Reciprocity is the concept that if one is given a gift, they are to return the favor.[8] The gift of Jesus is not a sacrifice in vain. God expects a return on the investment. Jesus expects us to give our lives, since he gave his own (Rom 12:1-2). With reciprocity there are no free gifts because all carry responsibilities. While this seems to suggest manipulation in many Americans' minds, it was necessary so that ancient communities could work together and share responsibility.

The prophets tell us that God did reconcile with the Israelites. God eagerly desired to forgive them and brought them home from Babylon. The nation's repentance (Jeremiah 29; Daniel 9) and desire to be faithful to God renewed their covenant and brought the promise of hope and peace to those abandoned by God. This promise came, by the grace and mercy of *Yahweh*, as a new start (Jer 16:14-16; 33:31-34; Ezek 37:1-14; Hag 2:6-8; Zech 3:1-10). But God still expected them to continue in obedience and loyalty while in the covenant.

> If you will walk in my ways and keep my requirements, then you will govern my house and have charge of my courts, and I will give you a place among these standing here. (Zech 3:7)

The covenant requires faithfulness from both parties. The consequences of breaking the covenant rest on the offender. The offended party has the right to punish or forgive. When Israel broke the covenant with God, God many times forgave them. Yet other times God chose to punish by

---

[8]Having lived in rural Missouri, I found that this was a common concept among farming communities. No one expected pay for any work that was done, but we helped each other out and made sure that we returned favors with friendliness, baked goods, or help on another project. This was an unwritten code, but one my family quickly adapted to when we moved from the city to the farm.

divorcing the nation of Israel. God did this because the covenant had become dysfunctional and the nation of Israel was shamelessly violating the trust and loyalty that *Yahweh* had given to them. The same is true in marriage. Both parties are expected to be faithful to the covenant. When dysfunction rules the marriage, the covenant is in danger of being dishonored or violated. The offended spouse has the option to confront the other individual and call them to repentance. The abusive spouse has the option to repent and work toward healing in the marriage or risk being cut off from the relationship.

Doesn't God Hate Divorce?

Another theological objection to God divorcing Israel is the verse often quoted from Mal 2:16, "I hate divorce, says *Yahweh* the God of Israel."[9] Many, especially clergy and abusers, have used this text to tell victims that God does not approve of divorce. While I believe that divorce can be traumatic to a family, I find that *Yahweh* practiced divorce in Israelite history (Isa 50:1; 54:6-7; Jer 3:8). The text seems to be difficult to reconcile if we take the view that God is opposed to any divorce.

In the book of Malachi, the nation of Judah had returned from Babylonian/Persian captivity (538/535 BC). They had been challenged by Haggai and Zechariah to rebuild the temple of God (Hag 2:1-9; Zech 2:7-13). God reminded them that they could start over and become holy (Hag 2:19). As time passed, they began to return to the ways of their former generations by neglecting the sacrifices and practicing idolatry (Mal 1:1-6). While God was the offended husband in Hosea, God became the offended wife in Mal 2:11-16.[10] Israel had married a foreigner and

---

[9]There is an alternate translation of this verse suggested by other language versions of the Hebrew text. Some versions read, "If you hate her, divorce her." For more information on the validity of this translation one can consult the sources listed in note 12 as well as Adele Berlin and Marc Zvi Brettler, editors, *The Jewish Study Bible: Tanakh Translation* (New York: Oxford University Press, 2004) 1272.

[10]For texts that suggest God as mother/wife/female see Isa 42:14; 46:3; 66:9-13. While John 4 suggests that God is spirit, female imagery is used of God as well as male imagery. Mark S. Smith, *The Origins of Biblical Monotheism: Israel's Polytheistic Background and the Ugaritic Texts* (New York: Oxford University Press, 2001) 90.

begun to practice injustice. The people of Israel again practiced the same behavior that caused the previous divorce. How was God to respond to this behavior?

> Judah has acted treacherously (faithlessly) and committed an abomination in Israel and Jerusalem. Judah has profaned what is holy to *Yahweh* and loved the daughter of a foreign God. (Mal 2:11)

First, God did not discourage divorce against those who profaned the holy covenant. In Ezra 10:11, Ezra and the Jewish leaders encouraged the Jewish men, who were married to foreign women, to divorce their foreign wives. If Mal 2:11 suggests that the Jewish men may have been married to foreign wives, then what are the implications of this text?[11] If Mal 2:16 states that God opposes divorce, then God would not have approved of Ezra's decree. Neither Malachi, Nehemiah, nor Ezra indicate that the Lord was displeased with the abandonment of these foreign wives. God's displeasure with something does not mean that it will not come to pass by divine will. While God may not wish to condemn or punish the wicked, it does happen. In Mal 2:16 God is displeased with divorce, but God is willing to practice it.

Second, the Malachi text may not be discussing literal marriages.[12] The term "covenant" is used throughout Malachi to refer to the Jewish nation's relationship to *Yahweh*.

---

[11]Malachi 2:11 states, "Judah has married the daughter of a foreign god." This can have two interpretations. First, the text can suggest that the Jewish men were married to foreign women. Second, the text can mean that the Jewish nation is again involved in idolatry. Biblical scholars support both interpretations.

[12]For further discussion on this debate see: Andrew E. Hill, *Malachi*, Anchor Bible 25D (New York: Doubleday, 1998) 422–43; David Clyde Jones, "A Note on the LXX of Malachi 2:16," *Journal of Biblical Literature* 109 (1990) 683–85; Beth Glazier-McDonald, "Intermarriage, Divorce, and the *Bat-'el Nekar*: Insights into Mal 2:10-16," *Journal of Biblical Literature* 106 (1987) 603–11; David L. Peterson, *Zechariah 9–14 and Malachi: A Commentary*, Old Testament Library (Louisville: Westminster John Knox, 1995) 195–206. Against this interpretation see Gordon P. Hugenberger, *Marriage as a Covenant: Biblical Law and Ethics as Developed from Malachi* (Grand Rapids: Baker, 1998) 27–47.

1:2   I have loved you

2:4   warning about breaking the *covenant* with Levi

2:5   *covenant* of life and peace, Levi respected me

2:8   you have turned from me

2:10   Why do you profane my *covenant*?

2:11   Judah has *broken faith*

         married the daughter of a foreign god

2:12   The Lord will cut him (Judah) off

2:14   false tears, remember the wife of your youth (*Yahweh*)

         broken faith with your wife (*Yahweh*)

2:10   One God made them both

2:16   I hate divorce so

do not break faith

Figure 9: Malachi 2 Revisited

These texts (Figure 9) indicate that the Jews were dishonoring their master, father, and wife.[13] The wife of their youth was to be *Yahweh*. Judah had left *Yahweh* and cleaved to another woman or god (probably the goddess Asherah).[14] *Yahweh* was challenging Judah in court, like an angry hurt wife, and warning Israel that they were about to be divorced, something God did not wish to do. The final statement was: "Guard yourself in your spirit and *do not break faith*" (Mal 2:15b). This interpretation is more in line with God's view of divorce (an aggressive action to protect the sanctity of covenant), but it does not suggest that God will not allow divorce.

---

[13]In some cases *Yahweh* is referred to as the female partner. See Peterson, 203, and Mark S. Smith, *The Early History of God*, 2d ed. (Grand Rapids: Eerdmans, 2001) 97–103. In Proverbs, wisdom is seen as feminine and is also the first creation of God (Proverbs 8–9).
[14]In Jeremiah 44, the Judeans who were left after the third Babylonian captivity turned from God to worship the *Queen of Heaven* (Asherah). It seems that the Jews in Malachi's day are again returning to this deity. Othmar Keel and Christoph Uehlinger, *Gods, Goddesses, and Images of God In Ancient Israel*, trans. Thomas H. Trapp (Minneapolis: Augsburg Fortress, 1998) 294–95; Smith, *The Early History of God*, 109–10. O'Brien also believes that the Jews have again been involved in idolatry to Asherah. Julia M. O'Brien, *Nahum, Habakkuk, Zephaniah, Haggai, Zechariah, Malachi*, Abingdon Old Testament Commentary (Nashville: Abingdon, 2004) 300–302.

Another interesting point in this text is found in Mal 2:16. "I hate divorce," says Yahweh the God of Israel, "and [I hate] a man's clothing himself [or his wife] with violence," says *Yahweh* Almighty, "so guard yourself in your spirit, and do not break faith." While God may not wish to divorce the people, God equally hates violent individuals. Malachi indicates that the Jews were showing partiality in the law (2:9), committing injustices (2:17), oppressing the poor (3:5), and practicing evil (3:15). Many abusive men have failed to read these sections of the text. They claim that God is angry with their wives for filing a restraining order and filing for divorce, while few (if any) believe that God is angry with them for being violent and controlling.

Mal 2:16 does not suggest that God is angry with divorced people. The text is a warning to those who are unfaithful *and violent* in their relationships with *Yahweh* and *other humans*. The text is calling people back to God. The text confronts those contributing to violence and dysfunction in the covenant and relationship. While God hates divorce, God practices divorce. Divorce is not something that God is eager to do, but it is an option in order to keep the covenant holy and honorable. While God accused Israel of sexual promiscuity (idolatry), God equally condemned them for social injustice and violence. Israel was divorced not only for idolatry, but also for social injustice, violence, and oppression.

> See how the faithful city has become a prostitute! She was full of justice and righteousness lived there but now murderers. Your silver has become cheap metal, your choice wine is watered down, your rulers are rebels, companions of thieves; they all love bribes and chase after gifts. They do not defend the cause of the fatherless; the widow's case does not come before them. (Isa 1:21-23)

Jesus also spoke on the issue of divorce. In Matthew 19 he said, "I tell you that anyone who divorces his wife, except for marital unfaithfulness, and marries another woman commits adultery." To some this seems to be the only reason Jesus gives for divorce. There are a few considerations on this point. First, Jesus was speaking to Pharisees who were questioning him and trying to find a reason for divorce. This is evident in the collection of rabbinical writings and traditions circulating around the time of Christ.[15] The Jewish rabbis had developed a complex method of validating divorce that in many ways victimized the women. In Luke 16:15-18, Jesus accused them of trying to justify themselves and he used divorce as an example of this. Both texts suggest that Jewish men, especially Pharisees, sought reasons to divorce their wives and further victimize them. The Jewish practice of divorce had also become highly influenced by the Greco-Roman culture and its freedom for men to divorce their wives.[16]

Jesus' discussion about divorce and remarriage was not designed to be a discussion of all forms of divorce but a prohibition for men victimizing their wives, something that was common practice in the first century. The Apostle Paul further discussed issues of Christian marriage in 1 Corinthians 7. Paul suggested that marriage was important for men and women in order to share sexual intimacy and fulfill each other's sexual desires (1 Cor 7:1-6). Paul reminded the married Christians that the Lord Jesus had commanded them not to divorce (1 Cor 7:10-11). This prevented one spouse from neglecting the needs of the other and victimizing them.[17] According to Paul, marriage was still a covenant that required *both* husband and wife to work together for love, security, and faithfulness.

Concerning the issue of mixed marriages, a Christian married to a non-Christian, the Christian was not to seek a divorce if the unbelieving spouse was willing to stay in the relationship.

> To the rest,[18] I say not the Lord, that if any brother has a wife who is an unbeliever and she is willing to live with him, do not divorce her. And if a woman has a husband who is an unbeliever and he is willing to live with her do not divorce you husband. (1 Cor 7:12-13)

---

[15]The Mishnah is a collection of rabbinic writings from 200 BC to around 400 AD. The section, *Gittin*, is a large tract that gives suggestions concerning legal divorce and reasons one might divorce their spouse.

[16]Santiago Guijarro, "The Family in First-Century Galilee," in *Constructing Early Christian Families: Family as Social Reality and Metaphor*, ed. Halvor Moxnes (London: Routledge, 1997) 46.

[17]Instone-Brewer has an excellent section on this issue, pages 189–212.

[18]Paul is giving a list of teachings for various individuals in the church. He addresses the married (7:1-7); the unmarried (7:8); the married (7:10 but in light of 7:12 these would both be believers who are married); and then the rest (7:12 who are the ones married to non-Christians).

This became a problem because Roman society was quite different from the Jewish and Christian communities in regard to morality. This was especially true concerning husbands and their treatment of wives and children.[19] Roman men were sometimes encouraged to be promiscuous and harsh with their families.[20] Roman wives had also been given many freedoms and could divorce their husbands and remarry.[21] In Roman history there are many examples of married women having affairs and engaging in prostitution, drunkenness, and other forms of illicit behavior that would have been condemned by the early Christian community. Greco-Roman culture had so affected the family that divorce was common even among Jews.[22] Yet the Christian was to be different and practice faithfulness in marriage.

But the Christian also had the right to expect to be treated fairly and honorably even in a mixed marriage. Paul believed that the Christian spouse should still expect faithfulness, loyalty, and respect even from the non-Christian spouse. In 1 Cor 7:12-14, Paul suggested that keeping the marriage together (meaning that both people agree to live with each other) brought a sense of holiness to the family. Paul was calling the mixed marriages legal and ritually pure according to Jewish standards.[23]

> For the husband makes the unbelieving wife holy and the wife makes the unbelieving husband holy, otherwise your children would be unclean but now they are holy. (7:14)

Both Christian and non-Christian could work together to bring holiness, love, and purity to their families. The Christian was be encouraged to

---

[19]For more information on this distinction see Russ Dudrey, "'Submit Yourselves to One Another': A Socio-historical Look at the Household Code of Ephesians 5:15–6:9," *Restoration Quarterly* 41 (1999) 27–31.

[20]Winter, *After Paul Left Corinth: The Influences of Secular Ethics and Social Change* (Grand Rapids: Eerdmans, 2001) 82–85.

[21]Seneca suggests that some of the women counted time by the number of husbands they had married and divorced (*De beneficius* 3.16.2).

[22]Guijarro, 46. This is also evident in Herod's encouragement for Herodias to divorce Philip, his brother, and marry him (Luke 3:19-20).

[23]Moynihan Gillihan, 711–44.

communicate with their spouse to work out the relationship, which would be a great witness for Jesus.

This would not have been possible in every marriage. In mixed marriages where the unbelieving spouse was not willing to honor Jesus and live in a healthy covenant (as described in 1 Cor 7:1-9), the Christian spouse was not bound to the marriage. Actually, Paul wrote:

> But if the unbeliever wants to depart, let them depart. The brother or sister is not bound in this for God has called us to peace. How do you know, wife, if you can save your husband and how do you know, husband, if you can save your wife? (7:15-16)

In the Greek language this is a command to *"let them go."*[24] While this seems harsh to many, Paul was not as concerned about the state of marriage as much as he was about the health and peace of the family. Paul mentioned five times that they were to stay as they were called (7:17, 20, 24, 26, 40) and be devoted to God (7:32, 34). Paul did not want the Christians to be pulled away from God by a desire to be divorced, single, or married. Each of these life stages were to help them to focus on God rather than on others. If the unbeliever brought abuse and sin to the family and neglected the wife, Paul allowed for divorce.

Paul also mentioned that God had called them to peace. A home with abuse, alcoholism, drug addiction, pornography, fighting, affairs, or hatred of another's religious convictions is not a home of peace. Paul's concern was for the Christian who would be subjected to sin through the other spouse. I believe that Paul was challenging the Christian to take a stand and call their family to holiness. The Christian should set the standard behavior for the family. Christians are not expected to let their abusive spouses rule the home and bring violence to the children. The children need to be holy and live in a house of peace. The Christian has every right to demand and expect peace and respect in their home. The Christian has the right to confront an abusive, alcoholic, drug-addicted, or sex-addicted spouse and say, "As long as we are married, this behavior will not continue." Many times the underfunctioning spouse agrees and receives help. This

---

[24]In Missouri, Paul would have said, "If they want to leave, send 'em packing!"

can bring peace to the family. Other times the spouse manipulates or refuses to get help. Paul would say, "Send 'em packing."[25]

I understand that this is difficult for many to accept, but Paul's doctrine was grounded in a theology that wished to help others become more like God. I have known wives who have confronted their husbands and have seen peace restored. I know of husbands who have addressed sin in their marriages and reunited with their wives.[26] I do not believe Paul was pushing for divorce; he was pushing for healthy families. For Paul, as with God, divorce was an aggressive action that protected the sanctity of the covenant as well as the home. As God confronted the men in Malachi to return to their covenant, so wives have the right to call their abusive husbands back to the covenant.

A New Context For Marriage

Traditionally, we have viewed the marriage covenant as beginning at creation when male and female were joined in the Garden of Eden.

---

[25]One way for a woman to find out the severity of abuse in their relationship is to view how her husband reacts when she confronts him over his controlling or abusive behavior. While a woman needs to be cautious she can challenge her husband on the sin of abuse. If he reacts even more violently or controlling, then there may be a problem. The Proverb "rebuke a discerning man and he will gain knowledge" (19:25) suggests that a righteous husband will listen to his wife if she challenges him concerning sin.

[26]The book by Paul Hegstrom, *Angry Men and the Women Who Love Them: Breaking the Cycle of Physical and Emotional Abuse* (Kansas City: Beacon Hill, 1999) seems to be a success story in this area. Although I have not met Paul and Judy Hegstrom at the time of writing this book, it seems that they have been able to reunite and reestablish a healthy marriage. It is also possible to coach couples to fight fairly, learn skills to resolve high-conflict discussions, and manage high-conflict situations. For an excellent article on this see: George F. Ronan, Laura E. Dreer, Katherine M. Pollard, and Donna W. Ronan, "Violent Couples: Coping and Communication Skills," *Journal of Family Violence* 19:2 (2004) 131–37. I am personally aware of many other success stories as well as relapse stories. Reunion is possible, but caution should be exercised and the victims must have a chance to heal and feel empowered enough to forgive and be confrontational if necessary. This can only happen after much work and counseling.

There was no helper found to complement Adam.[27] So God caused Adam to fall into a deep sleep and took a bone from his side/rib and closed the flesh from where it was taken. God built the rib, which he had taken from the man, into a woman and brought her to the man. The man said, "This is now bone of my bones and flesh of my flesh. This one is to be called woman/wife because she was taken from man/husband." So a man leaves his father and mother and cleaves to his wife so that they may become one flesh. The two were naked and were not ashamed. (Gen 2:20b-25)

The text tells us that the cleaving is a divine act and that husband and wife help complement each other. Since God has made them one (Mal 2:15), they should cleave together. As Jesus stated, "They are no longer two but one flesh. Whatever God has yoked[28] together man should not separate/divide" (Matt 19:6). Marriage is not just a uniting of two people; it is a partnership that depends on two people working together. Jesus' warning is not just to outsiders who may try to divide a couple; it is also to those in the marriage who refuse to treat the other spouse as a partner. Jesus' concern with the Pharisees was that they were taking advantage of women by looking for reasons to end their marriages and the marriages of upper-class Jews such as Herod and Herodias (Luke 3:19-20).

The Genesis 2 passage has been used to suggest that marriage began with the creation. Yet marriage, even the joining of male and female in Genesis 2, began with God's concept of covenant with humans. This plan was established before the foundation of the world (Eph 1:4) and is shown

---

[27]The Hebrew word for "opposite," "fit," "suitable," or "complement" is *neged*. This word means "opposite," "south," or, literally, "in front of someone or something." A derivative of the word also means "leader," "ruler," or "one who goes before someone." The image of Genesis 2 suggests that alone, man will struggle (2:18), but the woman/wife is a helper who is like or complements the man.

[28]I have chosen to translate this word "yoked together" since it is similar to Phil 4:2 (yoke fellows). I think that this suggests that the marriage is a partnership and working relationship as well as an emotional and sexual union. Jesus is angry with the Pharisees' view of divorce as a way to manipulate women, while the Genesis text, quoted by Jesus, suggests that the marriage is a partnership where husband and wife complement and help each other.

in Christ and the church (Eph 5:31-32). Marriage is a reflection of God's covenant with Israel as well as Christ's covenant with the church (Ezek 16; Eph 5:25). Since marriage is a reflection of the covenant, the question that should be addressed is, How does God want marriages to reflect the covenant?

As discussed earlier, God's covenant with Israel allows for blessings and/or punishment. But how do we view marriage as covenant? When Genesis 2 becomes the core of marriage, then the option of divorce is seen as a splitting or dividing of the one flesh. While this is partly true, it also causes people to see divorce as the problem. This is how marriage and divorce have traditionally been approached. Marriage is the goal, and divorce signals the end of the relationship.

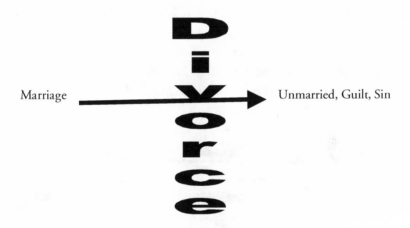

Figure 10: Traditional View of Marriage and Divorce

According to this view, the main problem for a marriage is divorce. As long as a couple does not divorce they assume that they are doing God's will. The recent rise in divorce, among American married couples, has caused the church to react by focusing on keeping marriages together. While addressing the divorce issue is a great need among our churches, the problem is not divorce. Divorce is only a symptom of a bigger problem. Too many couples feel that they are reflecting God's covenant by just "staying together." They seem unconcerned about the fighting, dysfunction, and sin that may be lord of their marriage. In fact, they practice tolerance because they believe that God practices tolerance with us in the covenant.

This view is damaging to those who have left dysfunctional marriages and divorced their spouses. Once an individual is divorced, they enter a spiritual "no man's land" where they struggle with guilt and wonder if they could have done something differently to keep the marriage together. Divorce is seen as the problem and is blamed for the breakup of the family. When couples or individuals who are cohabiting come for counseling, I ask them why they do not get married. None of them tell me that they are afraid of divorce. They tell me that they are afraid of marriage. They do not describe marriage as a healthy, loving partnership. They point out that they see marriage as a relationship of fighting, arguing, forced celibacy, unfaithfulness, and abuse that cannot be broken. They see that marriage has an intended permanence to it, but as a form of slavery. Their mother or father could not leave, so they put up with the dysfunction. The children have learned that this is marriage.

This suggests to me that we should have a different view of marriage and divorce. We should address marriage and dysfunction.

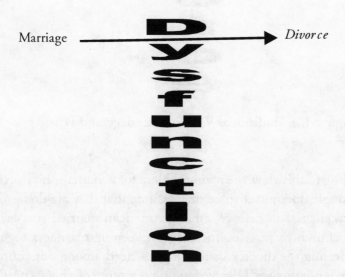

Figure 11: A New View of Marriage and Dysfunction

This view of marriage, dysfunction, and divorce shows us that the problem is not divorce, it is dysfunction. Dysfunction exists when a marriage is not healthy. Dysfunction exists when there is not mutual submission, shared power, or respect for each spouse. Dysfunction exists when the couple does not communicate, does not resolve conflict in a healthy manner, or shares little intimacy, if any. Dysfunction exists when the covenant is broken or is in danger of being broken due to the actions of one or both spouses. Dysfunction exists when one or both spouses practice behavior that is contrary to God's will. Is every marriage dysfunctional? No. Can there be dysfunction in an otherwise healthy marriage? Yes. My point is that healthy marriages seek to be godly while dysfunctional marriages try to "hang on to" or refuse to deal with the sin that exists between the couple.

Dysfunction can lead to divorce. It must be addressed in marriages or the marriage may dissolve. If it does not end, it may not be the type of marriage God has called the couple to have. Just as God did not tolerate a dysfunctional relationship with the children of Israel, so a couple should be willing to repent of anything that is sinful or damaging in their marriage. In the case of abuse, the abuser must repent and the victim should feel empowered to expect to be treated with love, respect, and mercy.

The church can be effective at addressing dysfunction in married couples by encouraging this model rather than bashing divorce. In the last thirty years, our attempts to address divorce have not been effective and we have seen an increase in divorce among Christians. Divorce recovery ministries have also increased and these ministries have been at the forefront of fighting the feelings of shame and guilt and trying to encourage members to see that divorce is not the end of their lives. Yet divorce continues even though the faith community has stood and condemned it. I have noticed that we blame society for divorce and the influence of society on our marriages. Yet we have not addressed or identified the real problem. Dysfunction is the problem. Dysfunction continues in marriages; but Christians believe they are doing the will of God as long as the couple stays together. We have had a hard time trying to condemn divorce and at the same time empower those who have been divorced. We have preached about a faithful God and Savior who will do anything to keep the marriage together, yet we have ignored texts, which suggest that God divorced those abusing the covenant. In some ways we have created confusion, caused resentment, or even worse, become dysfunctional in our own understanding of covenant and marriage.

Our role, instead, should be to encourage healthy marriages. Our churches should focus on addressing dysfunctional behavior in marriages by calling for marriages to reflect God's covenant. God's covenant is a model for marriages, and God's covenant expects the practice of mutual love, mercy, and justice within that covenant. We have a great opportunity to indirectly cause a decrease in divorce while at the same time strengthen marriages. We have the opportunity to call people to repentance before they go to the lawyer. Yet we also have the opportunity to call individual spouses to take a stand and be empowered to leave spouses who refuse to reflect the glory and love of God. These spouses can then grow stronger in their faith rather than become overcome with guilt.

Abuse and the Marriage Covenant

Abuse is a violation of a covenant between two individuals. A man who abuses his wife does not do so out of respect and love for her. He is attempting to control her. A man who verbally humiliates and degrades his wife is not trying to promote peace in the home; he is destroying the bond of peace that once existed. *Since the abuser is violating the marriage covenant, the abuser must be confronted, not the victim.* Too often the community of faith attempts to force the victim to keep the marriage together. This is impossible because no one keeps a marriage together by themselves. Covenant is a shared responsibility, and when it becomes one-sided, the underfunctioning partner violates it. Victims have been humiliated and shamed into returning to their abusive spouses. Faith communities give false hope that they can out-serve the evil in their partner. This is not theologically sound and is dangerous to victims. Holiness should be restored to the marriage covenant by addressing the abuse within relationship. Holiness comes by confronting sin rather than ignoring it.

Abusers and Confrontation

First, *the abuser must be confronted* concerning the sin of abuse and manipulation. Their commitment to the relationship and to God is reflected in how they treat their spouse. Questions such as "How does beating your wife glorify God?" or "How does God expect you to be in this marriage?" are important to address with an abuser. I have found that abusive men tend to point out why their wives cannot leave them, but they fail to admit that they are the cause of the marriage problems. In Mal 2:16, God confronted the dysfunctional partner in covenant, not the victim. Whether it is by the faith community and/or the victim, the abuser must be confronted for their behavior. They are the ones violating the covenant, not the victim.

Jesus' statements concerning marriage and divorce actually apply to abusers. Jesus' definition of adultery was a challenge to men to stop treating women as objects and victimizing their wives (Matt 5:27-30). Jesus' prohibition against divorce for any reason except sexual immorality (adultery) was another statement about husbands victimizing their wives (Matt 5:31-32; 19:1-9). Since any Jewish woman caught in adultery would be stoned, the realization that wives would be sexually pure was understood. Jesus was telling the Pharisees that they needed to stop looking for ways to find fault with their wives and be sexually faithful to them. Jesus clearly taught that marriage is a relationship where men are not to victimize their wives. The Apostle Peter carries this thought by reminding men that God will not hear their prayers if they are harsh with their wives (1 Pet 3:7).

Theologically, abusers violate many teachings of the Bible and the sanctity of the covenant if they are verbally, physically, sexually, and emotionally abusive and neglectful to their spouses. Marriage is not a relationship of enslavement, manipulation, control, or abuse. It is a relationship of empowerment, respect, support, and shared power. It is a relationship similar to that of God and Israel and of Jesus and the church. Abusers, rather than victims, need to be charged with violating the covenant. Abusers need to know that God, their spouses and families, the faith community, and our society oppose their behavior and will call them to repent. Victims need this support and should understand that leaving, seeking help and healing, and confronting this sin should be done because the marriage covenant needs to be made holy.

When confronting abusers it is important to remember that they can be manipulative and coercive. They may use minimization and denial concerning the sin of abuse. Abuse is not about anger; it is about control. They are not monsters; they are simply individuals who, like many of us, are afraid to get caught. They will resort to blaming the victims, police, their families, work and stress, you, or their background. They need to be reminded that repentance is not about them; it is about validating victims and making things right with God. While we all have sinned (past tense), *their sin* (present tense) is the focus. Once I had to confront a pedophile. He and his wife began to cry and explain how terrible it was that they could have no contact with children. They lamented the fact that they had been misunderstood. They felt that they had so much to offer a children's ministry, but because of "one mistake" they were not allowed to use their God-given gifts. I had to remind them that they were not the victims and that this was about their repentance and validating his victims. While confrontation is difficult, we must remain focused and keep the issue at hand. Abuse is a sin; no one deserves to be physically or emotionally humiliated. Our role in the faith community is to call them to repentance and turn them toward God. This means that we do not judge but that we confront them and give them the chance to repent. We have a legal system and many counselors who can make the decisions about the guilt or innocence of the abuser according to the law.

Victims Need Safety

Second, *victims need to know that leaving is well within their rights as a child of God.* God does not oppose their move to safety and healing. God confronts the sin of abuse. The victim does not need to feel guilty or ashamed for leaving and protecting themselves and their family. Marriage is not bondage, and the victim is not bound to stay in a relationship with one who practices evil rather than good. Victims should be encouraged to grow and develop a sense of self-worth in Christ as children of God.

My students in Albania were amazed to hear that an advocate, from their local abuse shelter, indicated that the women should submit to their abusive husbands with the hope of overcoming this abuse. My students had spent a week in my Gospel of Luke class and were well aware that confronting the abuser is a role for the church. They were surprised that their shelters had to help women in this way. I had to point out that at this time, many countries couldn't arrest an abuser due to cultural issues. One day that will change. Their role as young Christians is not to judge, but to speak out and call their society and government to address this issue and provide for the safety of women and children. They can also hold men accountable for their actions. Until societies change we all need to let victims know that they have rights.

One right victims have is *to be safe*. Since the covenant is to provide them love, support, and respect, they have the right to be in an environment where these needs are met. If their marriage provides the opposite or the works of the flesh (Gal 5:19-21), then they have the right to find safety. Victims have the right to call the police, bring in outside intervention, seek help from a shelter or family member, or press charges against their abusive partner. Sometimes outside intervention is necessary to provide balance and bring back shared power to an individual's life. A family caught in abuse has one person, the abuser, in control. Shared power has both partners working together to empower each other to develop. The victim needs to be empowered; there may need to be an equalization of power in their lives. This can only happen by breaking the abuse and dependency cycles and keeping the victim and family safe. Every woman has the right to sleep at night knowing that she is safe.

Another right is the victim's *right to choose*. Women who leave their abusive husbands commonly are immediately pushed by faith communities to forgive. *Forgiveness is a choice.* God chose to enter a covenant with humans. God chose to ignore the sins of a few people. God chose to punish the Israelites. God chose to forgive and bring them back to Jerusalem. God chose to send Jesus. Jesus chose to lay down his life. Jesus chose to forgive. We should never assume that God's forgiveness is forced. God can do whatever God wants (that's the advantage of being God). Yet, God overwhelmingly chooses to forgive. "But it is in God's nature to forgive," I am told. This is true, but the Bible shows us many times when God does not forgive. When we pray, we should thank God for choosing to forgive us and love us. God is not forced into a choice. God chooses to act and other times God chooses not to act. We should never assume that God will be forced into a decision and we should never assume we could manipulate God into forgiving.

Forgiveness is also a process. The Jews remained in Babylonian captivity for seventy years. God took time to forgive to allow them to reflect on their sin. In Dan 9:4-20, the righteous servant Daniel prayed for the sin of the people as well as his own. While he was a righteous man and highly respected by God (9:23; 10:11), Daniel took responsibility, as a leader, for the nation and their sins. Gabriel told Daniel that he would be given a vision and his prayers would be answered. The God who turned a deaf ear to the Jews when Babylon took them hostage (Jeremiah 11, 14) was listening to Daniel because of his righteousness (Dan 2:19; 9:23; 10:11). The seventy-year process helped the nation to repent and prepare for forgiveness and their return to Jerusalem.

Victims have the right to choose. They can choose to be angry and hurt. They can choose to prosecute and punish the abuser. When they first leave the abuser, they are hurting and full of fear and anger. With time they may choose to forgive, but it must be their choice. Forgiveness is a healing process. Forgiveness is a willing decision to *let go* of the pain and past sins of another. Forgiveness, however, is not the same as "reunion." David Livingston makes a distinction between forgiveness, reconciliation, and reunion.[29]

When one examines intimate violence as it actually presents itself, one finds that reunion of the violated and the violator is not always an appropriate response. The desire for reunion . . . is partly the consequence of a mythic view of reconciliation as reunion. This ideal of reunion has also been placed on the relationship of intimate partners and has become a model, at times even a "Christian expectation," that after violence one "should" try to reunite with one's abuser. As the church (bride) and Christ (bridegroom) have been able to reunite, so the survivor (bride) and the perpetrator (bridegroom) should also be able to reunite. This view does not take seriously the dynamics of intimate violence and does not take into account the physical and psychological scarring that has occurred. Reconciliation should not be confused with nor conflated into reunion.[30]

---

[29]Livingston, 81–82.
[30]Livingston, 66.

Reunion should never be the assumed solution, especially by a church, which often errs on the side of "saving marriages." Instead, reunion of the victim and the violator should be considered only after all precautions for the safety of the survivor are first met.[31]

A mimicry of reconciliation is present in the dynamics of intimate violence. It is, ironically, one of the most dangerous elements of the phenomenon we are exploring. Here we begin to see one of the dynamics disclosed at the mysterious center of the human being: a desire for reunion. Humans long to find relation after violation, and even if they may know that the relationship will continue to be violent, they will often seek some form of reunion instead of isolation. If the fundamental dynamics of intimate violence mock the fundamental goal of the Christian tradition, that is, forgiveness and reconciliation—then we as a theological and ecclesial community must be very cautious and aware that reconciliation is often misunderstood as reunion.[32]

Forgiveness, reconciliation, and reunion all suggest different levels of relationship. Forgiveness is the first step and has some preconditions. *Confrontation* is an important first step to forgiveness.

If your brother sins against you, go and explain this to him between you and he alone. If he listens, you have gained your brother. If not take one or two others with you so that by the mouth of two or three witnesses this is confirmed. If he doesn't listen to them then tell the church, and if he doesn't listen to the church treat him as a Gentile or tax collector. (Matt 18:15-17)

In this lesson, Jesus suggests that relationships can be strengthened or repaired through confronting the sinner. The one who has offended another must be made aware of their sin. Jesus calls us to confront the brother in order to help him to see his sin. Victims may never heal until they are able to confront their abusers with their sin. This is scary for victims. It takes time for them to feel adequately empowered to go to the one who has

---

[31]Ibid., 23.
[32]Ibid., 14.

offended them. The individuals whose abuser is dead may need to go to the cemetery to confront the abuser at the tombstone. There can be a liberating quality to speaking out about one's pain and telling the abuser, or representation of the abuser, how they feel. Society and the faith community must also confront abusers so that they understand that their behavior is unacceptable. Batterer intervention groups better provide this accountability to abusers, as opposed to individual counseling, since they provide a support network and the opportunity to form relationships with other men who confront abusive behavior. The prophets and prophetic books of the Old Testament are examples of this confrontation. God sent prophets to confront Israel so that the process of forgiveness could begin.

The parable of the unmerciful servant (Matt 18:21-35) occurs after the parable of the brother who sins against another. A king forgave an outstanding debt that his slave owed. The slave had begged for forgiveness and was freed from the debt. The slave then went and found another slave who owed him much less than he owed the king. The second slave also begged for forgiveness, but the first slave threw him into prison. The king found out about this and was angry and said,

> "I canceled all your debt because you begged me and you should have had mercy on your fellow slave like I had on you." The king was angry and turned him over to the jailers to be tortured until he should pay all he owed . . . "This is how my heavenly Father will treat each of you unless you forgive your brother from your heart." (Matt 18:32-35)

The unmerciful servant was a man who punished even after his friend repented. The point of the parable is that God will punish (and hand over to the torturers) those who refuse to forgive. While this verse is used to force victims to forgive, I believe that it suggests that victims should work toward forgiveness. Victims should not be forced to forgive but encouraged to choose to forgive.[33]

---

[33]Ibid., 67. "According to Matt 18:22, there is no limit to forgiveness within the community of Jesus. At the same time, the Gospels give clear denunciation of oppression at every level. Judgment is a reality within Jesus' ministry, but it is a judgment of the powerful and the religious elite. The balance between justice and forgiveness remains central to Christian theology throughout its struggle to embrace the truths revealed in the life and ministry of Jesus."

Repentance is the next step to forgiveness. When the nations heard the message of the prophets and repented, forgiveness followed close behind. Repentance is the point at which the victim is validated and hears from the victimizer. "I am the sinner, not you." "I chose to do evil, not you." When God warned Israel they were called to repentance. When Israel failed to repent, God did not forgive, God punished. Too often victims are told to forgive someone who is not repentant. Forgiveness can come without repentance, but reconciliation demands it.[34] Victims struggle with anger and fear not because they are weak but because they have not been validated.

> My point so far has been to suggest that it is not unreasonable to make forgiveness contingent on sincere repentance. Such repentance at the very least opens the door to forgiveness and often to reconciliation.[35]

Government batterer intervention programs and victims' services constantly find ways to validate victims and call abusers to repentance. Abusers providing financial support, avoiding harassment of the victim, attending counseling, and sometimes serving jail time are attempts to validate the victim. Churches must also encourage abusers to show their repentance and provide support for their families (2 Cor 7:8-12). Retribution and compensation suggest that the abuser takes responsibility for their sins and provide what they withheld from their spouses and children.[36]

---

[34]Kelman suggests that reconciliation involves the development of trust, transformation of the relationship to mutual responsiveness, and an agreement to address both parties' needs. It represents a change in each person's identity. This would suggest that the victim must change to become an equal partner within the relationship in order for there to be reconciliation. Herbert C. Kelman, "Reconciliation as Identity Change: A Social-Psychological Perspective," in *From Conflict Resolution to Reconciliation*, ed. Yaacov Bar-Siman-Tov (New York: Oxford University Press, 2004) 119.

[35]Jeffrie G. Murphy, *Getting Even: Forgiveness and Its Limits* (New York: Oxford University Press, 2003) 36.

[36]While Murphy suggests that retribution seeks to impose suffering on the abuser or criminal, I tend to feel that Livingston's view for this is related to calling the abusive husband to responsibility of his family and making sure that they are provided for. Schimmel suggests that vengeance and justice can be administered by neutral institutions, such as the legal system. Schimmel, 22–25.

One point of contention on this issue is the need for repentance. Can we forgive without repentance? Yes, it is possible. Can forgiveness substitute for repentance? No. Should we push repentance before forgiveness? Absolutely. We have three Major Prophets (Ezekiel, Isaiah, and Jeremiah) which contain extensive sermons from God about repentance. God calls for repentance and offers forgiveness. Our emphasis should be on confronting the abuser and calling him to repentance before we approach the victim and call her to forgiveness.

> Reconciliation, in situations of intimate violence, invites the perpetrator, the survivor, and the community to greater and fuller life through the healing of wounded relationships. The violator is welcomed into the community after he has been through the process of contrition, confession, and satisfaction. The victim/survivor is welcomed into a supportive community and is not told that she must reunite with her ex-partner but, rather, is invited to join a community of compassion, advocacy, and protection . . . Reconciliation must attempt to heal the internal brokenness of the perpetrator, allowing him to realize his own capacity to be loved by God, by others, and by himself. Healing in the interhuman sphere involves the perpetrator's relinquishing his desire to control or punish his partner and possibly his partner's capacity to forgive him. Yet, reconciliation, if it is to address the violation within the interhuman sphere, must also address the anger and resentment of the survivor of violence. To heal this resentment does not involve forgetting the violation, but creating the conditions for the survivor's being able to wish the well-being of the penitent batterer.[37]

Repentance makes it easier for a victim to forgive, and that is one focus of our ministry. If he chooses not to repent, she can choose to be angry for the rest of her life or to forgive.

Finally, the victim can *choose to forgive*. Forgiveness simply means to let go, and reconciliation means the reestablishment of the spiritual relationship of brother and sister in Christ. This is not the same relationship as in marriage. When a victim is validated, she can let go of the anger and pain caused by another.[38] Other times the victim is not validated but is

---

[37]Livingston, 82.
[38]Murphy, 36.

exhausted from the hatred and anger with which she has been living. At that point she can choose to let go of her anger and move forward. In both cases, it is a choice to forgive when they can. It is also a process that takes time and healing. Those who violate the covenant of marriage cannot force the offended spouse to forgive. Those who have not been in the victim's shoes cannot force them to forgive. But forgiveness is important to our healing. In the song *My Own Prison*, Scott Stapp sings about his anger and unwillingness to forgive his own past and pain. His anger has become a prison sentence. At the end of the song he sings, "I cry out to God seeking only his decision; Gabriel stands and confirms I've created my own prison."[39] Anger and vindictiveness can place all of us in a prison. We can let it go and forgive, but it is a process and a choice. Victims must move toward forgiveness, but they must also understand that it is something they choose to do.

Can people choose to forgive? It is possible, but it must be seen as a process. For all members involved in domestic violence, forgiveness will be part of their spiritual development. Victims should never be forced to forgive, but they can be encouraged to develop forgiveness. At the core of who we are as a faith community is forgiveness.

> For if you forgive people when they sin against you, your heavenly father will also forgive you. But if you do not forgive people's sins, your father will not forgive yours. (Matt 6:14-15)

> Father, forgive them because they do not know what they are doing. (Luke 23:34)

> Lord do not hold this sin against them . . . . (Acts 7:60)

Through forgiveness we call abusers to accountability and repentance. They have acceptance and someone who loves them enough to challenge them to become compassionate.

---

[39]Mark Tremonti and Scott Stapp, "My Own Prison," *Creed: My Own Prison* (New York: Wind Up Records, 1997).

What lies at the core of reconciliation is nothing less than the enchanting and overwhelming notion that even when a human has become so distorted and disfigured by egoism, rage, despair, and fear, that person will be embraced by the Christian community. The Christian community has within its treasure trove of symbols a call for reconciliation. We are called as Christians not to demonize those who act in evil ways but rather to call them to accountability and to love them. This required that we ferret out the true insights in this message of hope.[40]

Through forgiveness, victims, children, and families let go of their anger and hatred and pray that the abuser is transformed (although this will need to happen in a different church or counseling program). Through forgiveness, victims choose not to be like the abuser who is full of fear, anger, and confusion and low self-esteem issues. Victims and families can face the future with hope and choose not to let the abuser determine their happiness and spiritual choices. Through forgiveness, victims stop blaming themselves for the past and realize that their choice to be safe and protect each other was made through hope. Through forgiveness, victims realize that God is a loving God who empowers them to be compassionate and merciful with themselves and others.

Few abusive marriages have been salvaged. Hope is held out for couples who have reunited after intervention and extensive abuse counseling. Yet this process takes time and healing. What is important is that we protect victims and empower them to grow, heal, develop spiritually, and follow the journey to forgiveness. Abusers should be called to accountability and follow the journey to repentance. If reunion is not possible, there can always be hope of reconciliation and a relationship in which each parent becomes a role model for the children, one of courage through confrontation and the other of courage through repentance.

---

[40]Livingston, 65.

7

Abusive Families, Parenting, and Children

> We believe therefore that the psychological distress observed in children exposed to domestic violence results not only from their witnessing of periodic acts of violence but also from exposure to a batterer, and to his parenting style, in everyday life; in fact, we believe that the phrase "children exposed to batterers" is often more accurate than the current phrase "children exposed to domestic violence." For closely related reasons, we find that a batterer's parenting cannot be assessed separately from his entire pattern of abusive behaviors, all of which have implications for his children.[1]

This quote from two well-respected batterer intervention specialists comes as a result of growing concern over the presence of children in violent homes. The statistics on pages xii-xiii indicate that children in abuse homes are at risk of abuse themselves. Research continues to suggest that abusive parents have a detrimental effect on children. Witnessing acts of domestic violence,

---

[1]Bancroft and Jay G. Silverman. *The Batterer as Parent: Addressing the Impact of Domestic Violence on Family Dynamics* (Thousand Oaks, Calif.: Sage, 2002) 2

learning the process of power and control, and receiving emotional and physical abuse meant for their mothers, damages children every day. Three million children are exposed to acts of domestic violence each year.[2] Over one third of children in one study reported seeing violence used by fathers against mothers when a parent reported that no violence occurred. More than fifty percent of female victims of intimate violence live in households with children under the age of twelve. Children are killed in one-fifth of domestic violence homicides or attempted homicides each year.[3] Children in abusive homes are at great risk for emotional and physical abuse. When their mother leaves their father, they are at even greater risk.

I had taken the three boys to see their dad. This was my first real experience with domestic violence and divorce. I had recently finished college and was working at McDonalds while I figured out what I wanted to do with my life. I was a new Christian and was helping a small church in my hometown. One of my co-workers and her husband had been coming to church and had given their lives back to God. After a few months, he started drinking again and was emotionally abusive to his wife and three sons. He constantly threatened to kill himself and would hold a gun to his head and scream, "Daddy's goin' to kill himself!" He had attempted suicide regularly since he was sixteen and this thirty-two-year-old man lived his life drinking, changing jobs, and terrorizing his family.

She had had enough and finally left Joseph. The small church of mostly older people couldn't understand why she would leave her husband. Those of us at work tried to help her and the kids. We took turns, because the church would not help. I would take the boys one night a week while she worked. I also would take the kids to see dad every other weekend. As long as I was there, it was considered a supervised visit.

One afternoon I took them to see Joseph. I was playing with the two older boys (eight and six years old) and failed to see Joseph take the five-year-old into the house. Even when I realized that Joseph had the boy in the house, I stayed outside with the older boys because I didn't think anything would happen. Thirty minutes later Joseph yelled, "Ron, come here!"

---

[2]Ibid., 1.
[3]Ibid., 1.

I went inside and saw the youngest boy crying. "He don't want to go," Joseph said. All the boys started crying and began saying that they didn't want to go. Joseph was crying and wailing, which made the boys cry louder.

"Boys, I'm sorry, but the law says we have to go. We can see dad again, but mom's waiting for you," I said.

The boys stopped crying and went to the car. I could tell Joseph was mad at me. I told him that I didn't have to bring the boys by and that I was doing him a favor. "Next time don't play with their heads, or I'll stop bringing them by," I said. As we drove away, the boys quickly forgot about their sorrow and began to talk about seeing their mother.

Joseph was an emotionally abusive man. He continued to manipulate the children against their mother every opportunity he had. What I realized that day and many other days since then was that children can be abused even more when their mother leaves home. Visitation rights, weekends with an abusive dad, and phone calls from treatment centers or prison are not always in the best interest of the children. The following are quotes from sources concerning the effects of violence on children.

A 1999 Massachusetts Department of Youth Services study on children who witness domestic violence found that they are:[4]

1. Six times more likely to commit suicide.
2. Twenty-four times more likely to commit sexual assault.
3. Fifty percent more at risk for drug abuse.
4. Seventy-four percent more likely to commit crimes against others.

In general, the more frequent and intense the marital conflict, the greater the likelihood of child problems: witnessing unresolved marital conflict is more detrimental to children than witnessing satisfactorily resolved conflict, and conflict over children or childrearing issues appears to be more detrimental than conflict over other issues . . . children in families characterized by frequent physical marital violence display more behavior problems than do children in families characterized by less frequent

---

[4]Sheila Y. Moore, "Adolescent Boys are the Undeserved Victims of Domestic Violence," *Boston Globe* (Dec. 26, 1999) E7.

violence . . . children may misbehave in an attempt to end or prevent the escalation of marital conflict by shifting parental attention onto themselves. If children recognize marital violence as potentially lethal, they may be especially likely to act out in an attempt to alter the course of the conflict. [5]

Children's exposure to violence can cause them to adopt and practice violent interpersonal skills, become mediators or try to protect the abused spouse, and can experience Post Traumatic Stress Disorder.[6]

Children cry, express anger, freeze, evidence facial distress or bodily distress reactions . . . make requests to leave, or describe feelings of discomfort, anxiety, or concern . . . Children report feelings of anger, sadness, fear, guilt, shame, or worry . . . Physiological reactions also occur, including changes in heart rate, blood pressure, skin conductance, or vagal tone . . . Exposure to conflict also increases children's aggressiveness . . . and children's involvement in parental conflicts increases when there are high levels of marital conflict . . . A history of marital conflict in the home is linked with children showing greater emotional and behavioral reactivity, greater involvement in parental disputes, and more negative representations.[7]

Children learn to recognize ominous tones of voice and intimidating body language. They feel sharp pains when they see their mother humiliated or degraded. They are filled with an urgent desire to rescue her, but at the same time can feel paralyzed by fear, so they are left feeling guilty standing by and not intervening. Their innocence can slip away in the process . . . If their mother's partner is physically violent, they may shrink into corners trying to make themselves invisible, praying

---

[5] Jouriles, 178–79.

[6] Stephen A. Anderson, 5.

[7]Mark E. Cummings and Amy Wilson. "Contexts of Marital Conflict and Children's Emotional Security: Exploring the Distinction Between Constructive and Destructive Conflict From the Children's Perspective," in *Conflict and Cohesion in Families: Causes and Consequences*, edited by Martha J. Cox and Jeanne Brooks-Gunn (Mahwah, N.J.: Lawrence Erlbaum, 1999) 106–7.

for someone to come to lead everyone to safety. Or, if they are old enough, they may jump into the fray themselves and try to stop the fighting, hoping to be the peacekeeping force. If they happen not to be where an assault occurs, they still hear the screams and threats, the crashing of thrown objects, or the blows.[8]

Children are affected in normal activities, fear, sleep problems, explosive outbursts, poor interaction socially, poor conflict resolution skills, and other problems . . . Research has shown that witnessing adult physical aggression is more disturbing to children than observing other types of adult conflict . . . Children as young as one year begin to regress into states later diagnosed as "mental retardation" when they were exposed to parental hostilities that never went beyond the verbal abuse level. It is important to note for the question of contact with the abuser that the symptoms of retardation quickly disappeared after the parents separated.[9]

The effect of such abuse and neglect upon children is especially devastating. This is in part because a child's self-structure and defenses are weak and in the early stages of formation. Children also lack fully developed cognitive capacities, so they are even less able to understand what is happening to them than are adults in similar circumstances. Children are also more severely damaged by the tremendous power differential existing between themselves and significant adults.[10]

The sources of emotional and behavioral difficulty for children of battered women are many, with the actual seeing or hearing of acts of violence being only the beginning. The presence in the home of a batterer, usually in the role of parent or stepparent, has a wide range of implications for family functioning. Batterers tend to be authoritarian yet neglectful parents, with far higher rates than nonbatterers of physically and sexually abusing children. Battering changes the nature of children's crucial relationships with their mother, through mechanisms that include undermining her authority and interfering with her ability to provide

---

[8]Bancroft, *When Dad Hurts Mom*, 13–14.
[9]Straton, 5.
[10]Means, 24.

care. Batterers often engage in efforts to create divisions within the family and can be highly manipulative.[11]

The evidence seems clear. Children exposed to abuse and abusers are affected emotionally and physically. Bancroft and Silverman suggest that children of batterers also suffer from traumatic bonding.[12] When their mother leaves her abuser, she usually does not have to visit with him. She takes out a restraining order and he can have no contact with her—but this does not always include the children. Children then may be subjected to the same manipulative, authoritarian, and controlling father that their mother can now avoid.

Figure 12: Abuser's Impact the Children's Belief System and Values, which cause children to believe that:[13]

- Victims are to blame for the abuse.
- The use of violence is justified to impose one's will or resolve conflicts.
- Boys and men control, women and girls should submit.
- Abusers do not have consequences for actions.
- Women are weak, incompetent, stupid, or violent.
- The abuser's anger caused the violence and is an excuse for this behavior, rather than control and manipulation.

Children can learn unhealthy behaviors from batterers. While some children are resilient enough to be unaffected by abusive behavior, the majority are emotionally scarred by their abusive fathers. We must acknowledge that children exposed to abuse and abusers are at great risk for many problems. We have blamed children's behavior problems on the trauma of divorce rather than the modeling of dysfunctional behavior. Yet divorce is better than the daily exposure to the dysfunction of abuse.

---

[11] Bancroft, *The Batterer as Parent*, 2.
[12] Ibid., 37–41.
[13] Ibid., 48–51.

Women in abusive relationships should be willing to leave their spouses, and the church should see this as a way to protect their families. In 1 Cor 7:16, Paul allowed the unbelieving spouse to leave if they did not want to stay in the marriage and support the Christian spouse so that there could be peace in the home.

> Otherwise your children would be unclean, but as it is they are holy (7:16).

Keeping it together for the sake of the kids can be more destructive than leaving for the sake of the kids.

Issues of Parenting Roadblocks

Many times victims choose not to leave their abusive spouses because they feel they would be responsible for breaking up the family. Yet they are not the ones damaging their children. Abuse is contrary to God's plan for the family as well as contrary to the Spirit (Rom 12:9-15; Gal 5:20-26). The family is to be a place of peace, wholeness, and empowerment. Victims, especially mothers, need to know that they have the right to protect not only themselves but also their children. Rather than "keeping the family together," families in abuse need to be encouraged to work for peace in the home. Victims should be allowed to keep their children away from violence, manipulation, and controlling behavior.

I do believe that divorce is a traumatic event for children. The breakup of the home, the visitations, the transferring from home to home on weekends and during the summer all affect the emotional stability of children. Research is clear on this issue.[14] Fighting, arguing, confrontation among spouses, ex-spouses, and family and using children as informants

---

[14]"Divorce can involve feelings of guilt, rejection, and animosity on the part of the children. Children are required to accept a new milieu, new values, and new people in their lives," Gunilla Dahlberg, "The Parent-Child Relationship and Socialization in the Context of Modern Childhood: The Case of Sweden," in *Parent-Child Socialization in Diverse Cultures*, ed. Jaipaul L. Roopnarine and D. Bruce Carter. Advances in Applied Developmental Psychology 5 (Norwood, N.J.: Ablex, 1992) 128.

are some of the emotional tactics that couples experience in divorce that are equally as traumatic to children as the divorce. The effects of divorce or the attitudes surrounding abuse make divorce even more traumatic.[15]

> Children are far better off—as a number of studies demonstrate—living in peace with their mother than being exposed to a man who abuses her. In fact, the studies indicate that children are better off living with a single parent than being around parents who fight frequently even *without* abuse . . . The research that purports to show how damaging single mothering is to children has failed to control for income and for prior exposure to abuse, so that the difficulties observed are actually the effects of poverty and of the fact that many children witnessed abuse while their parents were together—and that is why the mother is now single.
>
> It is worth noting that we never seem to hear reports claiming that children are damaged when they are raised by single *fathers*. The reality is that single parenting is difficult, exhausting, sometimes isolating work, but both women and men can do it well, and the world is full of well-adjusted, successful people who grew up with one primary parent, male or female. What matters above all is to live in a home where there is safety, love, and kindness—and adequate economic resources.[16]

We attempt to call spouses to be Christian or moral in divorce by removing conflict from the presence of the children and agreeing not to place the children in the midst of their battle. While this is difficult, it is possible, and I find that when a sense of peace is established between ex-spouses, reconciliation is more likely.

I was asked to speak to a group of young mothers who were still attending high school in a special program sponsored by the public school system. The school provided child care while they attended classes. I was addressing healthy dating relationships and dating violence. Having a nineteen-month-old child myself, we spent time talking about our children (it made me feel old). One of the young women said that she knew her

---

[15]See Miller's quotes; notes 13 and 14, chapter 1, pages 10–11.
[16]Bancroft, *When Dad Hurts Mom*, 321.

son was going to have problems because she was a single parent. I began to share with them that parenting is harder for them, as a single parent, but not necessarily bad for the children. It was clear to me that they had been given the "anti-single-parent home" statistics. We were able to talk about healthy parent-child relationships as well as their responsibilities as a parent in dating and possibly marrying. I shared with them the research being done in Sweden and other countries on divorced families that has found that having a healthy family is better than having a dysfunctional two-parent family.[17]

Children can develop normally in a single-parent home, but parenting will be difficult.[18] In dysfunctional families (those with alcoholism, drug abuse, pornography, abuse, etc.), the continued exposure to these behaviors is more damaging than removing the children from the home.[19] While our government understands that children should not be exposed to these behaviors, our churches seem to be unaware of the damage that can be caused in the home. I have found that many ministers have preached on the "evils of divorce" but have never been willing to discuss how children can be "mentored in dysfunctional behavior." Divorce may be traumatic

---

[17]Dahlberg; E. M. Köhler, *HurMycket Ska Egentligen ett Barn Behöva Tala?* (Stockholm: Carlssons, 1990); L. Köhler, *Barn och Barnfamiljer I Norden* (Lund: Studentlitteratur, 1990); G. Lassbo, *Mamma-pappa-barn. En Utvecklingsekologisk Studie av Socialization i Olika Familjetyper* (Acta Universitatis Gothoburgensis, 1988).

[18]"It is difficult to make general statements about how children will react to divorce. It is my suspicion that some will have real difficulties due to instability, and conflicts within the family, while others will be able to handle the situation relatively well, and even gain new competencies. The parents' ability to cope with and frame the experience in a positive light seems to be of greatest importance. The capacity to effectively cope with transitional difficulties is closely linked to parent's material and cultural situation. More likely than not, divorce will be harder on parents and children living under conditions of economic scarcity and in families where parents have inflexible work schedules." Dahlberg, 129.

[19]In the past, pro-family advocates have presented statistics suggesting that children in single-parent homes are more prone to self-destructive behavior than those in two-parent homes. While these statistics are compelling, they do not take into consideration the following: 1) the exposure of the children to the dysfunctional behavior of the divorced parent, 2) the destructive and manipulative behavior of the divorced parents on the children and each other, 3) the counseling or lack of counseling given to the children, and 4) the effects of *parentification* on the oldest child. These issues have a greater affect on the behavioral development of children than divorce, and they can also be present in a two-parent family.

for children, but abuse, alcoholism, drug abuse, and other dysfunctional behaviors can damage them physically, emotionally, and spiritually. A clear examination of the evidence should lead us to a conclusion that a peaceful and holy home is preferable to one steeped in sin and dysfunction. Should churches support divorce? The question should be: "How can churches address dysfunction in the home?"

Victims Need to Be Empowered

Victims need to be *empowered to leave their abusive spouses,* since this is one way to provide peace and safety for all those in the home. One reason that victims must leave with their children is that the exposure to an abuser affects the children's emotional and physical development. Children living in abusive homes and witnessing violence can display the following behavioral problems:[20]

- Attention deficits
- Hyperactivity that interferes with learning and attention
- Learning delays
- Sleeping problems (nightmares, fear of sleep, bedwetting)
- Body pains (headaches, stomach problems and pains)
- Delays in language acquisition
- Poor academic performance
- Missing school often (truancy or sickness)
- Falling asleep in school
- Sibling rivalry or hierarchy

A second reason for the victim to consider leaving is that children who are in abusive homes have a greater risk of being physically abused themselves. The narcissistic belief system of the abuser increases the chance for a woman to be abused when she is pregnant. If abuse is occurring in the relationship, pregnancy can increase the frequency or intensity of the

---

[20]Bancroft, *When Dad Hurts Mom*, 76, 145–46; and Boston Medical Center <www.childwitnesstoviolence.org>.

abuse.[21] There is great risk for the baby during this time, and many victims have claimed that the abuser hit them in the stomach when they were pregnant. Abusive men also may abuse their children. Bancroft suggests that forty percent of abusive men carry their behavior pattern over onto other family members, and they have a higher rate of violating children's boundaries.[22] Children many times, in an attempt to protect their mothers, get in the way of the husband abusing his wife and receive the brunt of the violence.

Another reason to leave, according to Bancroft and Silverman, is that the strong similarities in the behavior of abusers and pedophiles warrant removing children from abusive homes.

> Multiple studies demonstrated that the mothers of incest victims are likely to be battered by the perpetrator. Other studies indicate that daughters of batterers have unusually high rates of incest victimization. These two sets of studies taken together suggest that exposure to batterers is among the strongest indicators of risk of incest victimization.[23]

While the studies do not suggest that all abusive men are pedophiles, the similarities between the two behaviors and high incidences of pedophilia by abusive men indicate that children in abusive homes are at greater risk of being sexually abused by their abusive parent or a step-parent. This evidence suggests that we should not always assume that the statement, "he abuses me but he wouldn't hurt the children," is true. Abuse victims must be encouraged and empowered to leave their spouse or have them removed. Abused women have the right and responsibility to protect their children and provide a peaceful home for them to grow and develop.

Finally, exposure to batterers increases a child's chances of being involved in abusive relationships in the future. Not all abusers were raised in abusive homes, and not all from abusive homes continue to abuse. Yet

---

[21]Rebecca L. Burch and Gordon G. Gallup Jr., "Pregnancy as a Stimulus for Domestic Violence," *Journal of Family Violence* 19:4 (2004) 243–47; and Sandra L. Martin, April Harris-Britt, Yun Li, Kathryn E. Moracco, Lawrence L. Kupper, and Jacquelyn C. Campbell, "Changes in Intimate Partner Violence During Pregnancy," *Journal of Family Violence* 19:4 (2004) 201–10.

[22]Bancroft, *When Dad Hurts Mom*, 53,55.

[23]Bancroft and Silverman, 84.

parents, the surrounding culture and media, and/or peer relationships or gangs can model abusive behavior.

> At the same time, many men who abuse women—roughly half, in fact—
> did not learn their values and behaviors from their fathers or stepfathers,
> but instead absorbed abusive attitudes from peers, from other male
> relatives, from television, or from pornography. So when we speak of
> stopping the 'cycle of abuse,' we need to broaden our thinking beyond
> just transmission from father to child, but also from the *culture* of each
> generation to the culture of the next. If we want to stop abuse, we have
> to transform social attitudes.[24]

Children need to be removed from an environment that supports power and control over another and encouraged to develop compassion, love, and a sense of encouragement.

Victims must also *be open with their children about what they have experienced*. Many of the abuse victims do not talk about the abuse with their children or families. Sometimes they are ashamed, and other times they believe that ignoring the problem may make it go away. Children, however, remember their experiences and try to process what they see and hear. They have questions that many of us wish to ask: "How can daddy be nice and then mean?" "Why did you stay with him knowing that he beats me?" "Why did you go back to daddy again?" "Are all people this cruel?"

> Avoiding the subject will not lessen their fear; in fact, children feel safer
> if they can talk to their mothers about how frightened they get, and
> discuss actions they might take next time their father erupts.[25]

Children need to know that what their father did was wrong and unacceptable. If children do not learn to make distinctions between right and wrong, they will be more likely to practice the same type of manipulation when they become adults. Children need to hear from their mothers that it was good for them to leave and that they will now be safe.

---

[24]Bancroft, *When Dad Hurts Mom*, 313.
[25]Ibid., 303.

They need to know that mom is doing what is best for them by leaving dad and trying to protect her family.

While I was in Tiranë, Albania, I met a very nice family one evening as I had returned from supper. The young woman and her mother and little baby were visiting at a table in the courtyard at the place where I was staying. I was feeling homesick for my sons, especially the baby, and stopped to see her baby. The young woman was a doctor and spoke English fairly well. Her mother spoke a tiny bit of English. My Albanian was good enough to get by with a nightly conversation. After a week of visiting, the mother told me that her father had been a well-known war hero and prime minister of Albania. His name was Haji Lexi. As I asked her questions about her father I turned to the subject of Enver Hoxha who was a partner with Lexi until Lexi died. Hoxha then became the prime minister of Albania in the 1960s, and as a communist dictator he proceeded to begin a countrywide persecution of all religious groups. Under Hoxha, the Albanian government tortured, murdered, and persecuted Muslims, Jews, and Christians during the 1960s. I asked the mother what she thought of Enver Hoxha. Was he a bad man or a good man? The daughter then entered into the conversation.

"You see, we have learned to look at the good in Enver Hoxha rather than the bad. So I would say he was a good man," she said.

"But," I replied, "He murdered many innocent people."

"Yes, yes, that is true," she said, "we feel that it is better to see the good in him rather than the bad."

When people experience the most horrible acts of cruelty at the hands of another human, the response is to dichotomize the character of that individual. In order to live with the memories of Enver Hoxha, many of the Albanian people have had to separate Hoxha's good deeds from his bad. Rather than saying that Hoxha was an evil man, it is safer for them to concentrate on the good and ignore the evil. Many times this is a coping skill used by victims of abuse. Since they feel helpless or feel there is no hope of repentance, they learn to adapt and accept the abuser. The problem is that this provides the opportunity for an oppressor to continue to victimize others. Since the oppressor is not called to accountability, they have the opportunity to seek out those who will not confront them on their sin. By condemning the actions of the abuser, the victim and her children have the opportunity to acknowledge good and bad behavior in their past and future relationships.

When women leave their abuser they provide the opportunity for the children to process and heal from the affects of domestic violence. Divorce/separation can be difficult and traumatic for children, but they need an environment in which they can discuss their feelings and what they have witnessed. Key elements that are helpful for children's healing from abuse are:[26]

- A close relationship with their mother
- A safe place to live
- A good relationship with their siblings
- A good connection to other loved ones, peers, and self
- The ability to talk and express their feelings openly
- The freedom to release distressing feelings through:
  * Crying
  * Raging
  * A deep release of fear
  * Laughing
- The ability to obtain good information about abuse
- Being empowered to:
  * Think critically at teachable moments
  * Address the culture and media issues that support abuse
  * Define how they cope with fear and discouragement

Victims and their children can heal together and form a united front so that they can approach their future and their abuser with confidence and courage.

Finally, victims must *work with an established domestic violence support system*. There is no shame in asking for help or receiving aid in order to become self-sufficient.

Without consultation plans are frustrated
but with many counselors they succeed. (Prov 15:22)

---

[26]Ibid., 269–70, 292–311.

A wise person listens to counsel. (Prov 12:15)

There is no shame in seeking advice from abuse counselors and advocates. Our government has provided our communities with grants, trainings, and programs to help domestic violence victims become independent and peaceful parents. Victims need to take advantage of abuse survivors support groups. These groups help women heal, forgive, find employment, practice non-violent parenting,[27] and find financial aid or rental assistance so that they do not have to return to their abuser in order to survive. Shelters, homes, centers, and women's groups provide a plethora of resources for abuse victims seeking help and support. Prevention is still the best medicine for abuse.

Churches Must Become Involved

Churches and faith communities must also *encourage victims to protect their children*, even if it means being a single parent. Churches can help women who have been victims of abuse overcome the shame associated with being a single mother and empower them to stand on their own and provide for their family. Single mothers struggle with a deep sense of shame and guilt from feelings that "I couldn't make my marriage work." Women who take a stand and leave or remove their dysfunctional spouses should be commended for their courage and desire to provide a peaceful and safe home for their children as well as themselves. Jesus warned the disciples about "causing little ones to sin" (Matt 18:5-6). When we allow children to be exposed to violence and abuse, and do not try to protect them, we commit a great crime against God. Churches and ministries must stress that protecting children and encouraging them to "be children" is the desire of Jesus.[28]

---

[27]This is important since many times the abuser uses physical discipline on their children. Victims will need to find non-violent forms of discipline for their children so that they will not find themselves accused by their husband of physically abusing their children.
[28]For a discussion of the Lukan text and challenge to act on behalf of children (Luke 18:15-17), see my article: "Kingdoms, Kids, and Kindness: A New Look at Luke 18:15-17," *Stone Campbell Journal* 5 (2002) 235–48.

Churches *must work with government agencies in order to provide victims with the best resources possible*. Many churches distrust government agencies and believe that they will actually make the problem of abuse worse and break apart the family. The email from the victim's advocate (Figure 1, pp. xxi–xxiii) suggests that it is the faith community that is complicating the problem of abuse in families. Churches can work with government groups and provide what they cannot provide, spiritual support. Women's groups and divorce recovery ministries can support victims by reminding them that God loves them and that they have a safe spiritual home. The children can develop relationships with other children and see healthy, loving families worshipping God and practicing peace and forgiveness. Churches may also have access to financial aid and personal donors who can help the women provide for their families.

Youth ministries also have a great opportunity to work with young people in this area. Children who are exposed to domestic violence many times will talk about it with their friends. When young people address the issue of violence occurring in their home, youth ministry leaders become mandatory reporters. Many youth ministers have kept the issue confidential, yet this continues the negative effect on the child. The longer young people are exposed to this behavior, the more they are damaged emotionally and spiritually. Rather than ignoring the problem, youth ministries must help the children address the problem and find safety. While the Bible says to honor father and mother, it also tells us that ignoring the cries of the oppressed distance us from God (Prov 21:13). One college student asked me what I had to do by law if someone told me that their father had abused them. "What would happen to you legally if you did not tell?" he asked. "Well, legally there are many issues and circumstances involved, but I do know that God would punish me if I did not help the person," I said. At the core of what we do there is the love of justice and truth that leads us to protect anyone from abuse and oppression. There must be a realization that children who live in abusive homes are emotionally and physically at risk.

Youth ministries should also keep the issue of domestic violence in mind when addressing issues such as rebellion to parents and sex outside of marriage. I have listened to speakers at youth rallies speak out about respecting parents. How does a child of abuse hear this statement? How does a child who has been sexually molested respond to a lesson about sex outside of marriage and virginity? Children of domestic violence and abuse struggle with shame and guilt, and the way we approach these two topics is important if we want to minister to them. It is a good idea to assume that at least one of the teens who is listening to any sermon or devotional may be living in an abusive family. How we address these issues will affect how they see themselves and how they see God.

Abusers Must Be Called to Change

Since batterers have a tremendous affect on children, the process of repentance for an abusive spouse must include repentance to the children. Abusers must be challenged to *keep an emotional and physical distance from their families* until they are adequately progressing in their batterer intervention counseling. The temptation to manipulate and control will be hard to avoid, and it can only be overcome with intensive therapy and counseling. Children must be allowed to be children and no longer be a part of the power and control cycle of abuse.

Second, batterers must be challenged to *financially provide for their wives/former wives and children.* While visitation rights may one day be granted, it is important that the batterers heal and their families grow and develop in a peaceful environment. It is not their fault that they are living as a single parent family and trying to pay the bills and make ends meet. The abuser must take responsibility for his actions by providing them with financial help so that they can experience life free from violence and abuse.

Third, batterers must *support their wives in their own personal growth and development.* Their wives have a hard road ahead, and they must back away and let them heal. The temptation is to humiliate, criticize, and shame their wives, which are still processes of control and manipulation. Abusers must encourage and empower their wives to be the best that they can be, but this may only come by letting them leave and grow, as they desire. An abuser should put his main focus on becoming a man of God rather than getting his family under his control.

Conclusion

Victims of domestic violence struggle with single parenting issues. Past studies and statistics have been used to enforce the "keep it together at all costs" mentality that has enabled victims to continue to stay in an abusive relationship. This mentality has not been healthy for the victim or the children. The rate of divorce has been increasing in the United States and in churches, but there is still a sense of shame associated with it. The solution is not to encourage or discourage divorce; the solution is to discourage and address dysfunction in the family. If the abuser is willing to repent and go through the process of counseling to change behavior, then the future of the family may be brighter. If the abuser will not change, the wife may have no option other than divorce. Being a single parent should not be a curse; it should be a choice. The church can help the wife focus on herself and her family to rebuild self-esteem and peace.

The church can also give both the victim and her family hope that they can develop spiritually and emotionally even though they are a single-parent family. Studies in Sweden suggest that there is little difference in the cognitive ability, social adaptability, and personality development of children brought up in single-parent or two-parent homes.[29] The church can provide resources and a place of acceptance for children who have come out of abusive homes. Rather than condemning divorce, the faith community should address dysfunction. Rather than judging single-parent homes, the church should support them and offer help. Rather than feeling sorry for these children, the church can empower their parents to be compassionate, strong, and merciful parents.

If the church is in the position of working with the abusive parent, it can accept the batterer and call him to accountability. It can encourage the abuser to take responsibility for his actions and to provide for his family. He should pay for their temporary housing, counseling, and medical bills. While this places a tremendous strain on the abuser, the church can be there to encourage him and let him know that this is the just action and part of the repentance process. The church can support him in attending counseling and confessing his sins to his spouse/ex-spouse,

---

[29]Dahlberg, 128–29.

children, and other family members. The faith community can help him to change his behavior in order to be the compassionate and loving father that God has called him to be.

8

Issues of Victimization

Have you ever noticed that our society seems to focus on victims rather than oppressors or abusers? This may seem like an odd statement, but read the newspaper or listen to the news reports concerning crime. Notice how the reports are presented. "*Woman raped* by stalker." "*Man attacked* by thief." "*Child molested* by his father." "*Thousands killed* in terrorist attacks." What is wrong with these statements? They do not give an accurate picture of the event. They are passive accounts of the story. The real issue should be addressed by blaming the rapist, thief, or molester rather than the victim. What if the headlines read differently? "*Man stalks and rapes* woman." "*Thief attacks and brutally beats* man." "*Father molests* his own child." "*Terrorists kill* thousands."

Too often the reports, investigations, and charges focus on the victim, not the offender. This is why we hear people ask questions that seem to accuse the victim. "Why was she out at that time of night?" "Why was he in that part of town?" "Why didn't the child tell someone?" "Were these people in the wrong place at the wrong time?"

Compassion for abused women is building across the continent, but we are still a society with deep habits of blaming victims. When people

200

suffer misfortune, we jump to analyzing what they should have done differently: She should have fought back, she shouldn't have fought back; she was in an area where it wasn't wise to be walking; she didn't plan ahead; she didn't try hard enough or think fast enough . . . These judgments can tragically limit the support and compassion that an abused woman receives from her community . . . In addition to oversimplifying her options, blaming the mother has the effect of reinforcing the abusive man's own messages to her.[1]

Unintentionally, these questions suggest that it was the victim's fault or choice to be raped, beaten, molested, or killed. Yet, the victim is not to blame. The abuser is committing the crime and needs to be held accountable. Notice how many victims' services exist in our government programs. We help victims, but how often do we confront abusers? Are we afraid to address oppression, or do we have a preoccupation with victimization?

I experience the same situation in churches. Mel Gibson's *The Passion of the Christ* reminded me how, for centuries, Christianity has been obsessed with the victimization, suffering, and pain of Jesus. While my wife and I appreciate the work that has been done by the director, it seems that the movie is an example of how Christianity has become overly focused on the cross and the victimization of Jesus Christ. The graphic display of the suffering of Jesus seemed to be overdone, and at times I felt like I was watching a cross between *Braveheart* and *Rocky*. The movie suggested that Jesus suffered more than any other crucified individual, and it even took liberties to intensify the beatings, which seemed to move the audience to tears (me being one of them). It is important for us to understand the suffering of Jesus, but there is a reason why the Bible briefly tells the story of the crucifixion. There is a reason why the apostles did not dwell on the death and crucifixion of Jesus as much as they did on his life.

Necrophilia and Victimization

Necrophilia is a preoccupation with or love of death. While it may have sexual overtones, it indicates a romantic notion of death or dead things. I

---

[1] Bancroft, *When Dad Hurts Mom*, 313–14.

feel that sometimes the church may be guilty of necrophilia. This may be a major cause for the victimization that I tend to see in our ministry to victims. Why necrophilia? The church has focused on the cross for centuries. It has been the emblem of Christianity. It has become the center of our preaching and a place for us to return when we need to reflect on our spiritual lives. I am a member of the churches of Christ, which have a Biblical tradition of celebrating communion every Sunday morning. People tend to complain about the communion devotionals if they do not emphasize the death and suffering of Jesus. In communion talks there is a strong emphasis on the death of Jesus and remembering his sacrifice and a sense of remorse and sorrow as we take the emblems. We are reminded weekly that Jesus suffered for us. Sometimes communion talks will focus on the last few hours of Jesus' life and include a graphic description of the flogging, crucifixion, or beatings from the soldiers. I have heard speakers tell us that we should shed a tear or hang our head during this time. If we do not, something is wrong with us. So often these reminders cross the line and tell us "we killed Jesus," something that the Bible does not suggest.[2] At times, communion becomes a funeral service, and if its not, people get concerned.

This same emphasis is in our Christian literature. What is the problem with Christianity, they ask? We are arrogant, proud, cocky, rebellious, or materialistic. What is the solution? We need a healthy dose of the cross to keep us in line. Many popular books have been written to call us back to the cross, which is supposed to represent who we are as Christians. We are reminded that those crosses on our necks are not real crosses. Real crosses are hard, painful, and shameful. Volumes of books have been written lamenting the fact that we have forgotten the value of the cross. We need

---

[2]Peter is the only one to state, "you killed" Jesus directly to his audience (2:23; 3:14-15; 4:10,27; 5:30). This statement occurred in the presence of the Jerusalem Jews and religious leaders who played a role in the trail and crucifixion of Jesus. Neither Peter nor Paul made this accusation to the apostles, those Jews not in Jerusalem during the Passover/crucifixion, or to the Gentiles who had no knowledge of the Messiah. Peter told the Roman Centurion, Cornelius, that "they crucified" Jesus, referring to the Jews in Jerusalem (10:39). It seems unbiblical to charge all people with the sin of crucifying Jesus. I feel that *indifference* and *abandonment*, rather than murder, have typically been the sins of God's people, including those of the Old Testament, as well as the early disciples in the Gospels.

to be reminded of the old rugged cross, the authors tell us. The cross keeps us in line, like a good switch. The cross humbles us and knocks us to our knees, like a good kick to the groin. The cross keeps us focused on our sin and its consequences, like that disappointing glance from mom or dad when we've done something bad. The cross is there to keep us from ever feeling too good about ourselves. It is a reminder that we are nothing, we are worthless, and we are worms (*for such a worm as I* . . .).

Yet, after all is said and done, we are supposed to find peace in the cross. God sent Jesus to die for us, and we should find comfort in the fact that Jesus received our beatings and death. He suffered for us so that we would not have to feel the wrath of God. Jesus and the cross are similar to the big brother who received the punishment that we deserved, and then reminds us of that every week. What a thrilling thought! One time Jesus took my punishment and for the rest of my life, every week, someone reminds me of that. Every time I come to church I am reminded that I should get a beating, but Jesus took it for me. I am reminded that I daily sin and kill Jesus. Does he still feel the nails every time I sin?

Not only this, but I am also reminded that we are all sinners (despite what the Bible tells us) and that everyday I commit a myriad of sins.[3] There is nothing I can do to stop this. I can try, but ultimately I will sin each day. To think that I can stop sinning is seen as arrogance and pride. The cross then becomes my whipping post. I am told that the cross reminds me that I have a substitute for my punishment who continues to suffer every day for my/our sins. Jesus is continually a victim, and every Sunday he is victimized. Not only is Jesus victimized, so are we. The story of the cross is told over and over again and we are forced to feel the horror and sadness that the apostles only briefly mention in their writings and sermons. In fact, our modern "cross historians" are more graphic than Matthew,

---

[3]Note that there is a difference between *all have sinned* (Rom 3:23, past tense) and *we are sinners*. There is a difference between *we are justified* (made righteous, present tense) and *we will one day be righteous*. There is a difference between *we are to put off sin* (Eph 4:17ff), *do not continue in sin* (Rom 6:1ff), and *put these sins to death* (Col 3:5) and *I cannot stop sinning*. One view is theological while the other is traditional. The Christian has hope that they are not a sinner, they are righteous, and that they can get rid of sin. James said that if we resist the devil he will flee from us (Jas 4:7). This does not suggest we are perfect; it suggests that we can become like Christ and conquer sin in our lives. We have hope *to stop sinning* and no longer live in it!

Mark, Luke, and John felt they needed to be! If we do not grieve, we may feel unspiritual or arrogant. If we want hope, we are told that the cross is where we find it. Is it a wonder that critics of Christianity have sensed this victimization and spoken out against it?

> When everything necessary to ascending life; when all that is strong, courageous, masterful and proud has been eliminated from the concept of a god; when he has sunk step by step to the level of a staff for the weary, a sheet-anchor for the drowning; when he becomes the poor man's god, the sinner's god, the invalid's god par excellence, and the attribute of divinity—just what is the significance of such a metamorphosis? What does such a reduction of the godhead imply?[4]

> Not their love of men but the impotence of their love of men keeps the Christians of today from—burning us.[5]

> "Love one another" it has been said is the supreme law, but what power made it so? Upon what rational authority does the gospel of love rest? Why should I not hate mine enemies—if I "love" them does that not place me at their mercy? Is it natural for enemies to do good unto each other—and WHAT IS GOOD? Can the torn and bloody victim "love" the blood-splashed jaws that rend him limb from limb?[6]

In my past studies and meetings with atheists, Satanists, and philosophy students, I find that, as with Nietzsche and LaVey, there is a distaste for Christianity. This distaste is not because we conquer sin and love others, but it is because we try to overcome sin by claiming to be victims to it! We have become hypocrites in their eyes.

There is compelling evidence that we have been wrong. First, have you noticed that the Gospel writers did not feel the need to tell us all the graphic details of the crucifixion? Have you noticed that only one chapter

---

[4]Frederich Nietzsche, *The Anti-Christ*, trans. H. L. Mencken (Tucson: See Sharp, 1999) 33.
[5]Ibid., *Beyond Good and Evil: A Prelude to a Philosophy of the Future*, trans. Walter Kaufmann (New York: Vintage, 1966) 84.
[6]Anton Szandor LaVey, *The Satanic Bible* (New York: Avon, 1969) 32.

of each gospel is devoted to the whole crucifixion story? From what we know about ancient Roman writings, some writers wished to defend their heroes who were unjustly killed. They wrote biographies that were similar to funeral eulogies. These biographies and *encomiums* were written to defend the nature, character, deeds, and unjust death of the individual.[7] The gospels also were written to defend the nature and death of Jesus.[8] The gospel message of the church is about the life of Jesus, not the death. This was evident in the preaching of Peter and Paul in the book of Acts.[9] What was their emphasis? Their emphasis was on the resurrection, not the crucifixion.

Imagine going to a funeral of a friend who died of cancer. When a friend stands up to speak, how do they talk about the deceased? Do they say, "She lived a great life but I want to talk about the agony she faced for six hours last week. I want to talk about her hair falling out, her screaming in pain, and her begging to die." Wow, what a downer! That is not what the eulogy is about, is it? In the eulogy people talk about her life, her accomplishments, and her courage. This was the purpose of the *encomiums* and the Gospels. The message of the gospel and resurrection brought hope, healing, forgiveness, power, and the work of the Holy Spirit, not guilt and depression.

---

[7] Craig S. Keener, *A Commentary on the Gospel of Matthew* (Grand Rapids: Eeerdmans, 1999) 20–22; Ben Witherington III, *New Testament History: A Narrative Account* (Grand Rapids: Baker, 2001) 16–23.

[8] Witherington points out that the Gospels are similar in length to an ancient biography. Witherington, *New Testament History* (Grand Rapids: Baker, 2001) 22.

[9] Notice that Peter's sermons (Acts 2:14-40; 3:11-26; 4:8-12; 10:34-48) and Paul's sermons (Acts 13:16-41; 17:22-31; 22:1-21; 24:10-21; 26:1-23) make a brief mention of Jesus' death, but they focus on his being raised as a testimony to God's power. I think that it is also interesting to note that the persecution and rejection that Paul faced was associated with his teaching on the resurrection. The Athenians scoffed at the resurrection (17:32). Festus stated that Paul was crazy concerning the resurrection (26:24), and Paul claimed to be on trial from the Jews over the resurrection (24:21). In Acts 5:34-39 the Jewish rabbi Gamaliel mentioned the death of revolutionaries and the scattering of their followers. He then seems to add support to the early church's mission. The test case was not in the death of the leader, Christ, but in the actions of the followers. Peter's statement to the Sanhedrin that God raised the one they killed (5:29-32) could only be proven, in Gamaliel's eyes, by the actions of the church. It was not the death of Jesus in question, but the resurrection. It seems that the emphasis of the resurrection is Luke's major theme in Acts. For Luke, the growth of the church in the world was not due to the cross but the resurrection.

But doesn't Paul tell us that the cross is the "crux" of Christianity? Paul does speak of the cross and emphasizes that part of his ministry, but even more so he discusses the resurrection.

1 Cor 1:23	We preach Christ crucified.
1 Cor 2:2	I desired to know nothing while I was with you but Jesus Christ and him crucified.
1 Cor 15	Paul ends the letter with a long discussion on the value and necessity of the resurrection for the Christian. Paul indicates that he preached also the resurrection, they believed in it, and that it gave hope for the church.
Gal 6:14	May I never boast except in the cross of our Lord Jesus Christ.
Gal 4-6	Paul emphasizes being born of the Spirit and living in freedom. Crucifixion is the putting away of slavery (circumcision and the law) but the Spirit gives life and freedom.
Eph 2:1-6	We died and are made alive, raised, and are seated with Christ.
Phil 3:10	Paul seeks to share and attain the resurrection of Jesus.
Rom 6:5	We are united in the death and resurrection of Christ.
Col 2:14-15	Christ triumphs through the cross.
Col 3:1-4	The Christian is told they have been raised with Jesus and need to put away sin.
Rom 1:4	Jesus was declared *with power* to be the Son of God by his resurrection from the dead.

While there are many references to the cross, Paul's point is that the resurrection provides the power, hope, victory, and justice for life on this earth and for the next life. The cross is important, but *it should never overshadow the resurrection.*

I spoke at a conference for Christians and domestic violence. As I spoke on this issue I pointed to the 100 foot cross, to my right, which was on stage by the choir section. I said, "No disrespect intended but I think we overemphasize the cross. What about the resurrection?" Isn't it interesting that this symbol has taken center stage, near the pulpit and choir section (area of praise and beauty). Has the cross dominated our worship, preaching, and sense of praise? My statements in churches, including the one where I attend, have evoked hostility at times. Why are we so upset with challenging our emphasis on shame and suffering? Many others, however, have come to me and said, "I have been feeling this way for years." My response to both groups is, "Why not the resurrection?"

This is what I believe we have missed. We are like the disciples on the road to Emmaus (Luke 24:14-32). This was the first sermon about Jesus given to an outsider after the resurrection. What was the lesson? Jesus was killed, and the tomb is empty. That was it! No hope, no joy, and no power. Yet Jesus revealed himself to them in the breaking of bread. In the breaking of bread and teaching of scripture, they recognized the risen Jesus rather than the dead Jesus. It was the resurrected Jesus that caused their hearts to burn!

And so it is with us. We are so overcome with grief, shame, and sadness in Jesus' death that we can't see the living Lord. Communion and Bible study have little life, because we only see the cross and an empty tomb with questions and a handful of testimonies. In our centuries of focus on the crucifixion and the cross, we have neglected the resurrection. In fact, it seems that we have completely ignored the resurrection. The very stage of the story that brought hope, healing, forgiveness, vindication, and freedom became a footnote to the story. In *The Passion of the Christ*, the resurrection was given a brief reference at the end of the movie. The resurrection is the heart of the gospel and should be the focus of the Christian faith. It makes Christianity different than any other religion. It illustrates the impossible and proves the power of God.

I don't want anyone to misunderstand what I am saying. I am not devaluing the cross, suffering, and death of Jesus. Those actions show the love and passion that God has for all of us. I am not trying to minimize the sacrifice Jesus made for all humans. I am not despising the story of the passion of the Christ. I am trying to deflate what *we have done* with the crucifixion and inflate what *we should be doing* with the resurrection. It is my contention that our fixation on the death, pain, and suffering has caused us to neglect the very power of the Gospel. It seems that we have become disoriented because of our fixation on the cross. Our symbol should be an empty tomb! It is my belief that communion has become a funeral service rather than a time of rejoicing. Rejoicing in the death of Christ? No! Rejoicing in the living Christ! "But Jesus says, 'do this in remembrance of me.'" How do you remember Jesus? Is Jesus a dead Lord or a living Lord? Is Jesus a victim or victorious?

"But shouldn't we mourn our sinfulness and the suffering of Jesus?" Yes, at least to some extent. I think that the early Christians, though, would tell us much more to praise God for our new life, get moving, and get rid of the sin in our life. Instead of enabling people to continue to sin and feel shame and guilt and reminding them that they are worthless, we should be calling people to holiness and healing. Which causes people to heal—guilt or hope? What causes our hearts to burn?

> In him you were also circumcised, in the putting off of the sinful nature, not with a circumcision done by human hands but with the circumcision done by Christ, when you were buried with him in baptism and *raised with him through your faith in God's power, who raised him from the dead.* When you were dead in your sins and in the uncircumcison of your sinful nature *God made you alive with Christ, he forgave us all our sins . . .* (Col 2:11-13)

An example of this type of victimization is seen in how we have portrayed the terrorist attacks on New York City on September 11, 2001. I remember the day well. I came in from my morning run and my wife told me what happened at the World Trade Center with the first tower. We watched the news reports together and later saw the second plane crash into the other tower. We saw people jumping and finally the towers crumble. Hour after hour we watched the news play the gruesome event over and over. We were mesmerized and victimized not just by the terrorists but also by the media. We relived the horrible event for months and felt the anger, pain, and grief continually. It was a reminder that we were helpless and hopeless victims. Yet how many of us only think of the attack when we hear about New York City or 9/11? I can tell you what I think about. I remember the concert afterward. I remember watching *The Who* play to a full audience. I also remember the joy of the citizens when they received news that New York City had become a finalist to be host to the 2012 Olympic Games. I remember seeing the stores and buildings near Ground Zero after they had remodeled and reopened. One of the greatest rock bands sang, "We won't get fooled again," and months later the city climbed out of the ashes to rebuild and again compete with the rest of the world. They won!

Yet the media seems to throw the horrible image of death and destruction before us as if to say, "Don't forget the horror of that day." I feel that very few people have any other image of New York City. I find that some get uncomfortable when I suggest that we need to go on. Are we made to feel guilty if we mention that we do not want to see again the airliner crashing into the building? Are we told that we are insensitive and cruel if we focus on something else every September 11? Is there any other vision that should be put before us as a memorial to the families? Visions of hope and healing drive people forward. While I will never forget the tragic events of 9/11 and the tremendous emotional pain of the victims, families, and police and fire-fighters, I will always remember the vision of hope and courage shown as New York City climbed out of the ashes and chose to rebuild. It is this vision that gives us hope that faith, love, courage, healing, and community win!

Abuse Victims and Victimization

I would like to suggest that a third major roadblock to the healing of victims of domestic violence is *victimization*. If a woman who is abused comes to worship in some of our churches, the image of a victim is continually before her. If suffering is our main calling, then her calling is to suffer at home. If Jesus suffered and won, then her victory comes through her submission to an abusive husband and looking for a victory through this suffering. If Jesus was helpless and a victim of sin, then she is also helpless and a victim of sin. If we are unworthy, sinful, or flawed humans, then she is even more so. Remember, her husband has told her how unworthy she is. If he attends church with her, then his cross is to keep her in line and her cross is to obey him.

I remember once hearing a minister hold up a bag of trash and say, "Without God we are all garbage." Wow, what an uplifting thought! Yet Gen 1:26-27 says we are in the image of God. This is another ploy to remind us to stay in line and hang our heads. In spite of this, we should be happy that Jesus died for worthless trash like us. Is there any difference between our churches and abusive homes? Our images of death, suffering, and shame will only enable victims to continue to be victims. Our preoccupation with shame and guilt will never empower the world to become what God wants it to be. Our passive reports of the story of Jesus make us all victims in the end.

> Communities and cultures use shame to keep people in line, to protect the traditions of the culture, and to keep religious laws sacred . . . People who are shame based don't have the ability to separate their guilt about unjust or unkind actions from shame about unworthiness made evident by shameful actions. If you've ever tried to tell a shame based person that his or her behavior was unacceptable to you, you've felt the difference right away. The shame based person won't be able to see the action as the issue. He or she will feel condemned to the core by your very mention of any mistake. This deflects the conversation away from the guilt-producing behavior and reinforces the shame.[10]

The glorification of Jesus' suffering also leads to a theological sadism and an image of God as a violent, angry, sadistic father. When the cross becomes the goal of love, love is distorted and perverted.[11]

A suffering Savior is an incomplete savior. Like the men on the road to Emmaus, we only see a dead Jesus and empty tomb. Victims see a victimized Savior and an empty tomb that only causes questions. They will find scriptures that support their suffering and suggest that they can serve their tyrant spouse into salvation. They will take to heart the sermons that give them a sense of false hope that they can overcome abuse by patient submission. They will *amen* when preachers tell them that abuse is their cross and that they must carry it alongside Jesus. They truly love God, but they believe that if they could be more submissive (or Christ-like in their eyes) they could save the marriage. They feel that God has called them to suffer and their abusive marriage is their cross. As Jesus told the disciples to pick up their crosses daily, so she daily shoulders the burden of shame, rejection, abuse, and guilt (Luke 9:23-27). She feels

---

[10]McClintock, 27–29.
[11]Gill-Austern, 308.

that spirituality is *overfunctioning* and out-serving the *underfunctioning* spouse. She is like Hagar sent back to abusive Sarah. She is like David returning to violent Saul. She is like Tamar begging Amnon, her half brother and rapist, to take her back.

Oksana had called to tell me that she wanted anger management training for her husband.

"Why don't you have him call me," I said.

"Well, he really doesn't think he has a problem," she said. "He says that I am the cause of this."

"Oksana, when you told me earlier that there was abuse, what did you mean?"

She immediately responded with, "Pushing, shoving, holding me down, verbally abusing me, pulling my hair."

"Has he ever hit you or assaulted you?"

"Yes," she said. "I know this is not right, but I have been living with this for eight years. His son verbally abuses me now. My family wants me to get out."

"Oksana, God does not want you to be treated this way. You deserve to be respected and loved by your husband."

"Yes I know. I love God. I go to Evergreen Community Church, and I heard a great sermon about marriage yesterday. I really feel I can commit to this and make it work. I can be a better wife . . . "

"Hey Oksana," I interrupted, "God does not expect you to stay in a marriage where you are being abused. Evergreen Community Church has not been open to what we teach about abuse and marriage. The Bible teaches that your husband is breaking the marriage vows by abusing you. Your family and your Lord love you and want you to be safe, as well as the children."

"I know," she said. "It's hard."

"You can come in and talk anytime. We won't force you to leave, and we will just listen. But we want you to be safe. God wants you to be safe!"

Oksana was like many other women with whom we talk. She knew that her safety and self-respect were to be priorities, but her faith community reminded her that being a Christian meant being a victim.

Somehow they had convinced her that by serving and taking it on the chin she would be able to change a violent and controlling man. She was also wrongly taught that God expected her to be a victim and suffer abuse at the hands of a man who did not love her.[12] That church taught her that the way Jesus changed the world was to die for us. Is that all that is needed for transformation?

Children can also be affected by this victimization. If they have witnessed abuse, they have learned that bullying is a means to get what they want. They have also seen that the abused find a way to survive by being good and catering to the abuser. In the church, submission will be viewed as a means of survival rather than a willing and loving attitude of love and sacrifice. Serving may become a compulsion for children of abuse, because they do it out of fear rather than love. They will also have a view that God is powerless to help victims, and their anger will be seen as they wrestle with a God who saves Shadrach, Meshach, and Abednego from the fiery furnace, but does not respond to the cries of their mother or themselves to be saved from their fiery and abusive parent. Victimization in the church will force them to keep their feelings and questions to themselves and will propose a false reality in their world of abuse and trauma. They will learn that bullies must be served, abusive parents must be supported, and victims receive no power from God to protect themselves.

> Children pick up on the threats, whether implied or explicitly stated, that are communicated by the abusive man's explosive outbursts and aggressive body language, and your flinching or frightened reactions. The research on children's exposure to partner abuse shows that they are aware of much more of their father's violence than the parents think they are, and can sometimes describe incidents in detail that both Mom and Dad didn't think the child even saw. These experiences are scary for children. They worry that their mother will get hurt, perhaps so severely

---

[12]"Disrespect and abuse are almost synonymous. You don't abuse someone you respect, and you don't respect someone you abuse. I have almost never had a client who didn't exhibit various kinds of contempt, superiority, and demeaning behavior toward his wife or girlfriend—it comes with the territory of abuse, and in many ways *is* the abuse." Bancroft, *When Dad Hurts Mom*, 30.

that she won't be able to look after them. They lie awake in bed staring into the dark or wake up later from nightmares. And they worry that someday he will turn his violent behavior toward them.[13]

Abusers and Victimization

Batterers who come to a church that has this "victim theology" will also have a hard time healing. First, abusers do *feel that they are victims* and that others are causing the unjust suffering. If they have been served with a restraining order or mandated to a batterer intervention program, they will feel victimized by "the system." Churches with a victim and shame-based theology will not be able to confront the abusers and call them to accountability. They will only enable abusers to play the role of victim and blame everyone else. Serving will be manipulation, and submission will become a means to coercion!

Second, abusers *may become predatory* in a church community and look for women who are victims. The reason many predatory ministers and church leaders have been able to practice pedophilia, physical and sexual abuse, and/or power and control over members is because they are in an environment that provides them with victims. It can be easy for those in religious leadership to manipulate women who have been victimized. They trust these leaders and seek advice, comfort, and guidance from them.[14] The victims need to be empowered. Empowerment helps victims become strong and self-confident. Victimization keeps them dependent on strong personalities. Abusers will pick up on this and victimize others. They need to be in an environment that promotes justice. This means that the community of faith has the responsibility to help the abuser overcome his nature and tendency to re-offend. They must remind abusers that they are expected to change, and that the Gospel calls them to transform into loving, peaceful, and compassionate men.

---

[13]Ibid., 34–35.

[14]This is why I question whether ministers who have had affairs or have been abusive should be restored to ministry without years of repentance and counseling. It is not just an affair or abuse, it involves victimization, it involves stalking, and isolation. It is an abuse of power.

Third, abusers *will be encouraged to stay victims*. Abusers must take responsibility for their actions and change their behavior. They are not victims and should not expect to be victims. They are to be reminded that the spiritual community is not a place of victimization but one of empowerment.

Steve was attending church with us. He had been released from prison for abusing his wife and mandated to a batterer intervention program. I referred him to a group that met at our building. He had a tough time at first. He was highly confrontational with his counselor and his parole officer. He came to church and I told him he needed to stick with the counseling and that we would provide a place for him to develop his faith. He found a listening ear with our members. Many began to empathize with him, feeling that we lived in a society that had been unfair to this young African American male and that his wife must have been a scheming witch. At times you could hear him get worked up as he retold the story and blamed his wife and the system. It seemed that many of those who listened to him became overwhelmed with his "mini sermons" and discussions about his mistreatment. Fortunately some of our men were familiar with our abuse ministry and encouraged him to stay with the program. I met with Steve to pray and reminded him that he made his own choices. With Steve it always seemed to be someone else's problem or fault. Everyone was against him. I would encourage him to turn to God and to remember that this was a long process. I reminded him that God was blessing our abuse ministry with the batterer's group and that this was the right thing to do. As time passed he accepted responsibility for his choices. He would begin by blaming his ex-wife but then would back up and say, "but I chose to do it and I am responsible." I found that Steve was growing only because he was continually reminded that he was not a victim. He always had a choice to make and the responsibility to choose a different path. The church needed to support the batterer's program and hold him accountable for his choices in life.

Steve will only move forward if he acknowledges that his choices are his responsibility. He must choose to do good rather than evil and remember that God has called him to be active rather than passive. He is not a victim of sin but a victimizer of others. He must choose to do what is right at any cost.

One way that churches can help abusers is by accepting that vindication can result in a positive feeling. Being overcome with anger and vengeance is unhealthy, and vindication can bring a sense of awareness to those who victimize others. This is a reflection of our moral commitment to a God of peace, who calls people to live in peace and justice.

> Moral commitment is not merely a matter of intellectual allegiance; it requires emotional allegiance as well, for a moral person is not simply a person who holds the abstract belief that certain things are wrong. The moral person is also motivated to do something about the wrong—and the source of our motivation lies primarily in our passions or emotions.[15]

> Those who have vindictive dispositions toward those who wrong them give potential wrongdoers an incentive not to wrong them. If I were going to set out to oppress other people, I would surely prefer to select for my victims persons whose first response is forgiveness than persons whose first response is revenge . . . If we do not show some resentment to those who, in victimizing us, flout those understandings, then we run the risk . . . of being "complicitous in evil."[16]

As Murphy suggests, the community of faith should present a sense of morality by reflecting a sense of vindication for victims. Abusers should be accepted and loved but also reminded that they are not the victims and they need to change. The community can be a source of tough love for abusers by their expression of anger for their actions and sins. This anger will not be motivated by personal pain but by a sense of moral justice, holiness, and spiritual devotion. The community can be stern yet loving.

> No longer will individual victims of wrongdoing be free to pursue individual—and thus unpredictable and socially dangerous—revenge. Rather the community will, as it were, take on the personae of victims

---

[15]Murphy, 19.
[16]Ibid., 19–20.

and act in their names—act in the regular, procedural, proportional, and predictable manner that we associate with the rule of law.[17]

Abusers can feel a sense of stability in a community that loves them yet condemns their actions. But they must be willing to change and face the long road of pain, suffering, and struggle that is necessary to modify their abusive behavior.

Was/Is God a Victim?

Much of what I have written may disturb the reader if Jesus is seen as a victim. Was Jesus a victim? Has God ever been a victim? I think that the answer to these questions begins with a definition of a victim. First, a *victim suffers unjustly*. What happens to them is not their fault or their choice. Victimization is not punishment. The victim receives pain and suffering that is undeserved. What is happening to them is unfair and should be stopped. Second, a *victim is not in control of the situation*. They have no power to start, stop, or change the amount of suffering. While they may feel a false sense of control in the cycle of domestic violence, it is the abuser who is practicing the control. Victims many times are helpless and powerless to change the situation. Finally, *victims suffer because of the works of evil*. There is no value in what is happening to them. God is not punishing them or acting upon them. They suffer because evil is active. Victims cannot make something good come out of their suffering because nothing good has been in their suffering from the start. A victim is being affected by evil.

While in this unjust world of suffering, victims may find a way to survive. Much of their survival depends on reframing their view of reality. If one is victimized and cannot change the situation, then they will change their outlook. They will have to believe that God has a *purpose for/to their suffering*. Since God is in control of all things, God has a plan for this process. God is seen as one who ordains this suffering. The victim is to *endure* this suffering and *find meaning to* the suffering. Like Job, they assume that God has brought evil upon them.

---

[17]Ibid., 20.

Yahweh gave, *Yahweh* took away,
blessed is the name of *Yahweh* (Job 1:21b).

Unfortunately, Job was not able to read the beginning of the book, as we have, so he was not aware of the war between God and Satan that went on around him. Because he was suffering, his perspective was that God brought suffering upon him. In fact, Job never even acknowledges that Satan exists. It is Satan who brought evil on Job, but Job was trying to find meaning *to* his suffering rather than meaning *in* his suffering.

The experiences of suffering, to those who try to find meaning *to* suffering, become a means to greater good and have an appearance of goodness. With this comes the desire for or glorification of suffering. While this may be a method of survival, it ignores the basic premise that victims suffer unjustly due to the work of Satan and evil choices by other humans. Suffering is experienced, accepted, and many times expected by victims.

> Sexual and domestic violence are forms of involuntary suffering. Neither serves any useful purpose; neither is chosen by the victim; neither is ever justified. Yet both cause great suffering for large numbers of people.[18]

Finding meaning to suffering is a passive form of spirituality and a passive resistance to evil in the world. The Christian, with this view, is not able to oppose various forms of evil or personal injustice. The Christian only learns to accept all things that happen as if they are by the hand of a mysterious God. With this view, suffering is expected and accepted as part of our spiritual growth.

Suffering that is chosen is not victimization. A person who chooses suffering for a greater good is not a victim. In Hosea, God chose to take unfaithful Israel back as a wife (Hos 2:14-23). God chose to be faithful in the covenant even when the people of Israel broke the covenant and were punished. God also chose to initiate a new covenant with those who rejected the Creator (Jer 31:31-34; Ezek 39:25-29). Yet, God's people again turned away and dishonored God (Mal 1:6). God called them to

---

[18] Marie Fortune, "The Transformation of Suffering: A Biblical and Theological Perspective," in *Christianity, Patriarchy, and Abuse, A Feminist Critique*, ed. Joanne Carlson Brown and Carole R. Bohn (Cleveland: Pilgrim, 1989) 143.

repentance and warned them to change their ways. God promised to visit them after Elijah turned them to their Lord (Mal 4:1-6). God continually initiated relationships with humans knowing that this might bring suffering. Yet this was by choice. God was not a victim because the Lord always has the ability and right to respond as the Lord chooses.

When Peter felt the need to fight, Jesus said, "Put your sword back in its place . . . Do you think I cannot call on my Father who will at once put more than twelve legions of angels at my disposal?" (Matt 26:52,53). Jesus made the choice to suffer. He willingly and knowingly chose to die. While the Romans and Jewish rulers felt that they had victimized Jesus, the Gospels defend the Son of God and suggest that he willingly chose to suffer.

Figure 13: Was Jesus a victim?

John 10:15	I lay my life down for the sheep.
John 10:17	I lay down my life only to take it up again.
John 10:18	No one takes it from me, but I lay it down of my own accord. I have authority to lay it down and authority to take it up again.
John 19:11	You would have no power over me if it were not given to you from above.

The Spirit also enters humans knowing that they can choose to go with or against the will of God. While it is possible for the Holy Spirit to be quenched or grieved by humans (Isa 63:10; Eph 4:30; 1 Thess 5:18), the Spirit is never a victim.

The suffering of God was not victimization. God was not powerless even though this suffering was unjust and the result of evil. Throughout the Bible, God was in control but chose not to act at times. When God decided to punish, God punished. God is never the victim. God sometimes made a conscious choice to be abused because there was a greater purpose or plan involved. God also made a conscious choice to judge the wicked after the suffering. Paul said this of Jesus and the resurrection:

Who [Jesus] being God in nature did not try to grasp at equality with God, but emptied himself taking the nature of a servant by being like a human. And looking like a man he humiliated himself (allowed himself to be humiliated) and became obedient in death, even death on a cross. *Therefore God has exalted him to the highest place and given him the name that is above every name, that at the name of Jesus every knee should bow, in heaven and on earth and under the earth, and every tongue confess that Jesus Christ is Lord to the glory of God the Father.* (Phil 2:6-11)

Because Jesus chose to suffer and be humiliated, God glorified him by giving him the name that is above all (*Yahweh*). Jesus showed us that he is God not because he died for us but because he has been exalted. But he was exalted because he chose humiliation over divinity. Again, God is not a victim but God willingly chose to suffer.

Abuse victims, however, do not have the choice to suffer. I have heard many people say that battered wives must want to be a victim, which is why they return to their abusers. This is not true. They return to their abusers because they are coerced, manipulated, and afraid. Their abuser doesn't say, "Come home so I can hit you again." Their abuser promises to change. They choose to return because they believe he will change. They are victims because the abuser lies and continues to control them. They are victims because they do not deserve to be abused. They are victims because they are not in control. They are victims because of evil. Many times they are victims because they are afraid to leave their relationship.

> Some people object to the systems approach precisely because it does not seek to apportion blame, and because it describes each participant's role in an interconnected network. This idea implies, critics say, that a woman who is beaten by her husband is as much to "blame" for his behavior as he is. It reinforces the view of woman as masochist: If she stays in a bad relationship, she must enjoy its pain. And it obscures the critical moral line between victimizer and victim . . . It is not masochism that keeps women (or men) trapped in destructive patterns, but the fear of greater pain or loss if they change the pattern or leave.[19]

---

[19]Tavris, 274.

Victims do not choose to suffer for a greater good, and they should never be told that being abused would serve a greater purpose. Their suffering is unjust and angers God. It is wrong for us to compare their suffering to Jesus' suffering! While Jesus understands their pain, Jesus does not approve of their suffering. God has always been a God who protects and vindicates the weak, poor, oppressed, and afflicted. God is angry over their abuse and does not call them to continue as victims. God chose to suffer so that they could be free (Luke 4:19). God expects the church to address this issue.

What about the persecution of Christians in the Biblical text as well as throughout the world today? Is that victimization? Yes, but there is a difference between living in a nation where you can do nothing about the abuses and living in America where it is illegal to abuse your spouse, children, or other family member. The church is not to encourage victims to stay victims; the church is to empower them to be strong. The church is to confront the oppressors and abusers. The church is to protect the oppressed and be the mouthpiece for God. Even in cultures or countries that tolerate abuse, the church must stand against it.

I shared this with my Albanian students. "It doesn't matter that the Albanian shelters can't address male violence; God has called *you* to confront oppressors." In the next chapter we will discuss the prophetic role of the church. God did not call us to be victims but to be strong. "*For God did not give us a spirit of cowardice, but of love, power, and self-control*" (2 Tim 1:7). God is not a victim and has not called the church to be a victim to evil in the world. The gates of hell cannot be stronger than the church, because the church is moving forward into hell to fight, resist, and break down the doors of evil (Matt 16:18).

What are the Results of Victim Theology?

I feel that a victim mindset (victim theology) has a dangerous effect on victims and abusers. This mindset can, and has, distorted how victims see their lives and their marriages. It causes them to seek a relationship with their abuser that is both unsafe and unhealthy. Victim theology can also affect the self-esteem of women and children who have experienced abuse in their lives. First, victim theology can be illustrated in the view that *we are all sinners.* Although we are all in the image of God, we have sinned and fallen from God. The Gospel calls us to come back to God and live for Jesus. When we come back to God and are in Christ, we are not sinners but are righteous.

> Since all have sinned and fallen short of the glory of God [past tense], they are justified [perfect tense, also righteous] by his grace through the redemption that came through Jesus Christ. (Rom 3:23-24)

The perfect tense indicates that we are now righteous because of past action—Jesus death and God's grace. Paul is not stating that we are all sinners but that Jews and Gentiles had all sinned and needed God's grace. Because of Jesus' death, Jews and Gentiles could become righteous just as those of us in Christ became righteous (present tense). In chapter 6 Paul reminded the Romans that their baptism was a past action that put them into Christ.

> Or don't you know that all of us who were baptized into Christ Jesus were baptized into his death? We were therefore buried with him through baptism into death in order that, just as Christ was raised from the dead through the glory of the Father, we too may live a new life. (Rom 6:3-4)

> In the same way, count yourselves dead to sin but alive to God in Christ Jesus. Therefore do not let sin reign in your mortal body so that you obey its evil desires. (Rom 6:11-12)

Because of this death and burial in baptism, they had put away their sinful lives. They were given a new life so that they would no longer be slaves or victims to sin. They had the potential to stop sinning and be holy before God. Victim theology, however, does not hold out any hope for holiness.

The second result of victim theology is the belief that *we cannot stop sinning.* While the Bible does teach that we all make mistakes and will sin, it also teaches that there is a possibility that we can stop a sin that has dominated our thoughts and lives. We are to stop being victims of sin and put sin out of our lives. James wrote that we could resist Satan and cause him to flee from us (Jas 4:7). Paul suggested that God believes we can resist sin and will not tempt us beyond that ability (1 Cor 10:13). Again, we are not victims to sin but have the potential and ability, through the grace of God and power of the Spirit, to walk away from sin and throw sin out of our lives.

Finally, victim theology reminds us that *perfection is impossible*. This reminder places us in a position to avoid setting goals about spiritual growth, Bible study, and holiness, because that would be considered self-righteousness. Because we are imperfect we avoid the feeling that we can remove sin. Yet perfection and maturity are translated from the same Greek word.[20] Instead of perfection we should expect *maturity* to be the goal of the Christian life. While perfection is something that we claim not to have or are not able to attain, maturity is possible for all humans. Maturity is possible, maturity is expected, and maturity is a process. All of us are expected to become mature; yet no one can be perfect. The church should encourage maturity rather than try to discourage perfection.

Victim theology sets us up to fail. Since we have "killed Jesus" and since "Jesus was a victim," we have prepared the church, as well as abuse victims, to expect suffering and injustice. Our worship services remind victims that our role in life is to expect suffering and to let others victimize us. We have suggested that true spirituality is seen not in transformation but in failure. We have held up fallen leaders as models and turned our heads to the sins of others. In our attempt to justify sin, we have forgotten holiness. In our attempt to comfort people, we have lost the power to transform them. Maybe this is why domestic violence advocates see the faith community as a hindrance rather than a powerful ally.

---

[20]The Greek word *telos* is translated complete, perfect, mature, and finished. Since the Jewish language does not have a future tense, it seems logical to believe that ancient Jews saw the future in a limited perspective. They based their time on life stages. People began as children, then later became mature, and then died. Maturity was seen as the goal of every individual or work of nature. To be complete, or mature, meant that you grew to what you were intended to be. I find that *telos* is used in Eph 4:13 to suggest maturity and growth. Leaders of the church are to help the members become mature or complete. This is an attainable state. Paul also discussed maturity in 1 Corinthians 13. He mentioned being a child and growing to adulthood. This transition was described as maturity (*telos*). Maturity is a better definition of *telos* than is perfection, because it suggests an attainable state *for all God's children*.

Abigail Abbot Bailey was a woman living in New England during mid 1700s. She was a devout Puritan and was very strong in her faith. Her husband Phineas Bailey was a harsh, cruel, and abusive man. Abigail's journal indicated that he was not a strong religious believer and that he emotionally and physically humiliated his wife through abuse, affairs, and neglect. Yet Abigail felt called to accept the abuse by her husband's hand as part of the plan of God. She once wrote:

> Now I pray God to make me truly humble to feel my unworthiness of the least mercy, and to see that every good gift is from God's free grace. May I give glory and praise to him for the many mercies I do enjoy, and for faith in Jesus Christ, though some deep affliction be laid upon me. I think I can truly say, "In my distress I sought the Lord" and "I found him whom my soul loveth." My complaint came before his throne. Oh, that I may ever have right thoughts of God, and adore him for his goodness, and his wonderful condescension to regard so vile a worm, as I feel myself to be. May I ever feel as nothing before him.[21]

Abigail Abbot Bailey's view is not unlike many women today. Christianity unfortunately has enabled victims to continue to submit to their abusive husband and through overfunctioning, attempt to out-serve them.

How Does the Resurrection Change This Approach?

If we place the resurrection as our main focus, our views of sin and spiritual growth change. First, we realize that while we live in a fallen world we are born again into a *risen kingdom*. The Kingdom of God is a place of resurrection, victory, celebration, and hope. Paul stated that the kingdom "is righteousness, peace, and joy in the Holy Spirit" (Rom 14:17). The kingdom is a place where God's justice and mercy reign. While the world may have corruption and sin, the kingdom is a place of retreat from the oppression of society. Love, justice, and compassion reign in this kingdom. Victims do not have to be abused and should be protected from their

---

[21]Ann Taves, ed. *Religion and Domestic Violence in Early New England: The Memoirs of Abigail Abbot Bailey* (Bloomington: Indiana University Press, 1989) 59.

abusers. Children can see healthy, loving, compassionate families. Abusers can acknowledge that they are meant to be better than they have been and have the responsibility to change and repent before God and the church.

Second, rather than guilt, shame, and sadness, the church becomes a place of *healing, forgiveness, and hope.* Victims can be protected and supported. We can empower them to be strong. The Spirit gives victims power and courage to transform their lives as well as the lives of their family. Victims are not told to carry their cross but to rise up and break free from captivity. The church must be acting by the Spirit and providing that hope, peace, and empowerment to women victims. Our greatest joys in this ministry are seeing the women get their children back and move into their own homes to raise and provide for their children. While divorce is always hard on their children, it is much more important that the wife provide for herself and her children by living in a house of peace. Abusers can find a place of acceptance as men and women created in God's image. When I baptize men who have been abusive, I tell them before the congregation that they are now to be men of peace. The Spirit can transform any abuser just as it did Saul of Tarsus.

Abuse Victims and the Resurrection

How does the resurrection affect abuse victims? First, it gives them a sense of *empowerment.* The same God who raised Jesus from the dead can also transform the lives of the women who come to us and are bruised, emotionally scarred, humiliated, and overcome with guilt and shame. They are encouraged when they hear that God wants them to be safe and strong. They do not have to be slaves in a marriage or relationship that brings violence, guilt, and manipulation. They are to be loved as humans in the image of God, their creator.

Second, the resurrection provides *freedom* for victims. The resurrected Savior illustrated that the death and suffering on the cross were not the end of Christianity. The new life and victory over the Savior's enemies illustrated that the church was to have a ministry of power and hope. Victims are not meant to live in guilt, suffering, and shame. They are to be free and live in safety with love, compassion, and respect. They are to experience justice, not humiliation. If they choose to be married they are to be respected and loved.

Finally, the resurrection provides hope that victims *can forgive.* Through time, healing, and validation, victims can one day forgive those who abused them. They do not have to live the rest of their lives with anger, bitterness, and guilt. They are not forced to forgive, but they can one day make that choice. They have the right to expect the abuser to repent, be accountable, and compensate them for their suffering and unjust treatment. They have the chance to move forward in their lives and allow the healing process to continue.

Batterers and the Resurrection

The resurrection tells batterers that the risen Savior may be their enemy. *They need to repent.* Jesus has risen from the dead and is the judge of those who oppose the will of God. Batterers can no longer hide behind a religious faÁade and claim that their wives are to "submit to their husbands" unquestionably. They learn that it is not their submissive wives or the "love of a good woman" that will change them. It is the conscious decision to change and be like Jesus. As illustrated earlier in this book, they cannot expect their wives to be slaves to a marriage covenant. Those who abuse their spouses are sinning against their families and against God. The resurrection brings a sense of judgment and accountability for their actions. God is the God of the victims and one who calls the abuser to change their ways or face wrath and judgment. As in the past, God confronts those who oppress others through the prophets and the faith community. Batterers must acknowledge their sin and begin the process of repentance.

Second, the resurrection means that *the abuser can change.* Paul told the early Christians at Corinth:

> And such were some of you, but you were washed, you were sanctified, you were justified in the name of the Lord Jesus Christ and by the Spirit of our God. (1 Cor 6:11)

The letter to the church at Corinth is a beautiful letter from a church leader to a congregation that is struggling with sin. Paul reminded them that they were to be in Christ and that they had the hope of being and were expected to be the type of people that God had called them to be. The conversion of Saul of Tarsus is an example of how the resurrected Jesus confronted and converted a violent man, who later became an apostle (Acts 9:1-19). Saul's conversion came with a price (Acts 9:16), but it was also a second chance at life.

Family and Friends and the Resurrection

Those who are close to victims or abusers must also know that the resurrection gives them a sense of hope in facing domestic violence. It is frustrating trying to help a family member or friend leave an abusive relationship, but it is helpful to understand that this is a slow process. Just as maturity is a process, so is healing. I have held men and women who have wept over their daughters, sisters, mothers, or friends who have returned to an abuser. They have listened and sacrificed hours of time in rescuing the victim and children only to see them return. They have visited her and seen the bruises. They have tried to call only to be cut off. They have initiated contact only to be ignored. They have been criticized for being too nosey. They mean well. They love her and have invested tremendous emotional, financial, and physical strength into helping. They weep because they feel helpless. They are angry, confused, and tired. They want to give up. While their pain is not the same as the victim's, they still suffer. They love her and want what is best for her and the children. They have listened to her, and been there for her and at times, they feel used. Yet, they still are called to act as if they love her partner.

The resurrection provides hope. The resurrection tells them that *God is still working*. Just as Jesus rose from the dead, the hope of resurrection is that she will one day leave the dead. She is overcome with fear and is confused, but all their efforts are not in vain. Just as God sent prophet after prophet over the centuries, so they send message after message over time. Some heeded the prophets and changed. Some finally hear their families and friends and leave for good.

God endured because someone would hear the call. Someone in another generation would respond. While the Manassehs and Amons ignore the pleas of the prophets, there always seems to be a Josiah who breaks the cycle of his grandfather and father and chooses the truth. While the Peters and Jameses of this world move to accepting the Gentiles a little too slowly, the Barnabases, Philips, and Sauls of this world are eager to go forward. The resurrection shows us the patience and endurance of God. The call of God is constant, and someone eventually hears and responds. Family and friends can endure with patience and hope, knowing that someday she may leave or someday one of the children may break the cycle. The resurrection provides hope concerning the patience of God to transform lives one at a time.

I believe that victim theology is bad theology. The church has too often preached the bad news rather than the good news. We have forgotten that the story did not end at the cross or the tomb. We have forgotten that Jesus is the risen Lord, not the dead rebel. We have forgotten that the center of the Apostle's preaching was that God did not abandon Jesus in the grave, not that Jesus was forsaken on the cross. While we were focusing on the tragic death of Jesus, we forgot to show the hope, healing, and justice in the resurrection. Maybe this is why we have shrugged our shoulders rather than stretched out our arms. The risen Lord calls for justice for victims.

Part 3
The Response of Faith Communities

If a culture's tribal rules deny a phenomenon,
then it is truly bound to silence.
—Susan Weitzman

9

The Prophetic Nature of the Church

How should the church respond to domestic violence and abuse inside and outside of the faith community? The first few chapters of this book discussed how the church has many times failed to protect victims and call abusers to accountability. It has been suggested that this is due to our theology concerning marriage, parenting, and the resurrection. It has also been suggested that the faith community has been guilty of ignoring or avoiding the issue of abuse. The Christian church is not alone in this problem. Similar problems exist in the Islamic and Jewish communities and other faith communities as well.[1] It is a problem that can be addressed by faith community leaders.

> "Do you speak Russian?" I said in Russian as I caught Alexander passing by (Alexander was a minister at a Russian church. I had met him at a community event and approached him afterward).

---

[1] Carol Goodman Kaufman, *Sins of Omission: The Jewish Community's Reaction to Domestic Violence* (Cambridge, Mass.: Westview, 2003) xii–xvii; Miles, 16–19.

"Da," he said smiling.

"Alexander, man am I glad to meet you. I am Ron Clark, the guy who called you on the telephone last month about abuse training for Russian ministers. I finally am glad to put a face with the name."

"Yes. I remember the call," he said as he slowly leaned away from me.

Leaning forward I said, "Hey, I know you are busy, but I would like to meet with you for coffee or a soda sometime. I would like to talk about a training for Russian-speaking ministers to address abuse issues in their congregations."

"Well, Dr. Clark, you see we Russian ministers all have full-time jobs outside the church. We do not have the privilege of getting paid by our congregations to preach. I am a mechanic by trade, and I have limited time to do my ministry. In fact, you will find that most Russian ministers have the same problem. We would rather spend our time teaching lost people who need Jesus," he said as he handed me his card. "I do still have your card. Thank you."

"I understand, Alexander, and I hope that we can meet sometime," I said smiling as we parted.

I understand that ministers are busy. They are constantly bombarded with new techniques to *better their ministries*. I understand that everyone who writes a book, has a ministry niche, or holds a doctorate degree seems to have a passion about their specialty and may try to sell this to others. With Alexander's comment, I didn't know whether to be insulted or simply accept that he is a busy man trying to be nice to one of the many salesmen that these ministers have to face. I chose the latter. I do, however, feel that this is the attitude of most of the male ministers that I meet. The female ministers have usually been willing to listen and discuss the issue of abuse. Isn't that interesting?

Two issues that Alexander mentioned should be addressed. These two issues help to define the role of the church in being prophetic. First, the issue of *evangelism* was mentioned in Alexander's response. He felt that dealing with domestic violence issues may not be part of evangelism. Most ministers struggle to define evangelism but suggest that we should be doing it. Church growth texts and classes teach ministers to be preachers in the community but not involved in local activism or community work.

We are told that it distracts us from the work of the gospel of Jesus. Does evangelism only mean preaching to people about Jesus? Is evangelism preaching only to those who are *lost*? Can evangelism involve family or social justice issues? According to Alexander, teaching men to be compassionate with their wives is not evangelism. Equally, social justice issues, such as the oppression of the weak, children, or women, do not fall under his definition of evangelism.

What is Evangelism?

Evangelism means *preaching a good message*. It is interesting that the first sermon Jesus gave in the synagogue was a good message that involved social justice. Luke wrote that when Jesus was given the scroll of Isaiah, he found the place where it was written and read:

> The spirit of the Lord is upon me, who has anointed me to preach good news to the poor, sent me to announce freedom for the captives and give sight back to the blind, to release those who have been wounded, and to announce the year of the Lord's favor. (Luke 4:18-19)

After Jesus read this text, he told the congregation that the scripture was fulfilled that day in their presence. Jesus was placing an emphasis on his ministry and those who were to receive the good news. The recipients of this good news were the poor, blind, and oppressed and those freed from captivity. His lesson seems to be a theme that carried throughout Luke and Acts. When John the Baptist was about to die, he sent two of his disciples to see if Jesus was the Messiah. At that moment Jesus was healing and curing the sick, blind, and demon possessed. What was Jesus' response?

> Go and proclaim to John what you have seen and heard. The blind see again, the lame walk, the lepers are cleansed, the deaf hear, the dead are raised, the good news is preached to the poor, and blessed is anyone who is not repulsed[2] by me. (Luke 7:22)

---

[2]Usually the text is translated "blessed is the one who *does not fall away* on account of me." The word for this phrase, *skandalon*, is many times translated stumbling block or

Luke's gospel and Acts were written to a community that needed to practice their ministry with outcasts. These outcasts included the poor, weak, sick, widows, children, Gentiles, Samaritans, and oppressed (Luke 5:30-31; 6:20-22; 7:34; 9:48; 11:41; 12:33; 18:22; 19:7). The gospel highlighted Jesus' work among the poor and oppressed in the community. He was known as the friend of sinners and tax collectors (5:30-31; 7:34). In Luke 4:18-19 and 7:22, the recipients of the *good news* were the poor and oppressed. Part of following Jesus meant accepting the ministry that he practiced. Evangelism meant bringing the good news to the poor, outcasts, and oppressed.

If this is evangelism, then isn't addressing spousal and child abuse also part of evangelism? Shouldn't the church be concerned about domestic violence? Even more, if twenty-five percent of women in America have been physically abused, how many people could we reach if we began to address domestic violence? If thousands of women in America are abused every year, how many of them need to know that Jesus wants to help them? If so many men abuse women, shouldn't we be calling them to repentance? If our missionaries were prepared to address domestic violence, how many thousands of captives would be set free? Can evangelism involve telling victims and abusers that the kingdom of God is a place of peace, healing, justice, and hope?

A second issue that Alexander mentioned involves those *lost people who need Jesus.* What should we do with those in the church who are being abused? If we *save the lost*, who are abused, what do we with them once they are part of our congregations? Are they supposed to be content with being *saved*? This has been much of the problem with the faith community and abuse. Women have come to Jesus for healing, been baptized into Christ, and then expected to continue in their abusive relationships. They are freed from the slavery of sin and abuse, but then they are expected to pick up their cross and again become prisoners. While their ministers and leaders are out *saving the world*, victims are physically

---

offense. The word means repulsed or offended. I have chosen to translate this phrase *repulsed* because it illustrates the struggle that Luke's readers would have faced by being called to work with the poor and outcasts. Jesus' ministry was offensive to those who separated themselves from the poor, and it is this attitude that Jesus and Luke sought to correct in the early disciples (Luke 5:31; 14:13; 15:1-2).

and spiritually dying at home. Abuse victims who attend church have indicated that they feel as if God is unconcerned about their suffering. I meet many people who have walked away from God because they have grown up in a religious family where the father was abusive. My own father was raised in a conservative church family where there was alcohol and physical abuse, and he later became an atheist. He made two vows. One was never to spank his own children, and the other was to walk away from God. He died not believing in God, and I saw the tension he continually faced over his childhood abuse issues and religion. I have come to regret that he confused the church's apathy about abuse as with that of God.

All people need Jesus, Jesus came to preach good news to the poor and oppressed. Evangelism means that we practice Jesus' ministry by bringing freedom and justice to all people who are oppressed, whether we consider them in or out of the church. This ministry must focus on justice issues that oppress any human being. Ray Anderson suggests that this social justice is an important part of evangelism.

> To separate evangelism and social justice as two issues to be debated and then prioritized is to split humanity down the middle. Theologically, it is a denial of the incarnation of God. In assuming humanity in its condition of estrangement and brokenness, Jesus produced reconciliation in "his own body," so that no longer can we see humanity apart from its unity in Jesus Christ. To approach persons in the context of their social, physical and spiritual existence, and only offer healing and reconciliation for the spiritual is already a betrayal of the gospel as well as of humanity.[3]

As Rauschenbush mentioned, social justice completes the gospel and ministry of Jesus and empowers the weak to experience the power of God's kingdom.

> There is nothing else in sight today which has power to rejuvenate theology except the consciousness of vast sins and sufferings, and the longing for righteousness and new life, which are expressed.[4]

---

[3]Anderson, 203.
[4]Rauschenbusch, 14.

Why have we had trouble equating social justice issues with evangelism? It seems that the church needs to return to the prophets to understand the prophetic nature of the kingdom. The prophets confronted the power structures of their day, including the kings, priests, and political officials. Notice that they confronted those in power and those who abused that power. The prophets did not preach repentance to the poor, orphans, widows, needy, oppressed, and afflicted. Amos, Jeremiah, Jonah, and Ezekiel challenged the government, whether it was in Israel or other nations of the world. The prophets challenged the political leaders to practice justice, righteousness, mercy, and compassion with the oppressed. Even Daniel challenged the Babylonian king, Nebuchadnezzar, to practice this form of leadership.

> Therefore, king, accept my advice: renounce your sins by doing what is right and your wickedness by being kind to the oppressed. Then your success may continue. (Dan 4:27)

Social justice is evangelism. Social justice requires courage. It involves confronting the abusers, oppressors, and power structures that humiliate and control others. It also involves comforting those who have been oppressed and abused. It is not about being a hero; it is about being a prophet, a friend, and a representative of God. It is about letting people know that a prophet/church has been among them (Ezek 2:5). This is not about condemning; it is about telling people that God knows what is going on. It is a sense of validation for victims and rebuke for abusers.

How is the Church Prophetic?

Jesus the Prophet

If the church is going to be evangelistic, it must be like Jesus. If the church is going to be like Jesus, it must be prophetic.

> The church achieves this goal [community witness] when it allows the eternal Word of God to shape its character. When the church fails to

conform itself to the true image of God, the incarnation remains merely an abstract idea.[5]

The Jesus in Luke's gospel was prophetic in that he called the early Christians to practice social justice. Luke 1:3 tells us that this Gospel was written to Theophilus. This means that the letter was addressed to a noble Gentile (possibly a Christian)[6] or to the Christian community.[7] Luke's intention was to reinvestigate the story of Jesus[8] and confirm what they had been taught.[9]

Luke reminded the reader that Jesus kept company with outcasts (5:30; 7:34; 19:7); touched lepers, demoniacs, women, and children (4:40; 5:13; 7:39; 8:35,44; 9:47; 13:13; 15:1; 18:15); and died with criminals (22:37; 23:33). Jesus challenged the rich to care for the poor (6:20-22; 11:41; 12:33; 14:13-24; 18:22; 19:31); the sinners (7:36-50; 15:24,32); and the sick (5:31). Jesus was highly suspect because of the company he kept. Luke's audience was also expected to keep the same company and face similar shame and humiliation from the world.

He said, "It is necessary for the son of man to suffer many things and be delivered over by the elders, chief priests, and scribes; and be killed, and

---

[5]Frederick D. Aquino, "The Incarnation: The Dignity and Honor of Human Personhood," *Restoration Quarterly* 42 (2000) 45.

[6]This is suggested by the phrase, "most excellent," which indicates that Theophilus may have been a well-respected official.

[7]Theophilus, lover of God, was also a term used of the Jewish community during the Diaspora.

[8]Luke indicates that he has "followed again" (*parekolouthekoti anothen*) or "carefully investigated" the stories of Jesus. It seems that Luke has done research on the story of Jesus and tried to present information that was not told in the other gospels. This may be evident in his discussions of Mary keeping events in her heart (1:29; 2:19,51) as well as the stories where only Luke (as compared to Mark and Matthew) emphasizes the command to take care of the poor (11:41; 12:33) and the stories about Jesus as friend to the sinners (7:34; 19:7).

[9]The phrase "the certainty of the things you have been taught" comes from a legal financial term (*asfaleian* which means certainty or safety) which occurs in Acts 5:23; Phil 3:1; 1 Thess 5:3; Heb 6:19; and Epictetus 2.13.7. It seems that Luke wanted to confirm the teachings that the church had concerning Jesus. It also seems that Luke wished to add to the teachings by emphasizing social justice.

be raised up on the third day." But he said to all of them, "If anyone wants to come after me he must deny himself and take up his cross every day, and follow me. If you wish to save your life you will destroy it and if you destroy your life for me you will save it. For how will there be a profit if one gains the whole world but destroys their life? Whoever is ashamed of me and my words the son of man will be ashamed of him when he comes in his glory, and the father, and the angels." (Luke 9:22-26)

Carrying the cross did not only mean following Jesus in death; it meant following Jesus in life. It meant going where Jesus went and not being ashamed of his life and ministry, regardless of where he preached.

Jesus the prophet challenged those in power to attend to the needs of victims. Jesus did this directly by challenging the religious leaders and wealthy elite to open their hearts to the rest of humanity. Jesus also does this indirectly in Luke's gospel as every generation experiences the parables, stories, and lessons that lift up the poor and criticize those who look down on them.

The Prophets of Old and New

Traditionally, prophets are seen as individuals who were crazy, magicians, or isolated from their communities. The television shows concerning Jesus of Nazareth display John the Baptist as a loud, confrontational, and erratic preacher. Others see the prophets as fortune-tellers. In the ancient world prophets were equated with mystics, fortune-tellers, magicians, and diviners.[10] The Israelite prophets were described by their character and work for *Yahweh*. The prophet Samuel was called a seer in ancient Israel

---

[10]Lester L. Grabbe, "Ancient Near Eastern Prophecy from an Anthropological Perspecitve," in *Prophecy in Its Ancient Near Eastern Context: Mesopotamian, Biblical, and Arabian Perspectives*, ed. Martti Nissinen, Society of Biblical Literature Symposium Series 13 (Atlanta: Society of Biblical Literature, 2000) 13–32; and Victor H. Matthews, *Social World of the Hebrew Prophets* (Peabody, Mass.: Hendrickson, 2001) 19–21. Matthews also writes that the equivalent for prophet (in the Mari language) is epileptic. Egyptian hieroglyphics also describe the prophet as one having convulsions.

(1 Sam 9:9). They held a deep conviction that they were called by *Yahweh* and brought a message directly from the Lord. Their prophecies began with "this is what *Yahweh* says," and many times ended with "declares *Yahweh*." Their courage and conviction was based not in themselves but in their calling from God.

The prophets represented ordinary people, such as sheepherders or farmers (Amos 7:14; 1 Kings 19:19), scorned husbands (Hosea 1:2), and young men (1 Sam 3:1; Jer 1:7). They were men in touch with common people. Whether they came from small towns (Jer 1:1; Amos 1:1; Mic 1:1; Nah 1:1), the larger cities (Isa 1:1; Hab 1:1; Zeph 1:1), cities in ruin (Hag 1:1; Zech 1:1; Jer 40:1) or foreign nations (Ezek 1:1; Dan 1:1-3; Jonah 1:2), these prophets knew the events of everyday life and the people in their neighborhood. When Amos and Micah prophesied about the abuse of the poor, it was something that they saw daily. When Jeremiah challenged the people to help the children and women of his day, he was speaking of what he saw in the streets. The judgment from *Yahweh* was the revelation, but the description was of crimes seen firsthand. Ezekiel was the only prophet who was transported out of his community and shown the hidden sins of idolatry occurring behind closed doors (Ezekiel 8).

Were the experiences of the prophets divine? Yes and no. While the call and authority came from God, the prophets described events that they knew about. While the rest of the religious leaders of the day had become hardened to the corruption, greed, and oppression that they saw daily, the prophet was *compelled by God* to address the problem. Most of the experiences the prophet faced were not new, but the authority and responsibility to preach were. This is part of Jeremiah's complaint to *Yahweh*:

> Whenever I speak, I cry out saying violence and destruction. The word of *Yahweh* has brought me insult and reproach all day long, but if I say, "I will not speak of God or in God's name," the word is in my heart like a fire, a fire closed in my bones. I am tired of holding it in; I cannot. (Jer 20:8-9)

The burden that Jeremiah faced was one that people face when they realize that they cannot turn their heads from injustice and oppression. It is the burden that has caused so many of us to bite our tongue and then speak out with a swollen tongue. No matter how hard we bite, our tongue prevails. The Jewish prophets usually preached what others already knew, but they did it with authority and conviction. They preached not only what people saw, but also what *Yahweh* saw. They were sent to tell the leaders that God saw what was happening and was expressing judgment or pleasure.

Does the one who planted the ear not hear? Does the one who formed the eye not see? (Ps 94:9)

Yahweh's eyes are on the righteous and ears are attentive to their cry. (Ps 34:15)

I know where you live—where Satan's throne is, but you are faithful to my name. (Rev 2:13)

Being prophetic does not mean that we preach a new revelation, a futuristic view, or a magical spiritual power. It is a reference to authority, calling, awareness, and a representation of God's heart. The prophets were those who felt called to do something about the injustice that they saw. While their community and leaders may have been corrupt, they had encountered the Holy One who was incorruptible. They had experienced the presence and voice of God. They met a King whose ethic was vastly different than that of their community and leaders. They were driven by the conviction that God wanted someone to respond to what was happening. They were driven by an ethical code that told them that ignoring sin was just as wrong as practicing it. They were also driven by their own human emotions concerning the issues that they faced. The prophets were emotional people who cried, shouted, screamed, cheered, and stared people down. They were emotionally invested in the problems because it was their community. They knew the heart of God because their hearts had united with *Yahweh's*. They spoke for God, represented God, and became more like God. To see the things that God sees may be a curse to some or a blessing to others, but it is an experience that purifies and motivates an individual to act for God.

When examining the literature of the prophets and their character, one can find some interesting qualities in their message. The prophetic literature and nature of the prophet had six similar characteristics.

Figure 14: Typology of prophetic literature and prophecy[11]

1. The prophet had an intense experience of the deity.
2. The prophet spoke or wrote in a distinctive way (prose or poetry).
3. The prophet acted in a particular social setting.
4. The prophet possessed distinctive personal qualities = charisma.
5. The prophet was an intermediary.
6. The prophet had a distinctive message.

The main focus of the Jewish prophets was the authority, message, and context in which they spoke. The messages were not complex, exclusively futuristic, or far removed from the daily lives of their audience. The messages were directed toward those in power who were usually the cause of problems among the people of God and their covenant.

> The books of Amos, Micah, Jeremiah, Lamentations, Baruch, Habakkuk, Zephaniah, and Ezekiel all have as one of their central concerns justice for those who suffer profound injustice at the hands of others whose inordinate need for power and control has caused unnecessary oppression—when Torah is disregarded, covenant is broken, God is forgotten, and the ways of justice and righteousness are abandoned.[12]

The prophets were men and women who were called by *Yahweh* to act on the injustices that they had seen. They were not given a new vision but a new responsibility. They heard the judgment from *Yahweh* and were now called to speak for God and open the eyes of others.

---

[11] David L. Peterson, "Defining Prophecy and Prophetic Literature," in *Prophecy in Its Ancient Near Eastern Context: Mesopotamian, Biblical, and Arabian Perspectives*, ed. Martti Nissinen, Society of Literature Symposium Series, 13 (Atlanta: Society of Biblical Literature, 2000) 33–44.

[12] Dempsey, *The Prophets*, 5.

Just as Jesus called his disciples to respond to what they had seen, so the new prophets are called to respond to the injustices and sins of our neighborhoods. Those of us who have learned to turn our heads to the injustices of society have also learned to turn our hearts away from the pain and anguish that God expresses to us in the scriptures. The Bible reveals to us that abuse, oppression, and humiliation are unacceptable to the one who has created all of us in the Divine image. The new prophets are men and women who have an encounter with God and with evil.

The alarming statistics presented earlier in this book suggest that abuse is more common than we wish to admit. Yet, being prophetic suggests that admission is not the issue—the voice of God is the issue. God has called all of us to be prophets, and God expects the church today to be prophetic in our neighborhoods and communities.

How Does a Church Become Prophetic?

Churches have the unique opportunity to be prophetic in many areas of social justice. If the church believes that it is the arms and hands of Jesus, then it has the responsibility to go where Jesus went. It has the responsibility to see what God sees. It has the responsibility to speak what God wants spoken and to preach what Jesus preached. If Jesus preached freedom for the captives, then the church must preach the good news of freedom to those who are caught in domestic violence and abuse. Our attempts to build churches like Christian malls for Jesus, travel afar to do revivals, and build schools as fortresses for our children have been noble but have not fully reflected the passion and heart of God for the little people. We have tried to create empires of power for God rather than kingdoms of justice for the Prince of Peace. We have been prophetic in the sense that we speak our mind but not in the sense that we represent the mind of Christ. Are we ashamed that our Savior is a friend of sinners and tax collectors?

If the church is going to be prophetic, it must be like Jesus. When we observe the ministry of Christ, we see that his ministry involved preaching and healing. The preaching of Jesus was meant to teach the good news of God. Jesus informed the world that God had come to enact justice, mercy, and judgment upon sin and darkness. But Jesus also healed the sick and demon possessed. By healing and casting out demons, Jesus was confronting the powers of darkness and showing us that Satan was defeated.

> The seventy-two returned with joy and said, "Lord, even the demons submit to us in your name." He said, "I saw Satan fall from heaven like lightning. I have given you authority to trample on snakes and scorpions and to overcome all the power of the enemy; nothing will harm you. However, do not rejoice that the spirits submit to you but rejoice that your names are written in heaven." (Luke 10:17-18)

While we often try to debate whether miraculous power and casting out demons exist in churches today, we forget that Jesus confronted all forms of evil. The disciples also were part of the fall of Satan in their ministry (Luke 10). Who of us feel called to be responsible for causing Satan to fall?

Jesus told the apostles, as well as us today, that he has defeated Satan and that we can trample on evil. We have been sent to confront evil and attack Satan in our ministries. The spirits submit to us if we are doing what God wants, and our ministries must confront evil on every front. This evil is not limited to sickness. When I look around my neighborhood, it is not cancer, leprosy, or blindness that I see gripping my neighbors. It is pornography, abuse, oppression, adultery, drugs, and alcoholism that are ripping people apart. Regardless of my theology on miraculous works in the church, I have to acknowledge that Jesus has given us the power to defeat these forms of evil. Does the church believe this? The church can be prophetic by preaching against evil and trampling evil for Jesus.

Awareness

The church must create awareness by preaching, teaching, and speaking out concerning domestic violence. This means that the church must look to its leaders, especially those who carry the role of prophet, which are our preachers. They are the ones who must first have the encounter with God and open their eyes to it. They see the problem, but they have not addressed it. Awareness cannot happen unless the preachers of our churches alert us to the problem. This will involve three steps.

First, preachers *must acknowledge that there is a problem.* We also must acknowledge this. In the beginning of this book, the statistics were given to inform you that domestic violence is an epidemic in our cities. Yet this is not what I mean by acknowledgement. Acknowledgement means that we state that it is a problem. We do not make excuses for the violence, we do not ignore it and hope that it goes away, and we do not justify it. Acknowledgement means that we call it what God calls it. Evil. Domestic violence is evil and it is not the work of God but Satan and people choosing to do evil. As Jeffrey Means suggests, we must acknowledge that abuse is not only a sin but a great evil upon our land.

> One of the few places evil has been consistently mentioned has been within communities of faith. At the same time, the church and religiously committed individuals have tended to leave evil unacknowledged as part of their own worlds and to ignore and deny the depth of evil's impact on people. When evil has been acknowledged, it too frequently is pushed outside.[13]

If preachers would communicate that domestic violence is evil, then the congregation would listen. Those who are victims would know that they are not to blame, and abusers would be called to repent. The church must acknowledge that abuse is a sin and the work of evil.

The church must also acknowledge that God is angered by abuse. My wife and I have had people ask why we are heavily involved in dealing with domestic violence. One reason is that we believe God leads victims and abusers to us. This is because we have publicly taken a stand concerning abuse and domestic violence. We are convinced that God has spoken out against abuse and will judge not only abusers but also those who ignore the problem. We fear God. We love God. We want to please God. For us it is theological and personal.

> On account of this we want to please [God] whether here or there. We all will appear in front of the judgment seat of Christ in order that each of us will receive what we deserve for our works whether good or bad.

---

[13]Means, 9.

Knowing the fear of the Lord we persuade men because we have appeared
to God. (2 Cor 5:9-11a)

Because Paul feared God, he tried to please God and persuaded people to
do the same. Likewise, ministers must seek God's will in addressing
domestic violence and abuse. We can be sure that if preachers feel passionate
about an issue, they will address it from the pulpit. It is unfortunate that
too many preachers wait to address abuse until someone close to them is
violated, and then it sometimes becomes more personal than theological.
Are we comfortable with our theological stance on domestic violence?

Second, we *must learn about this problem*. One of the biggest
frustrations that domestic violence service providers communicate with
me about churches is that the leaders do not know how to work with
those involved in abuse. Too often abusers manipulate counselors,
ministers, and church leaders because they are not prepared to work with
them. We, as human beings, place a great deal of trust and hope in humans
who have the potential to lie to us. We "strain at a gnat" when it involves
trusting God, but seem to "swallow a camel" when it comes to trusting
other humans. A pedophile goes before a congregation and says he's sorry
for his sins, and the church assumes that he is cured and will not re-
offend. An abuser confesses abuse to his wife and children and states that
it only happened once, and the church fully believes him. Yet the same
congregation chides victims because they just, "can't get over it and get on
with their lives." Church members push the victim to forgive and forget
as they have. They do not live in the same house with the abusers. We
need to understand the dynamics of abuse, power and control, and family
dysfunction. In order to work with victims, their children, and abusers,
we must be aware of the issues that are present in the home.

The bibliography at the end of this book is designed to provide
ministers and churches with material that can inform and educate them
concerning the dynamics of abuse and family violence. Local police
departments can be contacted for information about domestic violence
service providers in the area and most safe houses and batterer programs
are willing to offer trainings and provide information to churches, Sunday
schools, and groups concerning abuse prevention. Ministers should invest
the money needed to attend workshops and seminars in order to learn
how to recognize potential abuse problems and refer them to trained

providers. A simple search on the internet under domestic violence can provide many resources for ministers and other members in abuse prevention. The National Domestic Violence Hotline (1-800-799-SAFE), National Coalition Against Domestic Violence (www.ncadv.org), and Hot Peach Pages: World-Wide List of Abuse Agencies (www.hotpeachpages.net) provide local resources in your area. We live in a time when access to resources is easy, and information is readily available. Finally, once preachers have acknowledged the problem and learned about the issues, they should *preach and teach about God and domestic violence*. Biblical texts are full of stories about domestic violence and abuse including the rape of Dinah (Genesis 34), uncovering family nakedness (Deuteronomy 27), child sacrifice (Lev 20:1-6), the Levite and his concubine (Judges 19), the rape of Tamar (2 Samuel 13), and household codes (Ephesians 5; Colossians 3; 1 Peter 3), as well as other texts. Ministers have a great opportunity, given by God, to bring a text before the congregation and illuminate the issues of violence in the ancient world as well as today. God has spoken, in many of these texts, to the community concerning intimate partner violence and abuse. The Biblical writers and prophets illustrate God's judgment and protection.

According to victims, the sermon is one of the most encouraging mediums to inform them that God grieves over their suffering. I have heard some abuse advocates grieve over the fact that their minister will not publicly denounce abuse. Some say that their minister alludes to, refers to, or touches on the topic. But I have heard very, very few tell me that their minister has given a full sermon on domestic violence and the Gospel. Is it because so many ministers are male? Is it because this has been seen as a women's issue?

> Domestic violence and sexual abuse should not be made as "women's issues" but issues of the church. One result of the segregation of these important issues is that they remain outside regular activities of the church, such as theological education, scriptural reflection, liturgical practice, and even worship. Another result is that leaders of the church can more easily avoid addressing these issues "seriously and responsibly."[14]

---

[14]Ibid., 11.

Abuse is a serious issue. Unfortunately, it has not become a serious issue to preachers. Yet the number one compliment that I have received from others is that I do publicly address this issue in my sermons. Amidst the griping that "You preach too much about abuse," (never from victims) is the encouragement from many others to keep preaching about it and face the problem head on. It is those outside of our church that have been the most supportive. They have been my cheering section, and it is a great honor for ministers when their community stands behind them and pushes them forward. If a congregation wishes to create abuse awareness, it must first come from the pulpit.

Ministers can also create awareness in Bible classes, premarital counseling sessions, marriage classes, marriage counseling sessions, youth programs, dating classes, children's classes, small group meetings, and retreats. Domestic violence can be addressed in these informal or intimate settings, which provide a non-threatening environment for victims, children, and abusers. Members can also be empowered to help friends, family, and neighbors whom they suspect are in abuse. A church that integrates abuse prevention and addresses family violence issues will be a church that is healthy, evangelistic, and a light to the community.

Seminaries can require ministers to attend one or two workshops in domestic violence. Graduate schools can require reading for their students that exposes them to domestic violence. I had no training in abuse until one of my counseling classes in my doctoral work. I am thankful for Dr. Ed Gray of Harding University Graduate School of Religion in Memphis, Tennessee, who gave us a seminar on abuse. Accreditation committees can push for abuse prevention to be part of the curriculum of all seminary students. I have also been working for over five years on a project that introduces victims' testimonies to the students of my Biblical studies and religion classes.[15] The students indicate that these interviews and testimonies have created a desire to search the text for answers and made

---

[15]See my articles, "Victims' Testimonies and Prophetic Literature," and "Apocalyptic Literature and Testimonies of Suffering," in *Teaching the Bible: Practical Strategies for Classroom Instruction,*" eds. Mark Roncace and Patrick Gray (Atlanta: Society of Biblical Literature, 2005) 171–72, 393–94; and "Associating with the Humiliated: Victimization as a Tool for Teaching Biblical Studies in a Christian College Setting," *Journal of Religion and Abuse* 7 (2005).

an emotional connection with them. The project has received support from fellow colleagues in the Society of Biblical Literature at conferences and in publications. College students can be the ones to continue the grass roots movement in faith communities to address abuse, both theologically and socially.

Sin breeds in secret, but the light that shines into the darkness exposes evil. Awareness is a chance to expose, shed light, and inform a congregation about evil in the world. When evil is acknowledged, it can be confronted. When we expose it, we can confront it and become the servants of King Jesus.

Confrontation

Once we have become aware of the problem and are creating awareness, then we go to the next step. The church must confront the power structures of society. Abuse must stop. Abuse must cease to exist in our families, culture, and communities. This is a big goal, but transforming cultures has always been the goal of Jesus. Since God is in a battle with Satan, a battle between good and evil, then evangelism means joining God in battle. If we join God then one power structure that we must confront is *Satan and sin*.

> Moving beyond trauma to evil helps us shift our thinking. It encourages us to consider the powerful forces within persons and our culture that set the stage for potential acts of cruelty against others, without losing sight of the tremendous impact that violence and abuse have on particular persons.[16]

> Genuine evil is the abuse of power that destroys bodies and spirits; evil is produced by personal actions and intentions which are denied and dissociated by individuals; evil is organized by economic forces, institutions and ideologies, but mystified by appeals to necessity and truth; evil is sanctioned by religion, but masked by claims to virtue, love, and justice.[17]

---

[16]Ibid., 1.
[17]Poling, 110.

The Apostle Paul tells us that our battle is not against flesh and blood but against spiritual forces (Eph 6:12). Therefore, churches must decide to confront Satan and sin in regards to abuse and domestic violence. We must name this as a sin rather than a condition. We must clarify that it is wrong and not part of God's plan for the family. We cannot turn our heads, since we have set our faces to address the problem (Ezek 3:8-9).

Second, *we must be willing to confront abusers face to face*. This can be done with compassion, but it must be done. Too often churches confront only the victims. This is easy and safe, because there is little risk involved in confronting them. Confronting abusers is risky, but it is the right thing to do. Abusers are manipulative, aggressive, and confusing, but the church must be confident. Just as the prophets felt the courage of God's call, we also must believe that God has called us to call abusers to repentance. We must believe that God has called us to protect victims but also to firmly love abusers so that they can repent and change their lives.

> When those of us in the church deny and ignore the potential for evil that resides in every person, we contribute to the church's failure to address evil in its most basic form and to provide leadership in confronting evil. When those of us in the church ignore evil in the world, we contribute to the church's failure to look at all of life, as well as to the church's collusion in propagating the delusion that the world is a safe and benevolent place. When the church fails to confront evil at any level, it ultimately robs those touched by evil of the faith resources for which they so desperately long.[18]

We should protect victims and provide them with resources rather than confront them. They are not the ones who have been practicing sin. They have been surviving. The abusers are the ones who need to be confronted and challenged to stop their abusive behavior.

The third power structure *is the government and its leaders*. Ministers can take the lead by speaking out in their communities about abuse and domestic violence. They can also take the lead by providing a voice to the overworked, underpaid, and emotionally burdened abuse advocates. Law

---

[18]Means, 10.

enforcement, government programs, and school systems all have decisions to make concerning their budgets and fiscal responsibility. Too often abuse prevention programs are cut, because these organizations feel the need to conserve and work in a *crisis mode*. It is unfortunate that they don't devote ten years to prevention with the realization that a generation could be changed as a result. Yet the reality is that our government agencies are financially stretched.

God has not only called government agencies to address abuse, God has also called the church to lead the work in addressing this issue. It is time that we stood up and supported our government workers and provided the voice of holiness to our communities. We should call our community leaders to budget financial resources into abuse prevention, since this would address most of our community problems. We should encourage our leaders to provide resources to service providers, victims, and abusers in an effort to heal and become a society of peace. We should remind our leaders that we are praying for them and available to serve and help so that they do not have to carry the burden alone. We should rally our churches and faith communities to be involved with our government rather than fight against it, and let them see that the church is a vibrant resource rather than a museum. We should challenge our leaders to be fair, ethical, and honest in hearing the cries of the oppressed and victims.

Fourth, the church must confront *shame by providing resources and hope for victims*. Domestic violence victims and their children suffer tremendous scars and shame from their trauma and experiences. The church has the opportunity to enter their lives and aggressively love them and remind them that they have hope in God. We can empower them to become independent and know that Jesus loves them. They can stand on their feet and have the dignity that they have as children of the Almighty God. They can say, "I do not deserve to be beaten nor mistreated and will not let anyone humiliate me." The church can become a place that knits their hearts and souls together so that they can lift their eyes to heaven and see a powerful, merciful, and compassionate God.

This can only happen when ministers take the first step. When preachers acknowledge that there is a problem, they begin the journey of reform in a world where abuse and domestic violence are epidemic. For far too long faith community leaders have ignored the problem and hoped it would go away. It has not. It has continued to grow. Why have ministers not addressed these issues? According to Al Miles' ministers do not get involved with addressing domestic violence because of 1) denial, 2) fear and helplessness, 3) lack of involvement in the issue, 4) misconceptions about abuse, 5) sexism in male ministers, and 6) a lack of appropriate training.[19] Kaufman also provides similar evidence in the Jewish community by suggesting that some rabbis: 1) feel that it is permissible to punish a woman, 2) deny that the problem exists in their synagogue, 3) try to defend the Jewish community as not having as big a problem as the rest of the world, or 4) feel helpless with the problem.[20] While both Miles and Kaufman indicate that there are clergy who confront abuse, the majority has fallen silent on the issue.

> The magnitude of pastoral neglect . . . jolted me out of my own state of denial into reality. No longer could I think that pastors weren't coming to seminars on violence against women and children because they had scheduling conflicts or emergencies to tend to, the two most common excuses clergy had been giving me. I was forced to face the fact that many clergy people were willfully choosing to avoid these issues.[21]

This cannot be the case any longer. God has called faith communities to respond to the cries of the church. God has called faith community leaders to be God's voice and move the community forward. The community must have leadership that is not afraid and that understands the heart of God. If the faith community will not do the work of God, then the government is left to do the divine task (Romans 13).

The Prophetic Church and Abuse

The prophetic church is one that calls the members and community to an awareness concerning the damage and dysfunction of domestic violence. The church, by creating awareness, can empower a community to take a stand against violence and help others to heal, forgive, and spiritually

---

[19]Miles, 153–55, 166–72.
[20]Kaufman, 64–71.
[21]Miles, 17–18.

grow and develop. The prophetic church forms a community within its doors and outside in the local community. A community of peace and safety becomes a community that can seek God.

Second, the prophetic church, through awareness, becomes evangelistic. Too often churches try to avoid the outside communities and see government workers as the enemy. The same can be true in how our communities view the church. Yet the prophetic church embraces the community and works together with the government to help eradicate violence and abuse. The prophetic church does not attempt to build its own shelters or raise its own money to help victims and abusers. The prophetic church does not create its own way of counseling batterers or victims. The prophetic church understands that God is active in our government and that the abuse service providers are doing what we should have been doing for centuries. We should work together to provide families with the best resources possible. We should work with providers to offer spiritual counseling to families and should support the professionals who have devoted their lives to helping men and women caught in violence. Our outreach should be to all people, and we should let our communities know that God works through humans to advance the kingdom and bring peace to all families.

The Prophetic Vision of the Church

I had one of our Portland Bible scholars, Dr. Carol Dempsey, come and speak to my college class on the seventh to fifth-century prophets. She encouraged the students to be prophets and asked them how they could fulfill this role today. At the end of the discussion she said, "Remember, the prophets weren't warriors, they fought with their tongues. They also painted a vision for their communities that gave them hope. Be those prophets." Dempsey has touched on an important issue for the prophetic church. Is our role to fight, abuse, control, or manipulate? The prophets did not do this. Isn't our role to paint a vision for our churches and communities that includes peace, hope, justice, and compassion? The church has a great opportunity to paint a picture for all victims, abusers, and children that provides them with hope and peace. Hope that they can be compassionate like God. Hope that we as a community are going to replace violence and control over others with empowerment and encouragement. Hope that people can change and that love involves shared power and mutual respect and submission. Peace that comes when we live in hope and see our hope becoming reality.

In the past, the church has not painted this vision for God's people. Jesus provided this vision and called the world to respond, but he depended on his disciples to carry this hope and vision to all people. Jesus' vision was for the world. He knew that even though he was *Lord of all* he was not *Lord to all*. The disciples proclaimed that this Lord brought true peace as opposed to the Lord Caesar who brought Roman peace and power (*Pax Romana*). Has the church fulfilled this vision and prophetic call? Have we brought the peace of Jesus or the peace and power of Rome?

The church's worst problem is that it practices power and manipulation. It acts as the abusers do in how it treats others. Paul Kivel wrote that abusers respond to their power and control issues by practicing denial, minimizing the abuse, or redefining the violence.[22] The church has denied that abuse is a problem, blamed the victims, or claimed that they are over-exaggerating, and/or suggested that abuse is not a sin. We have done this because we, like the abusers, are afraid. We fear the truth, and we are not willing to confront abuse and the abuser. While the apostles took on the power structures and kingdoms of their day, we tend to build *straw kingdoms* and fight harmless doctrines. We boldly claim to fight Satan while allowing men to molest their children, humiliate their families, and assault their wives or partners. Our enemy is a figment of our imagination. We claim that we love all people but we ignore the victims in society.

The movie *Kingdom Come* is an interesting portrayal of an African-American family that has been affected by dysfunction and an abusive father. The father had passed away and the children came home for the funeral. Conversations among the sons, daughters, mother, and other family members reflect the struggle they were experiencing due to their father's behavior. The movie is a comedy, but it provides some valuable insights from a family scarred by abuse and dysfunction. One scene that I remember was a conversation between the widow, played by Whoopi

---

[22]Kivel, 101–2.

Goldberg, and the minister, played by Cedric the Entertainer. The minister visited the widow and was concerned that she was angry with her husband. She told him what she wanted said at the funeral.

Goldberg: "He was mean as a snake. He was mean and surly."

Cedric: "Sister, I didn't know brother Slocum well but to me he seemed a quiet man, a man of inner strength, a man that knew his own mind, kept his own council, and was at peace with the world, a wise, noble, gentle man."

Goldberg: "Well that's cause you didn't know him 'till he got old and sick, but he was mean and he was right surly."

Cedric: "Sister, in my experience its best to remember the happier times . . . "

Goldberg: "Well, they were few and far between."

In the minister's attempt to be nice and to encourage forgiveness, the widow was not allowed to be angry and see her husband for who he was. The minister, like many ministers, felt that forgiveness without repentance was important. Yet he did not understand that he was portraying a vision that was false and deceptive.

The church must portray a vision of hope, but we must also accept the truth and teach others that God is a God of justice. We cannot give hope to victims by painting over the abuse and sin that they have suffered. We cannot help abusers heal if we do not address the problem and call them to change. Children will resent us if we redefine, deny, or minimize what they have seen. The vision must be one that deals with reality. We are providing a vision of hope to all people, not an illusion.

Our vision is that God calls all people into a relationship. Our vision is that God calls all people to repent. Our vision is that God wants all to be saved, safe, and at peace. Our vision is that God can transform anyone to be a man or woman of peace, mercy, and love. Our vision is that God is a God of justice and will protect the innocent and hold the oppressor accountable. Our vision is that we practice God's will on earth. Sometimes the vision brings fear; other times it brings joy. But always the *vision brings hope*!

Conclusion

Domestic violence is an epidemic in the United States as well as in the rest of the world. The statistics tell us that twenty-five percent of women have experienced physical or sexual abuse by an intimate partner. The statistics for dating violence among teenaged females are almost the same. One in six men has been sexually abused as children. Yet these statistics are only reported statistics and only involve physical abuse. It is possible that the numbers are higher when it comes to emotional and verbal abuse. We have a problem in our society with power and control issues, and it needs to stop.

Theologically, God has addressed the problem. God is against oppression and stands for the rights of victims. God is a God of passion and mercy and has called the faith community to reflect this passion and mercy for victims. God has also called men to be like Jesus and to display the mercy, compassion, and courage that have been displayed in the ministry of Christ. God has called husbands and wives to live together in a covenant relationship that is healthy and supportive and practices shared power. This relationship is shown by God's covenant with Israel and by Christ's relationship with the church.

It has been suggested in this book that families caught in abuse develop a system of survival that is unhealthy for victims, children, and abusers. In the past, churches and service providers have found it difficult to help the members of these families. Today, providers are intervening and empowering families to become healthy and live with respect and love for each other. Unfortunately, many times the church's attempt to intervene has contributed to the problem. We have compounded the problems that victims face with our teachings concerning marriage, parenting, and victimization. Theologically, we have missed the opportunity to empower victims to be free and to confront abusers and call them to repentance. Theologically, we have failed to represent Christ in a world that seeks God. Theologically, our government has reflected the heart of God more than we have.

We now have two problems. One problem is the alarming presence of abuse, humiliation, and power and control in human relationships in our world and our churches. The other problem is the apathetic stance of the church in addressing abuse. God is addressing the first problem through the government agencies (Romans 13). God is addressing the second problem through other writers, ministers, theologians, and service providers whom I would call the modern prophets. Our legal system has responded to the first problem by providing aid, legal and emotional protection, and accountability to families in abuse. Has the church properly responded to the second problem? According to the modern prophets, the answer is NO!

> Many voices declare that the church has either caused men to be violent toward their wives or at least provided fertile soil for men's mistreatment of power within their families. They argue that since the church is part of the problem, it cannot be part of the solution. Thus when violence against women is being discussed, God's people are seldom consulted. Since we speak out so infrequently about violence, our collective voice is never heard on this issue. Generally speaking leaders in religious organizations and those involved in community pastoral care are never even invited to participate at the secular consultation table. The silence of our churches and our leaders is often interpreted in the public square as complicity with violent acts.[1]

---

[1] Kroeger, Nason-Clark, 16.

Conclusion

As long as Christian theology and pastoral practice do not publicly repent their collusion in sexual, domestic, and political violence against women and children, the victims of such violence are forced to choose between remaining a victim or remaining a Christian.[2]

It is men's work to unlearn violence as a response to need, to learn to acknowledge and express needs in healthy, nonviolent ways, and to form relationships of intimacy and interdependence rather than dominance and control.[3]

The modern prophets have confronted the church for years, and we have slowly begun to respond. Will we continue to move forward, or will we fall behind? Will we respond, or will we continue to be silent?

The solution to this problem is to return to our Bibles, seek God in prayer and repentance, and be prophetic. The faith community must respond to the plight of victims by responding to the call of God. God has called the church to be prophetic, because God is a God of justice. The church must represent the heart of God and stand for the victims, the oppressed, and the afflicted. The church must also confront those who oppress, abuse, and humiliate others. God has not called us to have power over others; God has called us to empower and practice shared power in our relationships. We have been called into covenant not only with God but also with each other. Our brothers and sisters should be living together in peace, compassion, and justice.

The church is to be prophetic by first creating awareness in our communities. We must acknowledge that abuse is a sin and that God wants it to stop. We must learn about the issue, and our preachers and teachers must address this in sermons, classes, and other venues. The church is then to confront evil, abusers, and our government and leadership structures that ignore the victims. The church must also confront shame by empowering victims to know they are loved and by calling abusers into a community of justice and love.

---

[2] Elisabeth Shüssler Fiorenza, "Introduction," *Violence Against Women*, ed. Elisabeth Schüssler Fiorenza and M. Shawn Copeland, Concilium (Maryknoll, N.Y.: Orbis, 1994) xviii.
[3] Pamela Cooper-White, *The Cry of Tamar: Violence Against Women and the Church's Response* (Minneapolis: Augsburg Fortress, 1995) 218.

Finally, the church is to create a vision of hope for families in domestic violence. Preachers, like the prophets of old, have the power to paint pictures of hope with their words. Ministers should lead the way in proclaiming peace, hope, love, compassion, and above all, justice. With these messages the church can be a light to their community. The church can call the government workers to endure, persevere, and practice justice. The church can call government leaders to make their budgets with hope and faith that prevention is the best medicine. The church can provide victims with hope that God and the disciples of Jesus do hear their cries. The church can remind abusers that God is not blind and that the risen Lord is a God of justice and power. The church can provide families with a healthy model of covenant and parental support. The church can remind the world once again that God is with us.

This begins with you. Hopefully, you have learned something in reading this book that will provoke a response. This book is not intended to be a complete guide to working with abuse, but it is intended to start the conversation. It is intended to move the minister to decide to investigate. I challenge and encourage you, one prophet to another, to do the following:

1. Read some of the books listed below:

   Adams, Carol J. *Woman-Battering*. Creative Pastoral Care and Counseling Series. Minneapolis: Fortress, 1994.

   Bancroft, Lundy. *Why Does He Do That? Inside the Minds of Angry and Controlling Men*. New York: Putnam, 2002.

   Engel, Beverly. *The Emotionally Abused Woman: Overcoming Destructive Patterns and Reclaiming Yourself*. New York: Fawcett, 1990.

   Evans, Patricia. *The Verbally Abusive Relationship: How to Recognize it and How to Respond*, 2nd edition. Holbrook, Mass.: Adams Media, 1996.

Kroeger, Catherine Clark, and
Nancy Nason-Clark. *No Place for Abuse: Biblical and Practical Resources to Counteract Domestic Violence.* Downer's Grove, Ill.: InterVarsity, 2001.

Livingston, David J. *Healing Violent Men: A Model for Christian Communities.* Minneapolis: Fortress, 2002.

Nason-Clark, Nancy. *The Battered Wife: How Christians Confront Family Violence.* Louisville: Westminster John Knox, 1997.

2. Attend one training and view one video or movie concerning abuse.

3. If you are a minister, commit to preaching one sermon in the next three months devoted to addressing domestic violence.

4. If you are not a minister, encourage your minister to address the issue. Pray with them and for them and push them to become aware of the problem.

5. Offer to start a reading group in your congregation that reads books written by survivors and that discuss the issues of power and control.

    Weldon, Michelle. *I Closed My Eyes: Revelations of a Battered Woman.* Center City, Minn.: Hazelden, 1999.

6. Invite a domestic violence advocate to speak to your group about intimate partner violence.

7. Never get in over your head! Always refer victims and abusers to professional counselors or domestic violence advocates. For the victim's safety, as well as your own, make sure that they are getting the best help possible. Working with advocates can build a strong

support bridge for the victim to cross in her journey to peace, safety, and healing.

If you are a minister, preaching on this subject will be a great experience for you. The first sermon I gave on abuse was well supported by the congregation. One young couple was visiting that morning. Three months later, I baptized the young woman and she told me she had left her husband because he was abusive. The woman told me that after my earlier sermon her husband accused her of telling me about their problem and beat her that afternoon. I was crushed. I said, "I am so sorry. If I would have known . . . " She interrupted me and said, "No, I am glad you did it. I never knew how God felt 'till then. You keep preaching about it." Since then, many women who sit in church by their abusive husbands have told me the same thing. "My husband doesn't like this . . . " or "My husband thinks you talk too much about social justice and abuse . . . " They all end with the same statement, however, "Keep preaching about it." Who would have thought that those who are oppressed and afflicted would be the ones to encourage the preacher!

This is my advice to you. When you come to understand how God feels about domestic violence, keep preaching, teaching, and telling others about it. You will see a great blessing in your ministries, not because of you but because those who seek God will be given what they need. God will lead victims, abusers, children, and domestic violence workers into the congregation. Those affected by domestic violence need support, hope, and justice. To whom will God send them?

How beautiful are the feet of those who preach good news!

Bibliography

Adams, Carol J. *Woman-Battering*. Creative Pastoral Care and Counseling Series. Minneapolis: Augsburg Fortress, 1994.

Amato, P. R., and A. Booth. "Consequences of Parental Divorce and Marital Unhappiness for Adult Well-Being." *Social Forces* 69 (1991) 895–914.

Anderson, Ray S. *The Shape of Practical Theology: Empowering Ministry with Theological Praxis*. Downer's Grove, Ill.: InterVarsity, 2001.

Anderson, Stephen A., and Darci B. Cramer-Benjamin. "The Impact of Couple Violence on Parenting and Children: An Overview and Clinical Implications." *The American Journal of Family Therapy* 27 (1999) 1–19.

Aquino, Frederick D. "The Incarnation: The Dignity and Honor of Human Personhood." *Restoration Quarterly* 42 (2000) 39–46.

Babcock, Julia C., and Ramalina Steiner. "The Relationship Between Treatment, Incarceration, and Recidivism of Battering: A Program Evaluation of Seattle's Coordinated Community Response to Domestic Violence." *Journal of Family Psychology* 13 (1999) 46–59.

Bancroft, Lundy, and Jay G. Silverman. *The Batterer as Parent: Addressing the Impact of Domestic Violence on Family Dynamics*. Thousand Oaks, Calif.: Sage, 2002.

Bancroft. *When Dad Hurts Mom: Helping Your Children Heal the Wounds of Witnessing Abuse*. New York: Putnam, 2004.

———. *Why Does He Do That? Inside the Minds of Angry and Controlling Men*. New York: Putnam, 2002.

Bartchy, S. Scott. "Families in the Greco-Roman World." In *The Family Handbook*, eds. Herbert Anderson, et al., 282–86. Louisville: Westminster John Knox, 1998.

Battaglia, Lisa Jeanne. "Conservative Protestant Ideology and Wife Abuse: Reflections on the Discrepancy Between Theory and Data." *Journal of Religion and Abuse* 2:4 (2001) 31–46.

Baum, Katrina, and Patsy Klaus. "Bureau of Justice Statistics Special Report: Violent Victimization of College Students, 1995–2002." *U.S. Department of Justice* (January 2005) 1–7.

Becvar, Dorothy Stroh, and Raphael J. Becvar. *Family Therapy: A Systemic Integration.* 2d ed. Boston: Allyn and Bacon, 1993.

———. *Systems Theory and Family Therapy: A Primer,* 2d ed. Lanham, Mass.: University Press of America, 1999.

Bennett, Harold V. *Injustice Made Legal: Deuteronomic Law and the Plight of Widows, Strangers, and Orphans in Ancient Israel.* Grand Rapids: Eerdmans, 2002.

Berlin, Adele, and Marc Zvi Brettler, editors. *The Jewish Study Bible: Tanakh Translation.* New York: Oxford University Press, 2004.

Bevan, Emma, and Daryl J. Higgins. "Is Domestic Violence Learned? The Contribution of Five Forms of Child Maltreatment to Men's Violence and Adjustment." *Journal of Family Violence* 17:3 (2002) 223–45.

Boston Medical Center Pediatrics. "Child Witness to Violence Project." <www.childwitnesstoviolence.org/care_givers/for_caregivers_facts.html>.

Boyd, Gregory A. *God At War: The Bible and Spiritual Conflict.* Downer's Grove, Ill.: InterVarsity, 1997.

———. *Is God to Blame?: Beyond Pat Answers to the Problem of Suffering.* Downer's Grove, Ill.: InterVarsity, 2003.

Bradley, Keith R. "Child Care at Rome: The Role of Men." In *Discovering the Roman Family: Studies in Roman Social History,* 37–75. New York: Oxford University Press, 1991.

———. "Remarriage and the Structure of the Upper-Class Roman Family." In *Marriage, Divorce, and Children in Ancient Rome,* edited by Beryl Rawson, 79–98. Oxford: Clarendon, 1991.

Browne, Angela. *Violence Against Women: A Majority Staff Report.* Committee on the Judiciary, U.S. Senate (Oct. 1992).

Burch, Rebecca L., and Gordon G. Gallup, Jr. "Pregnancy as a Stimulus for Domestic Violence." *Journal of Family Violence* 19:4 (2004) 243–47.

Bureau of Justice Statistics Crime Data Brief. *Intimate Partner Violence from 1993–2001* (Feb. 2003).

Bussert, Joy M. K. *Battered Women: From a Theology of Suffering to an Ethic of Empowerment.* New York: Division for Mission in North America, Lutheran Church in America, 1986.

Campbell, Jacquelyn, et al. "Correlates of Battering During Pregnancy." *Research Nursing Health* 15 (1992) 219–26.

———. "Why Battering During Pregnancy?" *Clinical Issues in Perinatal and Health Nursing* 4 (1993) 343–49.

Chapman, Gary. *Five Signs of a Functional Family.* Chicago: Northfield, 1997.

Clark, David K. "Faith and Foundationalism." In *The Rationality of Theism,* edited by Paul Copan and Paul K. Moser, 35–54. New York: Routledge, 2003.

Clark, Ron. *"Associating With the Humiliated: Victimization as a Tool for Teaching Biblical Studies in a Christian College Setting."* Journal of Religion and Abuse 7:1 (2005) 22–27.

———. "Code of Silence: Matthew 10 in a Context of Domestic Violence." *Journal of Religion and Abuse* 6:1 (2004) 235–48.

———. "Kingdoms, Kids, and Kindness: A New Look at Luke 18:15-17." *Stone Campbell Journal* 5 (2002) 81–98.

———. "Open Your Eyes." *Journal of Religion and Abuse* 4:1 (2002) 27–36.

———. "The Silence in Dinah's Cry: Narrative in Genesis 34 in a Context of Sexual Violence." *Journal of Religion and Abuse* 2:4 (2001) 81–98.

Clements, Caroline M., Caryn M. Sabourin, and Lorinda Spiby. "Dysphoria and Hopelessness Following Battering: The Role of Perceived Control, Coping, and Self-Esteem." *Journal of Family Violence* 19:1 (2004) 25–36.

Cummings, E. Mark, and Amy Wilson. "Contexts of Marital Conflict and Children's Emotional Security: Exploring the Distinction Between Constructive and Destructive Conflict From the Children's Perspective." In *Conflict and Cohesion in Families: Causes and Consequences*, edited by Martha J. Cox and Jeanne Brooks-Gunn, 105–9. Mahwah, N.J.: Lawrence Erlbaum, 1999.

Dahlberg, Gunilla. "The Parent-Child Relationship and Socialization in the Context of Modern Childhood: The Case of Sweden," in *Parent-Child Socialization in Diverse Cultures*, edited by Jaipaul L. Roopnarine and D. Bruce Carter, 121–37. Advances in Applied Developmental Psychology 5. Norwood, N.J.: Ablex, 1992.

Davis, R. C., Julia C. Babcock, S. E. Palmer, R. A. Brown, and M. E. Barrera. "Group Treatment for Abusive Husbands: Long-term Evaluation." *American Journal of Orthopsychiatry* 62:2 (1992) 276–83.

Davis, B. G. Taylor, and C. D. Maxwell, "Does Batterer Treatment Reduce Violence? A Randomized Experiment in Brooklyn." In *Report of the National Institute of Justice* (2000).

Dempsey, Carol. *Hope Amid the Ruins: The Ethics of Israel's Prophets*. St. Louis: Chalice, 2000.

———. *The Prophets: A Liberation-Critical Reading*. Minneapolis: Fortress, 2000.

deSilva, David A. *Honor, Patronage, Kinship and Purity: Unlocking New Testament Culture*. Downer's Grove, Ill.: InterVarsity, 2000.

Dixon, Cynthia. "Clergy as Carers: A Response to the Pastoral Concern of Violence in the Family." *Journal of Psychology and Christianity* 16:2 (1997) 126–31.

Dixon, Suzanne. *The Roman Family*. Ancient Society and History. Baltimore: Johns Hopkins University, 1992.

———. "The Sentimental Ideal of the Roman Family." In *Marriage, Divorce, and Children in Ancient Rome*, edited by Beryl Rawson, 37–75. Oxford: Clarendon, 1991.

Dudrey, Russ. "'Submit Yourselves to One Another': A Socio-historical Look at the Household Code of Ephesians 5:15—6:9." *Restoration Quarterly* 41:1 (1999) 27–44.

Dugan, Meg Kennedy, and Roger R. Hock. *It's My Life Now: Starting Over After an Abusive Relationship of Domestic Violence.* New York: Routledge, 2000.

Eckhardt, Julia Babcock, and Susan Homack. "Partner Assaultive Men and the Stages and Process of Change." *Journal of Family Violence* 19:2 (2004) 81–93.

Edleson, J. L., and M. Syers. "The Effects of Group Treatment for Men Who Batter: An 18-Month Follow-up Study." *Research on Social Work Practice* 1 (1991) 227–43.

Eichrodt, Walther. *Theology of the Old Testament.* Translated by J. A. Baker. Old Testament Library. Philadelphia: Westminster, 1961.

Eldredge, John. *Wild At Heart: Discovering the Secret of a Man's Soul.* Nashville: Nelson, 2001.

Ending Violence Against Women: Population Reports. Series L, No. 11, 27:4 (Dec. 1999).

Engel, Beverly. *The Emotionally Abused Woman: Overcoming Destructive Patterns and Reclaiming Yourself.* New York: Fawcett, 1990.

Engel, Mary Patten. "Historical Theology and Violence Against Women: Unearthing a Popular Tradition of Just Battery," in *Violence Against Women and Children: A Christian Theological Sourcebook*, edited by Carol J. Adams and Marie M. Fortune, 242–61. New York: Continuum, 1998.

Erickson, Millard J. *Christian Theology.* 2d ed. Grand Rapids: Baker, 1999.

Estrella, Rosa Emily Nina. "Effects of Violence on Interpersonal Relations and Strategies that Promote Family Unity." LaFamilia Unida: La Fuerza Del Futuro 4th Annual Power in Partnership Bilingual Conference. June 20, 2003, Portland, Ore.

Evans, Patricia. *The Verbally Abusive Relationship: How to Recognize it and How to Respond.* 2d ed. Holbrook, Mass.: Adams Media, 1996).

Everclear. *Wonderful.* Universal Records, 1997.

Eyben, Emiel. "Fathers and Sons." In *Marriage, Divorce, and Children in Ancient Rome,* edited by Beryl Rawson, 114–43. Oxford: Clarendon, 1991.

Fiorenza, Elizabeth Schüssler. "Introduction." In *Violence Against Women*, edited by Elisabeth Schüssler Fiorenza and Mary Shawn Copeland, vii–xxiv. Maryknoll, N.Y.: Orbis, 1994.

Fitzgerald, John T. "Domestic Violence in the Greek and Roman Worlds." Paper presented at the International Society of Biblical Literature Conference in Netherlands, July 24, 2004.

———, editor. *Greco-Roman Perspectives on Friendship.* SBL Resources For Biblical Study 34. Atlanta: Scholars, 1997.

Fitzmyer, Joseph A. *The Gospel According to Luke I–IX.* Anchor Bible 28. New York: Doubleday, 1981.

Fortune, Marie. "The Transformation of Suffering: A Biblical and Theological Perspective," in *Christianity, Patriarchy, and Abuse: A Feminist Critique,* edited by Joanne Carlson Brown and Carole R. Bohn, 139–47. Cleveland: Pilgrim, 1989.

Gabardi, L. and L. A. Rosen. "Intimate Relationships: College Students from Divorced and Intact Families." *Journal of Divorce and Remarriage* 18 (1992) 25–56.

Bibliography

Gazmararian, J. A., R. Petersen, A. M. Spitz, M. M. Goodwin, L. E. Saltzman, and J. S. Marks. "Violence and Reproductive Health: Current Knowledge and Future Research Directions." *Maternal and Child Health Journal* 4:2 (2000) 79–84.

Gill-Austern, Brita L. "Love Understood as Self-Sacrifice and Self-Denial: What Does It Do to Women?" In *Through The Eyes of Women: Insights for Pastoral Care*, edited by Jeanne Stevenson Moessner, 304–21. Minneapolis: Fortress, 1996.

Gillihan, Yonder Moynihan. "Jewish Laws on Illicit Marriage, the Defilement of Offspring, and the Holiness of the Temple: A New Halakic Interpretation of 1 Corinthians 7:14." *Journal of Biblical Literature* 121 (2002) 711–44.

Glazier-McDonald, Beth. "Intermarriage, Divorce, and the *Bat-'el Nekar*: Insights into Mal 2:10-16." *Journal of Biblical Literature* 106 (1987) 603–11.

Glazer, Sarah. "Violence Against Women." *Colorado Researcher* 3:8 (1993) 171.

Grabbe, Lester L. "Ancient Near Eastern Prophecy from an Anthropological Perspective." In *Prophecy in Its Ancient Near Eastern Context: Mesopotamian, Biblical, and Arabian Perspectives*, edited by Martti Nissinen, 13–32. Society of Literature Symposium Series 13. Atlanta: Society of Biblical Literature, 2000.

Gray, John. *Men Are From Mars, Women Are From Venus: A Practical Guide for Improving Communication and Getting What You Want in Your Relationship*. New York: HarperCollins, 1992.

Grenz, Stanley J. *Theology for the Community of God*. Grand Rapids: Eerdmans, 2000.

Guijarro, Santiago. "The Family in First-Century Galilee." In *Constructing Early Christian Families: Family as Social Reality and Metaphor*, edited by Halvor Moxnes, 42–65. London: Routledge, 1997.

Hamby, Sherry L. "Acts of Psychological Aggression Against a Partner and Their Relation to Physical Assault and Gender." *Journal of Marriage and the Family* 61 (1999) 959–70.

Hansen, Christine. "A Considerate Service: An Advocate's Introduction to Domestic Violence and the Military." *Domestic Violence Report* 6:4 (2001).

Harland, Philip A. *Associations, Synagogues, and Congregations: Claiming a Place in Ancient Mediterranean Society*. Minneapolis: Fortress, 2003.

Harris, William V. *Restraining Rage: The Ideology of Anger Control in Classical Antiquity*. Cambridge: Harvard University Press, 2001.

Hegstrom, Paul. *Angry Men and the Women Who Love Them: Breaking the Cycle of Physical and Emotional Abuse*. Kansas City: Beacon Hill, 1999.

Hellerman, Joseph H. *The Ancient Church as Family*. Minneapolis: Fortress, 2001.

Hill, Andrew E. *Malachi*. Anchor Bible 25D. New York: Doubleday, 1998.

Hobbs, T. R. "Reflections on Honor, Shame, and Covenant Relations." *Journal of Biblical Literature* 116 (1997) 501–3.

Hugenberger, Gordon P. *Marriage as a Covenant: Biblical Law and Ethics as Developed from Malachi*. Grand Rapids: Eerdmans, 1998.

Instone-Brewer, David. *Divorce and Remarriage in the Bible: The Social and Literary Context*. Grand Rapids: Eerdmans, 2002.

International Journal of Health Services 20:1 (1990).

Jeffers, James S. "Jewish and Christian Families in First-Century Rome." In *Judaism and Christianity in First-Century Rome*, edited by Karl P. Donfried and Peter Richardson, 128–50. Grand Rapids: Eerdmans, 1998.

Johnson, John M., and Denise M. Bondurant. "Revisiting the 1982 Church Response Survey," in *Violence Against Women and Children: A Christian Theological Sourcebook*, edited by Carol J. Adams and Marie M. Fortune, 422–27. New York: Continuum, 1998.

Jones, Christopher P. *Kinship Diplomacy in the Ancient World*. Cambridge, Mass.: Harvard University Press, 1999.

Jones, David Clyde. "A Note on the LXX of Malachi 2:16." *Journal of Biblical Literature* 109 (1990) 683–85.

Jouriles, Ernest N., Renee McDonald, William D. Norwood, Holly Shinn Ware, Laura Collazos Spiller, and Paul R. Swank. "Knives, Guns, and Interparent Violence: Relations With Child Behavior Problems." *Journal of Family Psychology* 12:2 (1998) 178–94.

Katz, Jackson. "More Than a Few Good Men: American Manhood and Violence Against Women." Keynote address given at the Justice and Hope Domestic Violence Conference, March 21, 2003, Kelso, Washington.

———. *Tough Guise*. Northampton, Mass.: Media Education Foundation, 1999.

Kaufman, Carol Goodman. *Sins of Omission: The Jewish Community's Reaction to Domestic Violence*. Cambridge, Mass.: Westview, 2003.

Keel, Othmar, and Christoph Uehlinger. *Gods, Goddesses, and Images of God In Ancient Israel*. Translated by Thomas H. Trapp. Minneapolis: Fortress, 1998.

Keener, Craig S. *A Commentary on the Gospel of Matthew*. Grand Rapids: Eerdmans, 1999.

Kelman, Herbert C. "Reconciliation as Identity Change: A Social-Psychological Perspective." In *From Conflict Resolution to Reconciliation*, edited by Yaacov Bar-Siman-Tov, 111–24. New York: Oxford University Press, 2004.

Kerr, Michael E, and Murray Bowen. *Family Evaluation*. New York: Norton, 1988.

Ketterman, Grace. *Verbal Abuse: Healing the Hidden Wound*. Ann Arbor: Servant, 1992.

Köhler, E. M. *Hur Mycket Ska Egentligen ett Barn Behöva Tala?* Stockholm: Carlssons, 1990.

Köhler, L. *Barn och Barnfamiljer I Norden*. Lund: Studentlitteratur, 1990.

Kroeger, Catherine Clark, and Nancy Nason-Clark. *No Place for Abuse: Biblical and Practical Resources to Counteract Domestic Violence*. Downer's Grove, Ill.: InterVarsity, 2001.

Lacey, W. K. "Patria Potestas." In *Family in Ancient Rome*, edited by Beryl Rawson, 121–44. Ithaca: Cornell University Press, 1986.

Lassbo, G. *Mamma-pappa-barn. En Utvecklingsekologisk Studie av Socialization i Olika Familjetyper*. Acta Universitatis Gothoburgensis, 1988.

Lassen, Eva Marie. "The Roman Family: Ideal and Metaphor." In *Constructing Early Christian Families: Family as Social Reality and Metaphor*, edited by Halvor Moxnes, 103–20. London: Routledge, 1997.

LaVey, Anton Szandor. *The Satanic Bible*. New York: Avon, 1969.

LeBlanc, Douglas. "Affectionate Patriarchs." *Christianity Today* (Aug. 2004) 44–46.

Levine, Samantha. "The Perils of Young Romance." *US News and World Report* (August 13, 2001) 46.

Livingston, David J. *Healing Violent Men: A Model for Christian Communities.* Minneapolis: Fortress, 2002.

Malina, Bruce J. *The New Testament World: Insights from Cultural Anthropology.* 3d ed. Louisville: Westminster John Knox, 2001.

Mananzan, Mary John. "Feminine Socialization: Women as Victims and Collaborators." In *Violence Against Women*, edited by Elizabeth Schüssler Fiorenza and Mary Shawn Copeland, 44–52. Maryknoll, N.Y.: Orbis, 1994.

Martin, Grant L. *Critical Problems in Children and Youth: Counseling Techniques for Problems Resulting from Attention Deficit Disorder, Sexual Abuse, Custody Battles, and Related Issues.* Waco, Tex.: Word, 1992.

Martin, Sandra L., April Harris-Britt, Yun Li, Kathryn E. Moracco, Lawrence L. Kupper, and Jacquelyn C. Campbell. "Changes in Intimate Partner Violence During Pregnancy." *Journal of Family Violence* 19:4 (2004) 201–10.

Mathews, Alice P. *Preaching that Speaks to Women.* Grand Rapids: Baker, 2003.

Matthews, Victor H. *Social World of the Hebrew Prophets.* Peabody, Mass.: Hendrickson, 2001.

McClintock, Karen A. *Sexual Shame: An Urgent Call to Healing.* Minneapolis: Fortress, 2001.

Means, J. Jeffrey. *Trauma and Evil: Healing the Wounded Soul.* Minneapolis: Fortress, 2000.

Miles, Al. *Domestic Violence: What Every Pastor Needs to Know.* Minneapolis: Fortress, 2000.

Miller, Mary Susan. *No Visible Wounds: Identifying Nonphysical Abuse of Women by Their Men.* New York: Random House, 1995.

Moore, Sheila Y. "Adolescent Boys are the Undeserved Victims of Domestic Violence." *Boston Globe* (Dec. 26, 1999) E7.

Morena, Naomi. "Cultural Specific Interventions for the Hispanic Domestic Violence Offender." Batterer Intervention Workshop, May 30, 2002. Portland State University, Portland, Oregon.

Moser, Paul K. "Cognitive Inspiration and Knowledge of God." In *The Rationality of Theism*, edited by Paul Copan and Paul K. Moser, 55–71. New York: Routledge, 2003.

Moxnes, Halvor. "Patron-Client Relations and the New Community in Luke-Acts." In *The Social World of Luke-Acts: Models for Interpretation*, edited by Jerome H. Neyrey, 241–68. Peabody: Hendrickson, 1991.

———. *Putting Jesus in His Place: A Radical Vision of Household and Kingdom.* Louisville, Ky.: Westminster John Knox, 2003.

———. "What is Family: Problems in Constructing Early Christian Families." In *Constructing Early Christian Families: Family as Social Reality and Metaphor*, edited by Halvor Moxnes, 13–41. London: Routledge, 1997.

Multnomah County Health Department. *Domestic Violence in Multnomah County*, February, 2000.

Murphy, Jeffrie G. *Getting Even: Forgiveness and Its Limits*. New York: Oxford University Press, 2003.

Nason-Clark, Nancy. *The Battered Wife: How Christians Confront Family Violence*. Louisville: Westminster John Knox, 1997.

National Center for Injury Prevention and Control. *Intimate Partner Violence* (October 2003) <www.cdc.gov/ncipc/factsheets/ipvfacts.htm>.

National Women's Health Information Center. *Violence Against Women*. (Sept. 2001) <www.4woman.gov/violence/index.htm>.

Nietzsche, Frederich. *The Anti-Christ*. Translated by H. L. Mencken. Tucson: See Sharp, 1999.

———. *Beyond Good and Evil: A Prelude to a Philosophy of the Future*. Translated by Walter Kaufmann. New York: Vintage, 1966.

O'Brien, Julia M. *Nahum, Habakkuk, Zephaniah, Haggai, Zechariah, Malachi*. Old Testament Commentary. Nashville: Abingdon, 2004.

Olyan, Saul M. "Honor, Shame, and Covenant Relations in Ancient Israel and Its Environment." *Journal of Biblical Literature* 115 (1996) 201–18.

Oregon Department of Human Services. *Intimate Partner Violence in Oregon: Findings from the Oregon Women's Health and Safety Survey* (February 2004).

Palacios, Maria Aracely Linares. "Strategies for Working with Latinos Who Have Experienced Family Violence." LaFamilia Unida: La Fuerza Del Futuro 4th Annual Power in Partnership Bilingual Conference. June 20, 2003, Portland, Oregon.

Perdue, Leo G. *Families in Ancient Israel*. The Family, Religion, and Culture. Westminster John Knox, 1993.

Peterson, David. *Zechariah 9–14 and Malachi: A Commentary*. Old Testament Library. Louisville: Westminster John Knox, 1995.

———. "Defining Prophecy and Prophetic Literature." In *Prophecy in Its Ancient Near Eastern Context: Mesopotamian, Biblical, and Arabian Perspectives,* edited by Martti Nissinen, 33–44. Society of Literature Symposium Series 13. Atlanta: Society of Biblical Literature, 2000.

Poling, James Newton. *The Abuse of Power*. Nashville: Abingdon, 1991.

Population Report Series L; National Women's Health Information Center: *Intimate Partner Violence* (Oct. 2003). <www.cdc.gov/ncipc/factsheets/ipvfacts.htm>.

Porter, Stanley E. *Katallasso in Ancient Greek Literature: With Reference to the Pauline Writings*, Estudios de Filología Neotestamentaria 5. Cordoba: El Almendro, 1994.

Rauschenbusch, Walter. *A Theology for the Social Gospel*. Nashville: Abingdon, 1917.

Rennison, Callie Marie, and Sarah Welchans. *Intimate Partner Violence*. Bureau of Justice Statistics Special Report (May 2000).

Resseguie, James L. *Spiritual Landscape: Images of the Spiritual Life in the Gospel of Luke*. Peabody, Mass.: Hendrickson, 2004.

Richardson, Ron. *Becoming a Healthier Pastor: Family Systems Theory and the Pastor's Own Family.* Creative Pastoral Care and Counseling Series. Minneapolis: Fortress, 2005.

———. *Creating a Healthier Church: Family Systems Theory, Leadership, and Congregational Life,* Creative Pastoral Care and Counseling Series. Minneapolis: Fortress, 1996.

Rink, Margaret J. *Christian Men Who Hate Women.* Grand Rapids: Zondervan, 1990.

Ronan, George F., Laura E. Dreer, Katherine M. Pollard, and Donna W. Ronan. "Violent Couples: Coping and Communication Skills." *Journal of Family Violence* 19:2 (Apr. 2004) 131–37.

Saller, Richard. "Corporal Punishment, Authority, and Obedience in the Roman Household," in *Marriage, Divorce, and Children in Ancient Rome,* edited by Beryl Rawson, 144–65. Oxford: Clarendon, 1991.

Schimmel, Solomon. *Wounds Not Healed by Time: the Power of Repentance and Forgiveness.* New York: Oxford University Press, 2002.

Shifflett, Kelly, and E. Mark Cummings. "A Program for Educating Parents about the Effects of Divorce and Conflict on Children: An Initial Evaluation." *Family Relations* 48:1 (Jan. 1999) 79–89.

Silvergleid, Courtenay S. "Research on the Effectiveness of Intervention Programs for Abusive Men." Presented at *Fundamentals of Working With Abusive Men* Workshop. Portland State University, Portland, Ore.; January 2001.

Simons, Ronald L., Kuei-Hsiu Lin, and Leslie C. Gordon. "Socialization in the Family of Origin and Male Dating Violence: A Prospective Study," in *Journal of Marriage and the Family* 60:2 (May 1998) 467–78.

Smith, Mark S. *The Early History of God: Yahweh and the Other Deities in Ancient Israel.* 2d ed. Grand Rapids: Eerdmans, 2001.

———. *The Origins of Biblical Monotheism: Israel's Polytheistic Background and the Ugaritic Texts.* New York: Oxford, 2001.

Stark, Evan, and Anne Flitcraft. "Spouse Abuse," in *Surgeon General's Workshop on Violence and Public Health Source Book* (1985).

Stone, Howard W., and James O. Duke. *How to Think Theologically.* Minneapolis: Fortress, 1996.

Stordeur, Richard A., and Richard Stille. *Ending Men's Violence Against Their Partners.* Newbury Park, Calif.: Sage, 1989.

Straton, Jack C. "What is Fair for Children of Abusive Men?" in *Journal of the Task Group on Child Custody Issues of the National Organization for Men Against Sexism,* 4th edition. 5:1 (2001) 1–10.

Szegedy-Maszak, Marianne. "Death at Fort Bragg," *US News and World Report* (Aug. 12, 2002) 44. "Physical Assault on Women by an Intimate Male Partner, Selected Population-Based Studies, 1982–99, Table 1." *Population Report Series L: Number 11.* <www.infoforhealth.org/pr/L11/L11tables.shtml>.

Talbot, Jennifer. "Children Witnessing Domestic Violence." Presented at the *Working with Abusive Men* workshop. Portland State University, Portland, Oregon, May 2002.

Taves, Ann, editor. *Religion and Domestic Violence in Early New England: The Memoirs of Abigail Abbot Bailey*. Bloomington: Indiana University Press, 1989.

Tavris, Carol. *Anger: The Misunderstood Emotion*. Rev. ed. New York: Touchstone, 1989.

Thistlethwaite, A., J. Wooldredge, D. Gibbs. "Severity of Dispositions and Domestic Violence Recidivism." *Crime and Delinquency* 44:3 (1998) 388–98.

Thompson, Barbara. "An Interview with James Garbarino on the Impact of Violence on Children." *World Vision* (April–May 1995) 8–9.

Tjaden, P., and N. Thoennes. *Full Report of the Prevalence, Incidence, and Consequences of Intimate Partner Violence Against Women: Findings from the National Violence Against Women Survey* (NCJ 183781). Washington, D.C.: U.S. Department of Justice, National Institute of Justice, 2000.

Treggiari, Susan. "Divorce Roman Style: How Easy and How Frequent Was It?" In *Marriage, Divorce, and Children in Ancient Rome*, edited by Beryl Rawson, 31–46. Clarendon: Oxford University Press, 1991.

Tremonti, Mark, and Scott Stapp. "My Own Prison." In *Creed: My Own Prison*. New York: Wind Up Records, 1997.

Tripolitis, Antonia. *Religions of the Hellenistic Roman Age*. Grand Rapids: Eerdmans, 2002.

Umberson, Debra, Meichu D. Chen, James S. House, Kristine Hopkins, and Ellen Slaten. "The Effect of Social Relationships on Psychological Well-Being: Are Men and Women Really So Different?" *American Sociological Review* 61 (1996) 837–57.

United Nations Children's Fund Innocenti Research Center. *Launch of the Innocenti Report Card 5: A League Table of Child Maltreatment Deaths in Rich Nations* (September 18, 2003) <www.uniceficdc.org/presscentre/indexNewsroom.html>.

Verner, David C. *The Household of God: The Social World of the Pastoral Epistles*. SBL Dissertation Series 71. Chico, Calif.: Scholars, 1983.

Violence Against Women. Sept. 2001. <www.4woman.gov/violence/index.htm>

Weems, Renita. *Battered Love: Marriage, Sex, and Violence in the Hebrew Prophets*. Overtures to Biblical Theology. Minneapolis: Fortress, 1995.

Weinfeld, Moshe. "*Berith*," In *Theological Dictionary of the Old Testament*, edited by Johannes G. Botterweck, Helmer Ringgren, and Heinz-Josef Fabry, vol. 2, 253–78. Grand Rapids: Eerdmans, 1974.

Weitzman, Susan. *"Not to People Like Us": Hidden Abuse in Upscale Marriages*. New York: Basic, 2000.

Weldon, Michelle. *I Closed My Eyes: Revelations of a Battered Woman*. Center City, Minn.: Hazelden, 1999.

White, Pamela Cooper. *The Cry of Tamar: Violence Against Women and the Church's Response*. Minneapolis: Fortress, 1995.

Wiedemann, Thomas. *Adults and Children in the Roman Empire*. New Haven: Yale University Press, 1989.

Willis, Timothy. "'Obey Your Leaders': Hebrews 13 and Leadership in the Church." *Restoration Quarterly* 36 (1994) 316–26.

Bibliography

Winter, Bruce W. *After Paul Left Corinth: The Influences of Secular Ethics and Social Change*. Grand Rapids: Eerdmans, 2001.

———. *Roman Wives, Roman Widows: The Appearance of New Women and the Pauline Community*. Grand Rapids: Eerdmans, 2003.

Witherington, Ben III. *New Testament History: A Narrative Account*. Grand Rapids: Baker, 2001.

Yarbrough, O. Larry. "Parents and Children in the Jewish Family of Antiquity." In *The Jewish Family in Antiquity*, edited by Shaye J. D. Cohen, 39–59. Brown Judaic Studies 289. Atlanta: Scholars, 1993.